World's End

World's End

Charlie Gere

Goldsmiths
Press

Copyright © 2022 Goldsmiths Press
First published in 2022 by Goldsmiths Press
Goldsmiths, University of London, New Cross
London SE14 6NW

Printed and bound by Versa Press, USA
Distribution by the MIT Press
Cambridge, Massachusetts, and London, England

Copyright © 2022 Charlie Gere

A CIP record for this book is available from the British Library

ISBN 978-1-913380-00-7 (hbk)
ISBN 978-1-912685-97-4 (ebk)

www.gold.ac.uk/goldsmiths-press

Acknowledgments

There are far too many people to thank properly, but the following must be mentioned; my father and mother, obviously, for making me, in Chelsea, and therefore making this book possible and also for choosing to live in such an aptly named district; my sister, Cathy, of course; Jenn Ashworth for her comments, as well as our ongoing conversations and her steadfast and generous encouragement of my writing; Matt Fuller and Arthur Bradley for their insightful comments; Ruth McLennan for graciously allowing me to quote her part of a private Facebook conversation; Sarah Cormack, for her comments, and for getting in touch out of the blue, and making me think about the more distant past; the editorial team at Goldsmiths Press, and their anonymous reviewers; and to all those friends, some of whom I have known since the 1970s or even 1960s, with and beside whom I have lived this life, especially my family Lucinda, Matilda and, above all, Stella, who says that I never talk about my past, and to whom I dedicate this book.

Contents

1

World's End

When making my will a few years ago I was asked to choose what should happen to my body after death. Without hesitation, I said I would like to be cremated and have my ashes scattered in London, in the river at the World's End at the wrong end of the King's Road, in Chelsea. In returning at, or after my end, at least in my imagination, to where I started, seemed right and seemed to exemplify the idea that life is a detour on the way to a return to where one starts. It was right that my world should end, where it started, at the World's End.

I rehearsed this final journey when Covid-19 struck in 2020 and we decided that it would be best if I went down to London to help my mother during the lockdown. This meant returning to my childhood home. The London I returned to was uncannily like the city of my youth, in that it felt empty, in marked contrast to its recent state of crowdedness. Before the virus, London had become almost unbearably full, choked with traffic and crowds. A bus journey that had taken twenty minutes in the 1960s or 1970s, now lasted a minimum of an hour and often longer. Now the streets were almost entirely devoid of traffic.

I recently came across some extraordinary images taken by Jon Savage, better known as a writer on Punk and related forms of music. They show North Kensington in the mid-1970s, an unrecognisable place of dereliction and emptiness.[1] That's the London I remember from my youth. I search archives of images of post-war London to confirm my memories. The sense of London being empty I remember and that Savage's photographs seem to confirm turns out to be accurate. London hit its peak population, 8.6 million,

---

[1] Savage, Jon, *Uninhabited London* (London: Rough Trade Editions, 2018).

in 1939, a figure only reached again in 2015. In the thirty years after 1939 the population dropped to 6.6 million, meaning that it was at its emptiest when I was a child and adolescent.

During the lockdown people mainly walked, alone or in pairs, with occasional family groups. Planes no longer flew over my mother's house, on the flightpath to and from Heathrow in the early morning. The city was strangely, eerily, silent. To prevent the spread of contagion, supermarkets only allowed a limited number of shoppers in at a time. People patiently queued, spacing themselves at the recommended two metres or six feet. The strangeness of the experience was compounded by the sight of police cars patrolling slowly around the streets, as if about to enforce the quarantine. I noticed that the police were armed with what appeared to be submachine guns, which added to the sense of foreboding. Under all this there was the continual sense of anxiety, the fear that some contact with another human, or even with a tainted surface, might cause infection, maybe mild or even asymptomatic, but possibly extremely painful or even deadly.

My return to London was motivated not just by the need to help my mother but for other, less noble, reasons. I was intensely curious to experience the city in which I had been born, and spent most of my life, under these unprecedented conditions. I wanted to witness this epochal event, which was bound to change the world entirely, close up, in one of the centres of the outbreak. To a great extent this was just a kind of car-crash voyeurism. I find catastrophes and disasters frightening but also exhilarating and fascinating. There was also a kind of atavistic pull of home, to return to the World's End, at what seemed at times to be the end of the world. It seemed to me that the current sense of dread caused by the virus was something I had felt all my life.

At the same time, I felt a curious joy all the time, which seemed entirely inappropriate in the circumstances. This was down to some extent to the sense of being on a kind of holiday, from the day-to-day banalities and repetitions of family and work, and also due to the extraordinary weather, with the beautiful spring greatly enhanced by the lack of traffic, cars and also airplanes on the Heathrow flightpath, and the general emptiness of the streets. I walked, with my mother, and with friends, all over the parts of London reachable by foot, seeing the houses and sights clearer than ever before. But it was something else besides these pleasures. Towards the end of my stay, after nine weeks, I had an at first unaccountable desire to re-read Thomas

Mann's *The Magic Mountain*. It seemed to me that London during Covid was a bit like the sanatorium in Mann's book, in which the mundane time of the valley below was suspended. However, this did not mean no time but many times co-existing in the emptied city. Something of this is caught by one of the characters in Michael Moorcock's London masterpiece *Mother London*.

We move through Time at different rates, it seems, only disturbed when another's chronological sensibility conflicts with our own. Choices as subtle and complicated as this are only available in a city like London; they are not found in smaller towns where the units, being less varied, are consequently less flexible. Past and future both comprise London's present and this is one of the city's chief attractions. Theories of Time are mostly simplistic... attempting to give it a circular or linear form, but I believe Time to be like a faceted jewel with an infinity of planes and layers impossible either to map or to contain; this image is my own antidote for Death.[2]

The name World's End has always struck me as having an appropriate apocalyptic implication for the context of my childhood. I was born at what was probably the zenith of the Cold War or at least one of its hotter moments. Like almost everybody of my generation, the threat of nuclear annihilation was a central fact of my existence, one that seemed to make the supposed solidity of our surroundings dubious, given that they could be destroyed in minutes, or even seconds. This produced what Jeff Nuttall called 'bomb culture', his term for the counterculture that emerged as a response to this threat. Reading his masterpiece *Bomb Culture* now gives me such a palpable sense of recognition as he tries to explain the devastating psychic effect of Hiroshima and the effect of possible nuclear annihilation on young people after the War.[3]

My friends and I suffered from that sense of doom described so well by Nuttall. His book is an impassioned account of the traumatic effect of the Bomb on a generation of young people for whom there appeared to be no future. It is a very personal book, recounting his early involvement with the Campaign for Nuclear Disarmament, and his subsequent disillusion with its efficacy. He became increasingly involved with both radical art and the Underground or Counterculture. What *Bomb Culture* captures, and which we allow ourselves to forget, to our peril, is the sheer insanity of nuclear

[2] Moorcock, Michael, *Mother London* (London: Weidenfeld and Nicholson, 2016), 520–21.
[3] Nuttall, Jeff, *Bomb Culture* (London: McGibbon and Kee, 1968).

weaponry and the horror of living in a world in which they exist. For Nuttall, the only sane response to this madness was through art that reflected it back to the surrounding culture. One of the great virtues of *Bomb Culture* is that it gives a picture of the 1960s and the Underground that is an immediate response and entirely lacking the nostalgia with which the 'Swinging Sixties' are now regarded.

Thus, that the area in which I was brought up was called the World's End appeared almost too apposite to be believable. It seems to me apt that one of the most apocalyptic Punk songs, the Clash's 'London Calling', was composed by Joe Strummer when he lived in the World's End. Between 1977 and 1980, Strummer's home was a fourth-floor flat in Whistler Walk, on the World's End estate between Whistler Tower and Greaves Tower, more or less next to the river. Strummer was inspired by a news item on the television about the possibility of the river flooding and submerging large parts of London, and also by near-catastrophes such as the nuclear accident at Three Mile Island in the United States in 1979.

That my parents chose to live in the World's End, rather than somewhere else, was mostly a matter of economics. They looked at houses in Little Venice (an area of West London between the Edgware Road and Notting Hill Gate, named after its proximity to the junction of the Regent's and Grand Union Canals), and in the more fashionable part of Chelsea in SW3. However, the World's End offered the kind of house they wished to live in at a price they felt they could afford. However, that entirely fortuitous decision has turned out to be a gift in thinking about how to write about my childhood and the cultural context in which I found myself.

To live with the threat of nuclear annihilation, however much it recedes into the background, is to live always with a certain dread anticipation. In his book *Tense Future: Modernism, Total War, Encyclopedic Form*, Paul Saint-Amour delineates what he sees as the continuous state of fearful anticipation that is a concomitant of our nuclear condition but which he dates back to the interwar period. He invokes the strange sense that the atomic bomb attacks on Hiroshima and Nagasaki were both entirely unprecedented and unimaginable but also the 'premonitory atmosphere in Hiroshima' before the attack, a sense that the city's strange good fortune at avoiding being bombed throughout the War was bound to change. He quotes Robert Lifton on the Japanese use of the word '*bukimi*', 不気味, meaning weird, ghastly or unearthly, to name this sense, which Saint-Amour describes as the 'nuclear uncanny'.[4] Those in Hiroshima experiencing this were the first

to experience a condition that, in a more explicit form, would come familiar to everyone living in a targeted city under the Cold War doctrine of Mutually Assured Destruction: the sense that the present security and flourishing of the city were at once underwritten and radically threatened by its identity as a nuclear target.[5]

I still feel that sense, of being in a target, even today. To a great extent I am surprised to have lived this long, to still be alive. It is as if our lives have been an endlessly deferred death sentence, or as if we have always already been deemed dead, and only given our lease of life through some act of sovereign mercy. As I write this I think of David Bowie's song 'We are the dead' from *Diamond Dogs*.

We lived in a house on the north of the King's Road, past the bend just a few yards west of Beaufort Street, which constitutes the beginnings of the World's End. It was sited in a grid of streets known as the Ten Acres, after the fields upon which they had been built in the 1860s and onwards. The name World's End is not a formal designation and its bounds are not that clear. In his memoir of his childhood there, Donald Wheal defines the area as 'very roughly [...] was and remains, the lower reach of riverside Chelsea, the furthest point in the King's Road from Sloane Square. Its southern limit is the river'[6]. According to Wheal, what was recognised as the World's End in the 1930s were 'the streets and houses on both sides of the King's Road for about three hundred yards in either direction from the World's End pub'. The point at which it

faded into propriety, and finally disappeared, was marked by a sharp S-bend in the King's Road and here the Chelsea of artists and aristocrats began, a Chelsea distinguishable by a difference in accent from ours, by freshly painted homes, by art galleries and expensive motor cars and the employment of hundreds of cleaning women – from, of course, World's End.[7]

[4] Saint-Amour, Paul K., *Tense Future: Modernism, Total War, Encyclopedic Form* (London, Oxford: Oxford University Press, 2015), 1–3.

[5] Ibid., 3.

[6] Wheal, Donald James, *World's End: Memoirs of a Blitz Childhood* (London: Arrow Books, 2005), 1.

[7] Ibid.

In his account of being a Jewish motor mechanic and antifascist campaigner in the World's End in the 1930s, Alf Goldberg also defines the area as starting after the double-bend in the King's Road by the old Chelsea Police Station and extending beyond Edith Grove and Chelsea Creek.[8]

According to Wheal, despite being part of the 'one of London's richest boroughs World's End was in the thirties and forties an area of mouldering dwellings, some of them rat-ridden slums, others with their own Victorian elegance, unpainted, broken-windowed and tatterdemalion as they were'[9]. Eighty years later, those same Victorian houses sell for millions of pounds, and the sharp divide between the World's End and the rest of Chelsea no longer exists, partly as the result of the gentrification of the area my parents and others enabled. Since it is no longer a byword for poverty, the definition of what constitutes the World's End geographically is a little more generous. The southern limit is, necessarily, the river. For me, the eastern limit is Beaufort Street, the Fulham Road is the northern, and the railway line that also marks the borders of Chelsea and Fulham the western limit. This means, incidentally, that Chelsea Football Club's Stamford Bridge Stadium, sitting on the western side of the railway, is actually in Fulham.

Despite these changes, some of the streets look more or less the same as they did when I was a child and, probably as they did from the late 19th century onwards. Nevertheless, I have a strong sense that 'my' London no longer exists. It is as if it has been buried under other people's Londons, new Londons that I no longer fully recognise or fully at am home in. But, of course, 'my' London sat on top of someone else's, most immediately the working class World's End described by Wheal, which my parents' generation's gentrification more or less destroyed. There are traces still but the world that Wheal describes had ended by the late 1970s. Similarly, my London and World's End has now ended, and what has replaced them, in the Ten Acres, is a London belonging to the poorer sort of multimillionaire, who cannot afford grander houses to the north and east, so treats the modest terraces of the World's End as if they were themselves larger and grander, not least by the addition of endless basements.

One of the anomalies of the World's End is that it is not near any tube stations. Neither my father nor mother could drive. This meant we all spent a great deal of time on buses, to work, to school, for shopping, to get to parties,

---

[8] Goldberg, Alf, *World's End for Sir Oswald: Portraits of Working-Class Life in Pre-war London* (Blackpool: Progressive, 2006), 14.

[9] Wheal, *World's End*, 1.

and to see friends. I became very familiar with all the local buses and their routes, which were, in numerical order, the 11, 14, 19, 22, 31 and 49 (all but one of these bus routes still operate in or near the World's End – the exception, the 31, now replaced by an imposter numbered 328). Strangely, I still talk of catching the 11 bus, as if there was one singular vehicle, rather than numerous buses with that number on the front, but in a way that's right. The 11 bus, like all the other buses, is a platonic archetype living in a kind of realm of ideal buses, and which is reflected in the earthly realm of actual buses. It doesn't matter, in the end, whether the 11 takes the form of the great Routemaster or the various single-decker, double-decker, and bendy buses, or even the travesty that is the New Routemaster, the so-called 'Boris Bus', masterminded by Boris Johnson, and designed by Thomas Heatherwick.

In April 2021, the last Routemasters in service were finally retired from the 15 bus route. This was the severing of a last connection to my childhood and the experience of travelling in these buses, with their interior colour scheme of 'Burgundy lining panels, Chinese green window surrounds, and Sung yellow ceilings', and their seats covered with tartan moquette of dark red and yellow.[10] The seats were edged with red leather, and were full backed to thwart pickpockets. The handrails and seat frames were tubular metal. The windows were quarter drop wind down for ventilation. Under the stairs there was a small luggage space.[11] Much of my childhood and youth was spent sitting on this kind of bus, always on the top deck, looking, reading, looking. The pleasure of travelling by bus was clearly appreciated by the Victorian poet Amy Levy in her 'Ballade of an Omnibus', published in 1889.

> In winter days of rain and mire
> I find within a corner strait;
> The 'busmen know me and my lyre
> From Brompton to the Bull-and-Gate.
> When summer comes, I mount in state
> The topmost summit, whence I see
> Crœsus look up, compassionate–
> An omnibus suffices me.[12]

---

[10] Elborough, Travis, *The Bus We Loved: London's Affair with the Routemaster* (London: Granta, 2005), 50–51.

[11] Ibid., 52–3.

[12] Webster, Augusta, et al., *Out of My Borrowed Books: Poems by Augusta Webster, Mathilde Blind and Amy Levy* (Manchester: Fyfield Books/Carcanet, 2006), 226.

Levy's romantic vision of bus travel is echoed in Rosemary Tonks' prose poem 'An Old-fashioned Traveller on the Trade Routes' in which she starts off 'cursing the waste of time, and pouring my life away on the one of those insane journeys across London', and ends up suggesting that the 'consistently idiotic' jogging of the bus 'induced a feeling of complete security', in which 'I gave up my complicated life on the spot; and lay screwed up like an old handkerchief screwed up in a pocket, suspended in time, ready to go to the ends of the earth. O trans-Siberian railways! Balloons! Astronauts'.[13]

The Routemaster was designed by Douglas Scott, who was also known for the Potterton Boiler, the redesign of the Aga, the K8 GPO telephone box and designs for Rediffusion radio sets. He had worked for the great American designer Raymond Loewy, who famously aimed for a clean, streamlined style for his products.[14] Scott, wishing to avoid a 'shoebox', and to produce an 'attractive piece of street furniture', gave the Routemaster a number of distinctive curves. Travis Elborough suggests that the arrival of the Routemaster coincides with the bursting into colour of life in the late 1950s. It first took to the roads in 1956 in the same year as the Clean Air Act, the exhibition *This Is Tomorrow* at the Whitechapel, with Technicolor being introduced a year later. The bus naturally became an icon of a London increasingly known for pop and youth culture, from the 1961 film *Summer Holiday* with Cliff Richard, through to Allen Jones' brilliant colourist 'Bus' series of paintings from 1962 onwards. The Routemaster also appears on one of the best paperback covers of the 1960s, that of *Nairn's London* by Ian Nairn, published in 1966 by Penguin Books. The cover is the perfect synthesis of the brilliance of Penguin design and of the bus's design. By the mid-60s, the Routemaster was a metonym of Swinging London. (Though, as Elborough points out, many of the buses in films and television programmes were not actually Routemasters.) The most explicitly swinging use of the bus was with The Who's single 'Magic Bus'. One sleeve design showed a double decker painted in psychedelic patterns, and another a Routemaster passing through Piccadilly Circus with the words 'Magic Bus' in psychedelic writing on the side. The lyrics, about a man buying a bus to visit his girlfriend, are also fairly trippy.

---

[13] Noel-Tod, Jeremy, *The Penguin Book of the Prose Poem: from Baudelaire to Anne Carson* (London, New York: Penguin Books, 2019), 254–5.
[14] Elborough, *The Bus We Loved*, 45–7.

Part of my fascination with buses had an erotic element, connected to the television programme *Here Come the Double Deckers*, about a group of six children who seemed, in my memory at least, to live an autonomous existence in a double-decker bus (not, it turns out, a Routemaster). Among the reasons I remember *The Double Deckers* is that I had a slight crush on Billie, the tomboyish leader of the group. Perhaps this was a kind of proleptic projecting forward to the kind of woman I would find attractive in the future.

The numbers of the routes thus also take on a quasi-mystical quality, especially given how they are, or at least should be, unchanging. In his memoir of the World's End, Donald Wheal describes people taking the 22 or 11 back in the 1930s and 1940s. This suggests a comforting, almost religious sense of continuity in a rapidly changing world. Even after the apocalypse, I would like to imagine the 11 and 22 still passing through the World's End, at the world's end. I imagine the buses Wheal mentions to be Routemasters, but this is impossible given they were not introduced until the early 1950s. However, the Routemaster's predecessors, the various Regents, are similar enough. The numbers themselves, in my mind, have an almost kabbalist significance, mystically compressing within a couple of digits whole worlds. For example, the number 22 for me always conjures up the places the bus went to almost to the degree that Proust's madeleine also invoked the past. Going west, the 22 would pass through the still-mysterious world of Fulham, then very much a working-class area, and less shiny than Chelsea, then over Putney Bridge, to the comfortable inner suburb of Barnes, where various girls, on whom I had hopeless crushes, lived. To the east, the 22 took a far more glamorous route, and those numbers still invoke for me the West End, with all its allure. From the World's End it went up the King's Road, then Upper Sloane Street, through Knightsbridge, and onto Piccadilly and the West End, before ending up in far off Homerton, a place as mysterious to me then as Tibet. Sadly, the 22 route has now been truncated, and now ends at Piccadilly Circus.

I found a curious account from the 1920s by civil servant and drama critic Arthur Bingham Walkley of the difference between Chelsea and Bloomsbury, and the experience of travelling by bus from one to the other.

Why those two names? Because they *are* names—names rather than areas, abstractions rather than concrete facts.... What I really mean is, you will not find them in those intriguing lists of London localities which decorate the fronts of our omnibuses, and which are a liberal education to most of us in metropolitan geography. For the 'bus-boards only indicate real places, such as 'Haggerston' and 'Ball's Pond Road,' whose authentic reality is their sole excuse. Thus M. Paul Morand, the ingenious author of 'Ouvert la Nuit,' assures us that Bus No 19 goes to Islington. I take his word for it. In my maddest moment of wanton caprice I have never been tempted to go to Islington. It sounds too real. If I could think it only a name, an idea, a dream, an aspiration, I should board No. 19 like a shot. 'Je m'embarquerais pour Cythére'. Now, there is an infrequent and elusive vehicle known as Bus No. 39, which takes you through (or alongside, for I don't want a letter of protest from the Secretary, L.G.O.C.) both Bloomsbury and Chelsea. The wonder of it The magic carpet superseded! And your kaleidoscopic changes of mood, as you bowl along, from 'inspissated gloom' at the corner of Tottenham Court Road, through a sense of bewilderment, as of having swallowed some stupefying drug and not having quite 'come to,' at Charing Cross, to your first fine careless rapture at the sight of a scarlet coat and cocked hat outside the Royal Hospital of, maybe, emerging from a handy pub thereabouts! Before you have done wondering why the Hospital clock is always five minutes fast you are already on the Embankment, where simple wonder turns to beatitude:

> Veramente quant' io del regno santo
> Nella mia mente potei far tesoro,
> Sard ora materia del mio canto,

you murmur to yourself ; and by the time you are opposite Don Saltero's you have attained the Higher Ataraxy.[15]

I have in my mind's eye an image of an earlier self, travelling down the King's Road, in the late 1960s or early 1970s, perhaps back from my school, which was then in Pimlico, and dressed in school uniform. The journey West on the King's Road, perhaps by the 11, 22 or 19 bus, was, in the 1960s or early 1970s, a trip from the heart of bourgeois respectability to something far more louche by the time you got to the World's End. The eastern extremity, the Sloane Square end, was (and, indeed, still is) dominated by Peter Jones, the department store, a wonderful example of 1930s modernism with its subtle curving shape. Peter Jones is, more or less, the secular cathedral of the London middle class, a perfect expression of a certain way of thinking and being, of soft furnishings, glassware, cutlery and private school uniforms. Opposite Peter Jones at the east end of Sloane Square is the Royal Court Theatre, in which *Waiting for Godot* and *Look Back in Anger* were performed,

---

[15] Walkley, A. B., 'Bloomsbury and Chelsea', in *The Crown & Anchor: A Chelsea Quarto, ed.* Reginald Blunt (London: The Chelsea Publishing Company, 1925), 6–7.

among other groundbreaking productions. (Respectable though this end of Chelsea may be, for a brief time, Pont Street, off Sloane Street on the way towards Knightsbridge, was the location of the World Psychedelic Centre, in which the taking of LSD was advocated, and practised.) A little further down, on the opposite side, is the site of Whitelands, now a block of flats. The building the block replaced, which was first a girls' boarding school and then a teacher training college, was for a moment in the 1930s the headquarters of Mosley's British Union of Fascists. On the corner of Royal Avenue, the Chelsea Drugstore, an extraordinary chrome and glass building from 1968, is still there, more or less. Based on Le Drugstore in Paris, on the Boulevard St Germain, it was originally a complex of different areas in which to eat and drink, shop or dance. Young women dressed in purple jumpsuits would deliver goods from the Drugstore on motorcycles. It is referred to, famously, in the Rolling Stones' record 'You Can't Always Get What You Want', in which Mick Jagger sings about going down' to the Chelsea Drugstore.

The record shop in the Drugstore featured in Stanley Kubrick's *Clockwork Orange*, as the Musik Bootik. It is there that Alex, the chief droog, played by Malcolm McDowell, picks up two young girls for the 'old in-out'. In his account of British record shops, Garth Cartwright points out both the names of the imaginary bands in the neon-lit top ten list, including Johnny Zhivago, Heaven Seventeen and The Sparks, as well as the actual records that are visible, among which are albums by Tim Buckley, The Incredible String Band, Pink Floyd, Canned Heat, The Beatles, John Fahey, Neil Young, Johnny Winter and Rare Earth, 'all favourites of London's hippie elite'.[16] There are also a couple of in-jokes in terms of records, the soundtrack to Kubrick's previous film, *2001: A Space Odyssey*, and *Missa Luba*, the Congolese mass that McDowell's character listens to obsessively in the film *If...* The pub it replaced, The White Hart, can be seen in Joseph Losey's 1963 film *The Servant*. The Drugstore, or what is left of it, is now, unfortunately, a McDonald's. (Apparently, at one time, before Kubrick made his version, Rolling Stones manager Andrew Loog Oldham tried to secure the rights to *A Clockwork Orange*, with the idea that the Stones would play the droogs.)

---

[16] Cartwright, Garth, *Going for a Song: A Chronicle of the UK Record Shop* (London: Flood Gallery Publishing, 2018), 128.

Beyond the Drugstore, Wellington Square, on the south side of the King's Road, has the strange distinction that both James Bond and Aleister Crowley lived there. Crowley was there sometime in the 1920s. Bond's creator worked with Crowley in the War, and it has been supposed that the Bond books reflect his fascination with Crowley and the occult.[17] Fascinatingly, John le Carré has George Smiley live very close, on the other side of the King's Road in Bywater Street. One can imagine Bond and Smiley meeting in some fictional metauniverse, maybe in the Sainsbury's that was more or less half way between their respective residences. Perhaps they might have also encountered the real-life spy Kim Philby, who lived very nearby, in Carlyle Square.

From there the bus passed the various boutiques and leafy squares for which Chelsea was famous. The boutiques and other shops included Mary Quant's Bazaar, Cecil Gee, I Was Lord Kitchener's Valet, Just Looking (with its silver modernist exterior), Blueberry Hill, Chelsea Girl, Kleptomania, Kweens Ministore, Top Gear, Countdown, Dandie Fashions, Apple Tailoring (the briefly lived boutique arm of the Beatles' empire), John Michael, Alkasura, and the Sweet Shop. Where the Marks & Spencer is now was The Great Gear Trading Company, a large space full of clothes stalls, and a head shop, selling, among other drug apparatus, dollar bill rolling papers. A couple of blocks down Antiquarius, built as a temperance hall, was full of antique stalls.

About a third of the way down the King's Road is the Pheasantry, an elegant building the name of which derives from a previous occupant of the site, from where pheasants were sold. The building itself was built in the mid-19th century, and was bought in the 1880s by Jouberts, an upholstery firm. In the 1960s it became a semi-commune, with various famous or notorious inhabitants, including Germaine Greer, Eric Clapton and David Litvinoff. It was also a concert venue where, among others, Lou Reed, Queen and Hawkwind played. Next to the Pheasantry was the Chelsea Classic Cinema, where *The Rocky Horror Show* was performed for a few months in 1973.

Near the Pheasantry, Flood Street was the location of Michael Cooper's photographic studio in which the photoshoot for what maybe the most

---

[17] Gardiner, Philip, *The Bond Code: The Dark World of Ian Fleming and James Bond* (London: New Page, 2008), 122–4.

famous album cover, that of the Beatles' *Sgt Pepper's Lonely Hearts Club Band*, took place. Flood Street was also where Margaret Thatcher and her husband, Denis, lived from 1968, until she was elected prime minister and moved to Downing Street. Just past the Town Hall is Oakley Street, which has a history of colourful residents, including Oscar Wilde's mother, Jane Wilde, who later named herself Speranza, and who chose to live there after the death of her husband, Sir William Wilde. Her house became a salon devoted to poetry, Irish nationalism and aestheticism. Extraordinarily, the footballer George Best later lived at the same address. He used to drink at the Phene Arms and I can remember seeing him, intoxicated, walking down the King's Road. Other notable Oakley Street residents include the discreetly homosexual novelist E. F. Benson, author of the highly camp books on Mapp and Lucia, the Cambridge spy Donald McLean, the actress Dame Sybil Thorndyke, Robert Falcon Scott, 'Scott of the Antarctic', David Bowie, and briefly and barely believably, Bob Marley and his wife, Rita, who moved there in 1977 after an attempt on his life in Jamaica. It is strange to think of Mrs Thatcher living a few hundred yards from both David Bowie and Bob Marley at various times in the 1970s. Marley features in the mock blue plaque on the front of the Cross Keys, which also lists Dylan Thomas, J. M. W. Turner, Agatha Christie, John Singer Sargent, James McNeill Whistler – as 'Celebrated figures drank here'. (Clearly not all at the same time, though the idea of a lock-in with all those figures is beguiling.)

Perhaps the most mysterious building on the King's Road was the dark, old mansion on the corner of Oakley Street, and opposite the Fire Station, in a block with three smaller but still old-fashioned terrace houses. It looked so out of place in the modern context, better suited to a Dickensian London than that of the 1960s. This was Argyll House, one of the original 'Chelsea Palaces', built in 1723 by a Venetian architect, Giacomo Leone, for a Huguenot merchant named John Pierene or Perrin. It got its name after the Duke of Argyll, who lived there in 1769 to 1770, just before he died. In the early 20th century the socialite and interior decorator Sibyl Colefax lived there. The mysteriousness of the house was dissipated for me when my stepdaughter and her husband were among a number of house sitters there before it was redecorated by its current owners. I was able to see what lay behind the dark façade, which turned out to be more or less what I expected, a shabbily grand interior looking much as might be expected for a house of its period.

The bus would also pass a number of more discreet locations, such as Bramerton Street, location of the Gateways Club, for gay women, which featured in the film *The Killing of Sister George*, the King's Road Theatre, where the *Rocky Horror Show* ran from 1973 to 1979, the Sound Technique Studio in 46a Old Church Street, where many important 1960s records were recording, as well as Robert Whittaker's studio at no. 1 The Vale, in which the extraordinary picture of the Beatles in butcher's coats, dismembering baby dolls, was taken.

Beaufort Street was the border to the World's End, and between the postal districts of SW3 and SW10. In the 1960s Quentin Crisp lived there, on the edge of the World's End, in a famously dusty flat in the part of the street that runs north of the King's Road. He was there from 1940 to 1981, when he decamped to New York, and, appropriately perhaps, the Chelsea Hotel. I do not remember ever seeing him. Perhaps he was not that exceptional in the general context of the King's Road and Chelsea in the 1960s and 1970s. If there was one place that Crisp's flamboyant appearance would not be that remarkable it was there and then. My sister does remember seeing him and her description is vivid. She passed him on Beaufort Street, and remembers him as 'small and slight, wearing a black velvet cape with a white satin lining and a broad-brimmed fedora, under which I caught a glimpse of his face, lined, melancholy, and heavily made-up, with clumpy mascara and dabs of rouge'. That Crisp chose to live in Chelsea was probably a question of expedience, rather than any sense of the area as especially gay. His room, a 'bedsit', was notoriously squalid. He famously refused to clean, claiming that, after a certain time, the dust got no worse. The nation was given a glimpse into his curious lifestyle in, of all things, a 1970 episode of the current affairs programme, *World in Action*.

Finally, the bus would get to the S-bend in the King's Road that signalled the beginnings of the World's End. At the south-eastern corner of the bend there is a single tower block, covered in yellow cladding, and known, rather prosaically, as 355 King's Road. It was built between 1968 and 1971, and was nearly demolished in 1983, owing to its core rotting. Instead, it was sold to a development company who dealt with its structural problems, including covering the original redbrick exterior with the cladding. Its original name, Moravian Tower, is more intriguing than its current one. It is actually named after the Moravian Burial Ground, a mysterious patch of greenery that sits behind a wall, and a pair of large wooden doors between the Tower and what was once The Water Rat pub (now a restaurant).

The Moravians buried in the Burial Ground were members of one of the oldest Protestant sects, founded in the mid-15th century by Gregory the Patriarch, following the reforming idea of Jan Hus, earlier in the century, in Bohemia, and known originally as the *Unitas Fratrum*. It endured and survived persecution, especially in the 17th century, when it went underground during the triumph of Catholic forces. In the early 18th century some fleeing Moravian families found refuge on the estate of the pietist aristocrat Count Zinzendorf in Saxony. Zinzendorf enabled the founding of the Herrnhut community on his estate and encouraged the Moravians to go out to proclaim the Gospel in all parts of the world. Moravians went and founded communities in the Caribbean, America and Britain, including Yorkshire, Bedfordshire, Wiltshire and Ireland. Zinzendorf bought Lindsey House in the World's End, intending it to be the international headquarters of the Moravian Church and the centre for its missionary activities. The stable yard was turned into a burial ground, 'God's Acre', with a chapel and a congregation house. However, after Zinzendorf's death in 1760, the Moravians sold Lindsey House in 1774, retaining only the burial ground and its buildings.

If the Sloane Square end of the King's Road is the most respectable then the World's End is its antithesis. It's where the most extreme manifestations of various forms of counterculture were found, from the boutique Granny Takes a Trip, the shop/commune Gandalf's Garden, the psychedelic shack of a record shop, Town Records, and the countercultural teashop The Flying Dragon in the 1960s, to the shop known variously as Hung On You, Mr Freedom, Paradise Garage, Let It Rock, Too Fast to Live Too Young to Die, Sex and Seditionaries, which is arguably the birthplace of British Punk. Thus, if the King's Road is, somehow, a royal road to the unconscious, then its end, the World's End, is perhaps the heart of the area's id. In his book on the King's Road, Max Decharné quotes Mick Farren on the World's End, and its cast of characters such as Hung On You boutique owner Michael Rainey.

Well in the King's Road up until say the mid-seventies there was a wealth of difference between Sloane Square and World's End, a real wealth of difference, you know ["laughs"]... Heading west, you kind of got to the Town Hall and the Fire Station, but after that there wasn't very much going on until you reached these almost kind of circled waggons at World's End. Rainey was an aristocrat, he was a lord. So you have all that – the sort of dispossessed Lord Alfred Douglas kind of characters, then you move over one step and you've got Quentin Crisp through to the Rocky Horror Show, then you move over three more steps and you've got the socialite end of the Krays and Richardsons like Johnny Bindon. [Chelsea] was fun when it was sort of crumbling, even though there were people who lived off weekly cheques from Daddy or whatever...[18]

In her account of coming to London as a young American and living and getting divorced in Chelsea in the mid-1960s, Phyllis Raphael describes her experience of the remoteness and difference of the World's End, when fleeing her marital home on Royal Avenue and turning left rather than right towards Peter Jones.

After a while I began to feel disoriented. Instead of taking a right turn at the Chelsea Drugstore and heading towards Sloane Square, Knightsbridge, and the parts of London that had become familiar to me in the few weeks I'd been there, I'd gone in the opposite direction, past the Chelsea Potter Pub, the Antique Market, and the Public Baths at Sydney Street and into an unknown area, a place I'd never been and wasn't likely to go. The cityscape of Chelsea was gone; no whitewashed terraces, very few small shops, pubs, or cafes. I was running past open spaces; vacant lots, looming behind them some dark buildings that were probably a housing project. I had seen only a few cars and one or two people since I started out, lonely figures walking rapidly in a barren landscape, heads down and inaccessible. I couldn't see much ahead of me. The streets were poorly lit. When I finally gave up, I was out of breath, sweating and panting, a stitch in my side, the damn coat half off on my arms. I was under a pub sign. "World's End," it said. Ahead of me the sky was almost imperceptibly beginning to lighten. A wavery line of pinkness glowed on the horizon and I had the thought that if I kept running towards it I might just fall off the earth.[19]

As late as the 1970s, in his short story 'World's End', Paul Theroux could describe the area as 'a bizarrely named but buried alive district called the World's End in London'.[20] Theroux's choice of the area for the story's title and location is clearly symbolic. The story is about an American who, having moved his family to London, discovers his wife's adultery. He has brought

---

[18] Décharné, Max, *King's Road: The Rise and Fall of the Hippest Street in the World* (London: Weidenfeld & Nicolson, 2005), 223.

[19] Raphael, Phyllis, *Off the King's Road: Lost and Found in London* (New York: Roadswell Editions, 2014), chap 3, Kindle.

[20] Theroux, Paul, *World's End and Other Stories* (New York: Houghton Mifflin Harcourt, 1980), 1.

them to the end of the world, 'so far from home', while his wife's affair is the end of his world.

Perhaps the strangest and most curious literary reference to the World's End is in William Burrough's notorious experiment in writing using cut-ups and other techniques, *The Soft Machine*. At one point the character Jimmy appears to be in Fulham and then in Chelsea.

Jimmy walked along North End Road—(Slow-motion horses pulling carts—boys streaked with coal dust)—A low-pressure area and the wind rising—Came to the World's End Pissoir and met a boy with wide shoulders, black eyes glinting under the street lights, a heavy silk scarf tucked into his red and white striped T-shirt—.[21]

It was, in many ways, extraordinarily fortunate, to have lived in this part of Chelsea in this time. I teach students about the 1960s and 1970s, which must seem unimaginably distant to them and reflect that I was there, and could have easily appeared, for example in the image I show them of the boutique Granny Takes a Trip, just round the corner from our house. When I talk about this period, it does seem very remote. I can remember bombsites, rag-and-bone men in horse-drawn carts, milk floats delivering milk from the diary depot in Hollywood Road, off the Fulham Road, which had come that morning from the country, a necessity before widespread refrigeration, and even a Frenchman on an old bike festooned with onions which he sold door to door. (Though it seems almost too good to be true, I seem to remember him wearing, yes, a striped singlet and a beret.) I remember black and white television, and 78 rpm records, which my parents still had. I remember pre-decimal coinage, pounds, shillings and pence, and even how such coinage worked (twelve pennies to a shilling, twenty shillings to a pound, or twenty-one to a guinea). I can also remember going with my parents to the Lyons Corner House in South Kensington and eating Battenberg cake, known as window cake for its distinctive appearance when cut of four squares in two different colours. (I later found out that Lyons pioneered commercial computing in Britain, with their Lyons Electronic Organiser, LEO, originally designed to manage the complexities of stock control.) I remember the curious resistance of the money slot in the phone booth as I pushed my two

---

[21] Burroughs, William S., *The Soft Machine: The Restored Text* (London, New York: Penguin, 2014), 51.

pence in. When I was a small child, homosexuality was still illegal and the Lord Chamberlain still censored theatrical productions.

My mother remembers the big flour mills and breweries on the river, the Watney's bottling plant, where the men still wore clogs, as well as the Lot's Road gasometers, which rose and fell, and which often gave out a strong smell of gas. When we were first there the Chelsea Palace of Varieties still existed on the King's Road, though by the time my parents arrived in Chelsea it was used as a studio by Granada Television. In 1959, in one of her last performances, Billie Holiday sang 'Strange Fruit' and two other songs for a programme entitled *Chelsea at Nine*. The same programme featured the first bare female breasts on British television, when the African dance troupe Ballets Africains performed one of their routines. Nobody had checked that this would happen and it caused panic in the control room. In the mid-1950s it was the venue for risqué burlesque shows such as those put on by pornographer Paul Raymond. Just up the road, Mary Quant had opened her boutique Bazaar. Quant claimed that 'We went once a week... the Chelsea Palace chorus girls wore very naughty fur bikini knickers.' In so many ways it was little changed from how it was before the War or even earlier. It is difficult to explain how dirty and dreary London was in my childhood. In her memoir of growing up in London in the 1960s and 1970s, Lavinia Greenlaw captures perfectly the feel of London in the period, and how

London was still dark. There were blanks and bomb sites and cratered backstreets where the lights that went out with the war had not yet gone back on. The Houses of Parliament were shabby with centuries of soot. Most people dressed quietly and sensibly. At school we watched chalk on blackboard and at home, black-and-white television.[22]

Photographs of London from the 1950s and early 1960s show a city for which the sense of being in black and white is not an artefact of the film stock, but an accurate reflection of how the city felt. One straightforward reason for this is that houses, neglected, necessarily, in the War, were often grimy and dirty, partly due to the widespread use of distemper paint, which discolours fairly quickly.

[22] Greenlaw, Lavinia, *The Importance of Music to Girls* (New York: Farrar, Straus and Giroux, 2008), 39.

Sometime in the late 1990s parts of the second film version of Graham Greene's *The End of the Affair* were shot near where I lived with my wife and family in Clerkenwell. A whole street of houses had had the white paint of their ground and basement floors replaced with the appearance of grimy distempered walls. So convincing did this appear that I persuaded my mother to come up to see and confirm that this was what London was like. She said that it was shockingly uncanny in its accuracy, and gave a strong sense of how gloomy London was during and after the War. However, the early 1960s was a period when this gloom began to be replaced with something more colourful and often more garish, which indicated how the post-war world was changing and being superseded by something new.

This is not just an artefact of the development and greater ubiquity of colour photography, Technicolour, colour television and other such phenomena. It was a palpable transformation in London at least owing to legislation that dramatically reduced the amount of aerial pollution. Heavy smog, fog and smoke combined, had been a major feature of London life since the 17th century, made much worse in the 19th by industrialisation. Repeated attempts had been made to mitigate these depressing and unhealthy phenomena, but little seemed to work. By the second half of the 20th century, the instances of heavy smog had diminished. However, as Lynda Nead describes in her excellent book *The Tiger in the Smoke*, in December 1952, a days-long smog episode occurred, known as the 'Great Smog of London', probably as a result of cheap coal, 'nutty slack', being taken off ration.[23]

The novel *The Tiger in the Smoke* by Marjorie Allingham, after which Nead names her own book, gives an extraordinarily vivid sense of what the smog felt like. The book starts with a description of it.

The fog was like a saffron blanket soaked in ice-water. It had hung over London all and at last was beginning to descend. The sky was yellow as a duster and the rest was a granular black, overprinted in grey and lightened by occasional slivers of bright fish colour as a policeman turned in his wet cape.[24]

Later on the detective her detective hero Albert Campion reflects that the 'evil smell of fog is a smell of ashes grown cold under hoses'. As Nead points out,

---

[23] Nead, Lynda, *The Tiger in the Smoke: Art and Culture in Post-War Britain* (New Haven, Yale University Press, 2017), 29–30.

[24] Allingham, Margery, *The Tiger in the Smoke* (Harmondsworth: Penguin Books, 1957), 9.

this seemed an uncanny return of Victorian gloom in a country desperate, in the post-war context, to embrace modernity. Nead cites Marghanita Laski's *The Victorian Chaise Longue* as a working through of this haunting of the present by the Victorian past. She connects the greyness of the smog to the characteristic black and white photographic representation of bombed and ruined buildings, or what she names as 'photography noir'.[25] By the time I was born in 1961, the Clean Air Act of 1956, passed in response to the resurgence of smog, had mostly transformed the city's atmosphere. However the need to give people time to move from burning the fuels that caused smog meant that it took time to entirely change. In December 1962, another major smog event took place, following smaller such episodes in the late 1950s.

The beginning of the 1960s was the moment when Britain began to recover from the terrible toll of the War and try to become a more modern country. This was part of a more general lurch into modernity throughout the world. In April 1961, the Russian cosmonaut Yuri Gagarin became the first human to venture into outer space. This was also the year in which construction started on the ultramodern Post Office Tower. Sometime later in the decade I remember crying, inconsolably, outside the Tower. I was there to help celebrate my best friend Paul's birthday. We had been to the Tower, and to the famous revolving restaurant at the top. I had somehow failed to communicate with Paul's father that I too would like something from the gift shop. He was exasperated but returned to the shop to buy me what I wanted, a scale model of the tower, with a tiny band for the revolving restaurant that can be turned by hand.

I search online for an image of this model and immediately understand why I wanted it so much. It is perfect, a Platonic archetype of the Tower itself, although made not in the real building's concrete and glass but in a translucent blue-green plastic that resembles a kind of crystal. It is packaged in a clear plastic box, with the words POST OFFICE TOWER LONDON running vertically on the front in a sans serif font, and 600 FEET 1991 METERS APPROX on the inner surface of the back, facing the front. The packaging is elegantly modernist, and exemplary in its fidelity to the building's own design ethos.

It was also about this time that the Anglo-French project to build a supersonic passenger airliner was formally initiated. The result, Concorde, was a

---

[25] Nead *Tiger in the Smoke*, 78–89.

technological success and a commercial failure. I owned a toy version made by Corgi, which was die-cast metal but had a plastic nose that could be dipped. It offered the pleasure, so vital for me, of something from the adult world reduced to the miniature. It was about the same size as other Corgi toys, which meant, of course, that it was at a far smaller scale. That this representation of Concorde was miniature was also apt, as it mirrored how we tended to see the plane itself, high up in the sky, and correspondingly apparently small. Thus, seeing Concorde in the sky became a strange kind of pleasure, a glimpse of the romantic, technological sublime, but which was increasingly also mixed with a kind of ironic understanding of the ultimate futility of the plane and all it promised.

In 1961 Britain, under the premiership of Harold Macmillan, made its first application to join what was then known as the European Economic Community. The application was vetoed by France's General de Gaulle. Thus, it turns out, my life has coincided more or less exactly with Britain's long and conflicted relationship with what is now called the European Union, from that first, failed, application to Brexit in 2016 and its continuing aftermath.

But the most vivid example of Britain's modernisation was just a few yards from our front door, the King's Road. As Paul du Noyer puts it in his history of London's popular music culture,

The King's Road is pop's cerebral cortex. In the 1950s it was the site of Mary Quant's fashion shop, perhaps the first sign of a distinctively modern pop culture. In the sixties it was the meeting point of pop music and high society. And in the seventies it became the cradle of punk rock.[26]

The 'King's Road' was a metonym for what *Time Magazine* described, in 1966, as 'Swinging London', that brief moment when the capital was the most fashionable place on earth. (The story on 'Swinging London' became one of the magazine's most well-known covers. Fascinatingly, the week before the cover had borne the famous question 'Is God Dead?', referring to a feature on the then fashionable form of religious atheism. That a feature on 1960s countercultural London should be preceded so closely by one on nihilism seems highly appropriate.)

---

[26] Du Noyer, Paul, *In the City: A Celebration of London Music* (London: Ebury Publishing, 2009), 93.

In 1960 came the introduction of the contraceptive pill, 'the pill', in the United States, and in Britain a year later. The pill supposedly liberated women in particular in terms of sex. (Other pills gained different forms of notoriety. My mother lost the thalidomide pills the doctor had given her to counteract morning sickness. The doctor, having realised that something was wrong with the pills, had, of course, called my father, rather than my mother, into the surgery to discuss the problem.) The period between 1960 and 1963 saw, inter alia, the Profumo Affair, the *Lady Chatterley* trial, the rise of satire with *Beyond the Fringe*, *That Was the Week that Was*, the Beatles' first LP, those phenomena that, for Philip Larkin, were the beginnings of sexual intercourse in 1963, between 'the end of the "Chatterley" ban/And the Beatles' first LP', which, he proclaimed, was 'a little late for me'[27]. Obviously, I remember none of these things, but they were part of the disruptive cultural forces that would form the world into which I came into consciousness. Actually, given that the Chatterley ban was ended on 2 November 1960, and the Beatles' first LP was released on 22 March 1963, and I was born on 15 December 1961, 408 days after the Chatterley trial and 462 days before the Beatles' record was released, I too began more or less at the same time as sexual intercourse. My birth more or less coincides with an event that may have more direct bearing on the coming of the emerging permissive society. Lord Denning, in his report on Ward's trial and the Profumo affair, quotes Keeler's description of a notorious party Mandy Rice-Davies and she went to at Ward's behest in December 1961.

One night I was invited to a dinner party at the home of a very, very rich man. After I arrived, I discovered it was a rather unusual dinner party. All the guests had taken off their clothes. There were both men and women there and the men included people I would not have suspected of ever doing anything improper. There was one well-known barrister who, I am sure, would be willing to make stirring speeches in court attacking that sort of thing. There were also some well-known actors and a politician whom I recognised. The most intriguing person, however, was a man with a black mask over his face. At first I thought this was just a party gimmick. But the truth was that this man is so well-known and holds such a responsible position that he did not want to be associated with anything improper. The guests were not just ardent nudists. Even I was disgusted.[28]

---

[27] Larkin, Philip, *Collected Poems* (London: Marvell Press and Faber and Faber, 1988), 167.

[28] Denning, Alfred Thompson, *John Profumo and Christine Keeler 1963. Abridged ed.* (London: The Stationery Office, 1999), 203.

This became known as the 'Man in the Mask Party'. Denning continues that

There is a great deal of evidence which satisfied me that there is a group of people who hold parties in private of a perverted nature. At some of these parties, the man who serves the dinner is nearly naked except for a small square lace apron round his waist such as a waitress might wear. He wears a black mask over his head with slits for eye-holes. He cannot therefore be recognised by any of the guests. Some reports stop there and say that nothing evil takes place. It is done as a comic turn and no more. This may well be so at some of the parties. But at others I am satisfied that it is followed by perverted sex orgies: that the man in the mask is a "slave" who is whipped: that the guests undress and indulge in sexual intercourse one with the other: and indulge in other sexual activities of a vile and revolting nature.[29]

The person doing the whipping was one of the most notorious figures in this particular demi-monde. Mariella Novotny, whose name was kept out of the report by Denning, was of Czech origin, and was reputedly a spy, an under-age prostitute, who had been white-slave trafficked, and had been expelled as a security risk from the United States, having slept with President Kennedy. We will meet her again.

For a child, the area was a perpetual source of fascination. This, along with a profound sense of futility in the light of possible nuclear destruction led, perhaps, to my tendency to drift, aimlessly and without direction through spaces, whether physical and intellectual. Sometime in the 1960s my mother bought me a Box Brownie from an Oxfam shop, which took surprisingly good photographs, despite the utter simplicity of its operation and the incompetence of its operator. I did not take photographs for aesthetic reasons, but simply to capture, tame and make sense of the plethora of tantalising things around me. I still have this sense of being tantalised by what I see, and hear, and read. Perhaps that is what this book is about, an attempt to both represent the great archive of stuff that accumulates over a lifetime and also to show how excessive it is, how impossible to fully make sense of.

The space of the city offered an alluring and endlessly frustrating display of phenomena that I sought to track down and subdue in endless peregrinations. The use of the camera was an expression of my desire to look at and capture everything, as was my restless moving around London. I was a bit of an infant *flâneur* or child psychogeographer. My mother claims

---

[29] Ibid., 203–4.

that I was so restless that I refused to wait for a lift to school from another parent, and insisted on making my own way from about the age of eight or nine. Having been given the freedom to roam on my own, I took full advantage beyond going to school, and she further claims that she would get calls from shocked friends saying they had seen me walking on my own in Piccadilly Circus.

My mother is discreet about what must have been the troubling experience of bringing up two difficult children. She only remarks that

our increasingly feral children knew far more about the ebb and flow of hippy and then punk Chelsea life than we did. Their formative years were spent in 'swinging' Chelsea when it was at its most notorious and they have a far better recall of it than I do. They lived quite dangerously in their feral explorations.

My sister has generously ascribed my early academic delinquency to, in her words, being overly dilated to the world, being far too interested in everything around me to pay attention at school. I often feel like Alex in *Clockwork Orange*, my eyes forced open to witness the world. A similar image is found in Virginia Woolf's essay 'Street Haunting'. Starting with a description of various objects that 'perpetually express the oddity of our own temperaments and enforce memories of our own experience', she suggests that when we leave the house for a solitary ramble,

when the door shuts on us, all that vanishes. The shell-like covering which our souls have excreted to house themselves, to make for themselves a shape distinct from the others, is broken, and there is left of all these wrinkles and roughnesses a central oyster of perceptiveness, an enormous eye.[30]

---

[30] Woolf, Virginia, *Street Haunting* (San Francisco: Westgate Press, 1930), 5.

2

The Angel Standing in the Sun

During lockdown I spent a lot of time walking around Chelsea and its neighbours, and particularly on the river. The river edge of the World's End extends from the end of Lots Road in the west to Beaufort Street, a distance of, perhaps, two hundred yards, at the beginning of Cheyne Row. It starts just beyond the very last remnant of the Cremorne Gardens, now a little riverside park, but once the name of a vast pleasure gardens stretching from the river to the King's Road. This stretch is always busy with traffic mostly either coming down from Edith Grove or going up Gunter Grove, which, in its successive incarnations as Finborough Road and Warwick Road, is a major conduit to west and north London and, indeed, the north and west of England and to Wales. The other direction goes along the Embankment to the West End and the City. To the West there are the great shapes of the World's End towers, the brutalist housing estate built in the 1970s, and the Lots Road power station looms and beyond them the tower of Chelsea Harbour, which has recently been joined by two more glass and metal tower blocks of private apartments. On the Chelsea side of the river itself are the famous houseboats, moored permanently as and lived in. Across the river in Battersea are numerous tower blocks and contemporary constructions, with the Battersea Old Church still visible among them. The view is positively science-fictional, or at least resembles a rapidly developing contemporary city such as Seoul or Singapore. Facing the river on the Chelsea side are a number of houses of all different ages, from the 17th century Lindsey House, one of the last of the great Chelsea palaces still standing, to 1950s low-rise social housing. At the Beaufort Street end, beyond Lindsey House is a row of three Georgian houses.

In the middle of the 19th century, the view would have been entirely different. The Embankment itself was not built until the 1860s. In the 1840s the river front was little more than a quiet country path. Snipe shooting took place up the creek that marked Chelsea's borders. Battersea Bridge was a massive timber structure. There is a beautiful description by Thomas Carlyle, in a letter to Jane Carlyle, of the riverfront in Chelsea in the first half of the 19th century.

Our row runs out upon a beautiful Parade (perhaps they call it) running along the shore of the River; shops etc., and a broad highway, with huge shady trees; boats lying moored and a smell of shipping and tar; Battersea Bridge (of wood) a few yards off; the broad River, with white-trousered, white-shirted Cockneys dashing by like arrows in their long canoes of boats beyond, the green beautiful knolls of Surrey with their Villages; on the whole a most artificial, green-painted, yet lively, fresh, almost opera-looking business such as you can fancy.[1]

Chelsea has always had a certain glamour owing to its royal connections. The King's Road is so called because it was quite literally that, a royal road, reserved originally for King Charles II to get to Kew, though people with connections could also use it. One of four gates into it was at World's End. Amazingly it remained a royal road until 1830, and still bears something of that distinction in its sense of its own dignity.

In his *Tour through England and Wales* Daniel Defoe described Chelsea as a 'town of palaces' reflecting the large number of great houses there, from Thomas More's Beaufort House, to Lindsey House, also on the river, Argyll House and Stanley House, Lawrence House, Sloane House, Shrewsbury House, Danvers House, Winchester House and many others, almost all of which have long disappeared.[2] (The exceptions are Lindsey House, Argyll House, Sloane House, and Stanley House.) In the late 18th century and into the 19th and the 20th centuries Chelsea was better known as the home of writers and artists. So many well-known authors lived in Carlyle Mansions on Cheyne Walk, including Henry James, T. S. Eliot, Somerset Maugham and Ian Fleming, that it was nicknamed the 'Writers' Block'. In the 1950s the

[1] Carlyle, Thomas, *Collected Letters of Thomas and Jane Welsh Carlyle. Vol 7: October 1833 to December 1834* (Durham: Duke University Press, 2007), 173.

[2] Defoe, Daniel, *A Tour through England and Wales. Vol II* (London: New York: J. M. Dent & Sons; E. P. Dutton & Co., 1928), 11.

area became known for the Chelsea Set, the loose grouping of aristocrats, designers and bohemians, or as Mary Quant put it in her 1965 memoir *Quant by Quant* 'painters, photographers, architects, writers, socialites, actors, con-men, and superior tarts', who preceded the full emergence of the counterculture in the area.[3] In Len Deighton's London Dossier, Jane Wilson is less generous, describing the Chelsea Set as 'a nasty and roaring offshoot of the deb world' who 'ten years ago' had 'moved in and opened up the stretch of the King's Road which extends from Sloane Square to the Six Bells, where Oakley Street turns down to the river'. This meant that 'the post-war bohemians were pushed gradually down towards World's End and cisalpine Fulham'.[4] By the 1960s the King's Road was one of the centres of 'swinging London'. However, the World's End has always remained a bit of an anomaly in relation to the rest of Chelsea, resisting its aura.

That the name of the World's End is apparently apocalyptic is, at one level, entirely coincidental, as it actually derives from the name of various inns that have been sited on the King's Road since the 17th century, marking the limits of habitation. The name of the inn thus suggested something about the area's sense of being the end of something, and also somehow disreputable. In 1873 in *Old and New London* Edward Walford mentions the inn.

In the King's Road, near Milman Street, is an inn styled 'The World's End'. The old tavern [...] was a noted house of entertainment in the reign of Charles II. The tea-gardens and grounds were extensive, and elegantly fitted up for the reception of company. The house was probably called 'The World's End' on account of its then considerable distance from London, and the bad and dangerous state of the roads and pathways leading to it. As it stood within a few yards of the river, most of the visitors made the journey in pleasure-boats.[5]

Though Walford is too coy to be explicit about this, the reception of company meant prostitution. William Congreve makes this clear in his comedy from 1695, *Love for Love*. In act II, scene IX, Mrs Frail and Mrs Fore, two women of the town, discuss the propriety of being seen with a man in a hackney carriage in various parts of London.

---

[3] Quant, Mary, *Quant by Quant* (London: Cassell and Co, 1966), 38.

[4] Deighton, Len, *The London Dossier* (Harmondsworth: Penguin Books, 1967), 30.

[5] Thornbury, George Walter, and Walford, Edward, *Old and New London; Illustrated. A Narrative of Its History, Its People, and Its Places, vol V* (London, Paris: Cassell, Petter, & Galpin, 1873), 87.

Mrs Frail: If I had gone to Knight's Bridge, or to Chelsea, or to Spring Garden, or Barn Elms with a man alone, something might have been said.

Mrs. Fore: Why, was I ever in any of those places? What do you mean, sister?

Mrs. Frail: Was I? What do you mean?

Mrs. Fore: You have been at a worse place.

Mrs. Frail: I at a worse place, and with a man!

Mrs. Fore: I suppose you would not go alone to the World's End.

Mrs. Frail: The World's End! What, do you mean to banter me?

Mrs. Fore: Poor innocent! You don't know that there's a place called the World's End? I'll swear you can keep your countenance purely: you'd make an admirable player.[6]

It's amusing to find the name of the World's End here being employed as an obvious sexual double entendre, and appropriate as well. A footnote in the New Mermaid edition of the play makes the meaning clear. 'World's End. In Chelsea. All the places referred to were resorts of doubtful character.' The area's reputation for prostitution was even greater in the middle of the 19th century, largely because of Cremorne Gardens, which opened in 1845. But before that the World's End was nothing but fields. In his oral memories, recorded later in the century, a local figure named John Munday recalled the Chelsea of his childhood and youth. Munday remembers an almost entirely rural scene, in which

there was a field then belonging to the Baron de Berenger and afterwards turned into Cremorne Gardens, and the Man in the Moon fields belonged to him, and he had two sons who used to ride about upon white ponies after the boys who would go to play in these fields. At the end of Lots Road were the lots upon which the poor folks were allowed to turn their cattle for six months in the year to graze; the other six months the lots were shut up and no cattle allowed on them.

He continues to describe the ubiquity of market gardens for which the area was famous.

And at the World's End Passage towards the water-side were a very few houses, and all the rest part was Trigg's nursery and market gardens, and they grew mangel-wurzels, etc., for his cows, and these gardens ran down to the water's edge, with a

6 Congreve, William, *Love for love* (London: Benn, 1969), 48.

hedge this side. The water here was famous for fishing in; the fishermen used to set their eel-pots here and caught a large number, and you would see a lot of people in boats against the Old Bridge fishing for roach, dace, and flounders.[7]

In October 1846, a couple calling themselves Booth rented, paying cash for a twenty-one-year lease on one of the cottages on the river front in the World's End. The man, in his seventies, short and stout, was known as Puggy Booth to the street boys of Chelsea, and Admiral Booth to others, as his habit of carrying a telescope led to the rumour that he was a retired admiral in reduced circumstances. Admiral Booth was actually the great painter Joseph William Mallord Turner, who had come to Chelsea to live with and be looked after by his mistress, the Margate widow and landlady, Sophie Booth. He still owned a house in Queen Anne Street in the West End of London, but this was in the care of his housekeeper Hannah Danby, and in an increasing state of disrepair and decay. Turner was careful to keep his new location secret, and it was only after his death that many in the area realised who he was and many of his friends found out where he had been. Turner was apparently content in Chelsea, being a 'waterfront person'. He had a balcony with a railing built on the roof so he could sit and look at the River. According to Mrs Booth, he called the view to the West his English view and that to the East his Dutch view.[8]

In his book *Old Chelsea: A Summer's Stroll*, published in 1889, the American visitor Benjamin Ellis Martin tries to capture the older Chelsea that drew Turner still discernible amidst the new.

The long summer afternoon is waning, and the western sky, flaming with fading fires, floods broad Chelsea Reach with waves of dusky gold. The evening mist rises slowly, as yet hiding nothing, but transforming even commonplace objects in a weird unwonted way. Those pretentious blocks of new mansions loom almost lordly now; that distant railway bridge is only a ghost of graceful glimmering arches; money-making factory chimneys and commercial wharves pretend to picturesque possibilities; clumpish barges, sprawling on the mud, are no longer ugly; and a broad-bottomed coasting schooner, unloading stone at a dock, is just what we would choose to see there. And here at the end of this bridge is a fragment of 'real old Chelsea,' left intact for our delectation – a cluster of drooping trees on the bank, an unaccountable boat-house, stone steps leading down to the bit of beach, whereon

[7] Blunt, Reginald, *Red Anchor Pieces* (London: Mills and Boon, 1928), 105.
[8] Bailey, Anthony, *Standing in the Sun: A Life of J. M. W. Turner* (London: Pimlico, 1998), 368.

are skiffs drawn up, and cordage lying about, and sail-wrapped spars. Out on the placid Reach there is but little movement; the river steamboats are anchored in a dark mass near the shore, and the last belated one edges up to its mooring beside them for the night; a burly barge drifts slowly by under its dusky brown sails, or a 'dumb-barge' floats with the tide, its crew of one man busied with his long skulls and his not-dumb blasphemy; a puffing tug with a red light in its nose drags tortuously a long line of tarpaulin-covered canal boats. As each of these moving objects breaks the burnished waves into bits of golden gloom, the whole still surface of the stream becomes alive for us with a fairy flotilla, born of the brain, yet real enough to our vision.[9]

Earlier in the same year in which he moved to Chelsea, Turner exhibited what must be one of the most extraordinary paintings of the 19th century at the Royal Academy. 'An Angel Standing in the Sun' is one of a number of square canvasses he produced at this late period in his life and career. Others include 'Shade and Darkness – The Evening of the Deluge', and 'Light and Colour (Goethe's Theory – The Morning after the Deluge – Moses Writing the Book of Genesis'. Apart from their distinctive shape these paintings share an intensity and strangeness, verging on the incoherent and even incomprehensible. As his biographer Anthony Bailey suggests, 'it seems to be an attempt to paint the unpaintable'[10]. It is an example of what Gilles Deleuze and Félix Guattari describe as the third period of Turner's paintings, in which

the canvas turns in on itself, it is pierced by a hole, a lake, a flame, a tornado, an explosion. The themes of the preceding paintings are to be found again here, their meaning changed. The canvas is truly broken, sundered by what penetrates it. All that remains is a background of gold and fog, intense, intensive, traversed in depth by what has just sundered its breadth: the schiz. Everything becomes mixed and confused, and it is here that the breakthrough—not the breakdown—occurs.[11]

The painting shows the eponymous angel, with its arms raised almost consumed by the radiance of the sun, with a number of figures below, all biblical exemplars of murder and betrayal, including Adam and Eve lamenting over the dead body of Abel, Judith standing over the decapitated body of Holofernes,

[9] Martin, Benjamin Ellis, *Old Chelsea. A Summer-day's Stroll* (London: T Fisher Unwin, 1889), 170–73.

[10] Bailey, *Standing in the Sun*, 386.

[11] Deleuze, Gilles, and Félix Guattari, *Anti-Oedipus: Capitalism and Schizophrenia* (London: Athlone Press, 1984), 132.

and Samson and Delilah. The gallery label in Tate Britain describes the angel as Archangel Michael appearing on the Day of Judgement with his flaming sword, though the online catalogue entry quotes John Gage's claim that Turner may have conflated the Angel of the Apocalypse with the Cherubim with flaming sword at the Gate of Paradise, enforcing the Expulsion of Adam and Eve.[12] The catalogue entry from the Royal Academy Exhibition in 1846 contains the following quotation from The Book of Revelations, chapter 19, verses 17 and 18.

And I saw an angel standing in the sun; and he cried with a loud voice, saying to all the fowls that fly in the midst of heaven, Come and gather yourselves together unto the supper of the great God;

That ye may eat the flesh of kings, and the flesh of captains and the flesh of mighty men, and the flesh of horses, and of them that sit on them, both free and bond, both small and great.

(*Revelation*, xix., 17, 18)

In the catalogue there is also a quotation from Samuel Rogers' poem *Voyage of Columbus*, taken from a section the subtitle of which is 'The Flight of an Angel of Darkness',

The morning march that flashes to the sun;
The feast of vultures when the day is done.

It also seems possible that Turner was influenced both by the 12th century *Beatus Apocalypse*, bought by the British Museum in 1840, which depicts an angel in the sun, and the first daguerreotype of the sun taken by Louis Fizeau and Leon Foucault in 1843, and which also showed sunspots and solar flares.

'The Angel Standing in the Sun' was shocking enough for Turner's great defender, the art critic John Ruskin, writing in 1860, to describe it as 'indicative of mental disease'. Strangely though, in 1843 in the first edition of his great work *Modern Painters*, Ruskin had described Turner 'as a prophet of God to reveal to men the mysteries of his Universe, standing, like the great Angel of the Apocalypse, clothed with a cloud, and a rainbow upon his head,

---

[12] Tate Britain, *Joseph Mallord William Turner: The Angel Standing in the Sun*, www.tate.org.uk/art/artworks/turner-the-angel-standing-in-the-sun-n00550, accessed 15 June 2020.

and the sun and stars given into his hand'[13]. This passage was left out of the second edition in 1846, perhaps as a response to *Blackwood's Magazine's* suggestion that it was blasphemous. However Ruskin's characterisation of Turner as the Angel of the Apocalypse suggests that the painting may be seen as a summation by Turner of his career, and perhaps even a kind of self-portrait. Whatever its meaning for Turner, it does appear to be a profoundly pessimistic work, even though it exemplifies his lifelong devotion to the sun. This was more than merely an aesthetic matter. Turner was familiar with the various works of late 18th and early 19th-century literature speculating on the origins of religion in sun worship. He had contact with, and worked for the antiquarian Richard Payne Knight, one of the first to make such speculations. A note in a sketchbook from 1808 about the 'worship of the Lingam or Phallus' suggests that he had almost certainly read Knight's notorious *Account of the remains of the Worship of Priapus latterly existing in Isernia*, in which Knight is 'concerned to identify Priapus with the sun itself, and to understand Greek ideas of creation and generation in terms of light as well of the animal organs'. For all its scholarly pretensions this book led to Knight's social disgrace. This would be of obvious interest to Turner given his solar and erotic preoccupations. In the same sketchbook from 1808 he also jots down a note from Alexander Dow's *History of Hindostan* from 1768, about Brahma creating the world by means of 'a spirit the color of flame', as well as other notes from the works of the orientalist Sir William Jones on the Gods of Greece, Italy and India embodying the notion of Vedic religion as sun worship.

The intensity of light in Turner's paintings was much admired. The sculptor Sir Francis Chantrey once pretended to warm his hands in front of a Turner painting, and then joked that Turner had been commissioned to paint a picture for 'the Sun Fire Office', an insurance company. In *Modern Painters* Ruskin claims that

the works of Turner are peculiarly distinguished from those of all other colourists, by the dazzling intensity, namely, of the light which he sheds through every hue, and which, far more than their brilliant colour, is the real source of their overpowering effect upon the eye, an effect so reasonably made the subject of perpetual animadversion; as if the sun which they represent, were quite a quiet, and subdued, and gentle, and manageable luminary, and never dazzled anybody, under any

---

[13] Ruskin, John, *Complete Works of John Ruskin: Vol. III* (New York; Chicago: National Library Association, 1903), 254.

circumstances whatsoever. I am fond of standing by a bright Turner in the Academy, to listen to the unintentional compliments of the crowd – 'What a glaring thing!' 'I declare I can't look at it!' 'Don't it hurt your eyes?' – expressed as if they were in the constant habit of looking the sun full in the face with the most perfect comfort and entire facility of vision.[14]

Bailey suggests that, as he got older, Turner 'wanted to paint pure light, the ultimate measurement and the final unity'. He speculates that Turner felt dread and despair from the 'horrible pointlessness that formed the backdrop to human striving and to his own compulsion and hard work in light of the fact that the sun would burn up all human achievement and art entirely in seven billion years, leaving our earth a 'dead cinder'.[15]

But perhaps there is something more than merely a love of light and an interest in solar mythology at play in Turner's devotion to the sun. Michel Serres sees Turner as the 'first... the very first' to see that the 18th century world of form and mechanics was being overturned by fire and energetics.[16] In Serres' words Turner is 'not an Impressionist. He is realist, a proper realist', 'the first true genius of thermodynamics'.[17] He understood the forces that were already transforming the world and would continue to do so in unimaginable ways. He anticipates Marx and Engel's great statement in *The Communist Manifesto*, that 'all that is solid melts into air'.[18] Bailey makes him appear darkly prescient. Bailey sees 'The Angel Standing in the Sun' as evidence of Turner's despair. 'He saw mankind ending in an all-consuming fire. It is the merciless light of this solar furnace that blazes behind the Angel'.[19]

In letter 45 of *Fors Clavigera* Ruskin famously claims that Turner said '"The Sun is God"', 'a few weeks before he died with the setting rays of it on his face. He meant it, as Zoroaster meant it; and was a Sun-worshipper of the old breed.'[20] Ruskin recounts his story of Turner's last words in the midst of a polemic about belief that has little to do with Turner, and it seems likely he

14   Ruskin, *Works: Vol III*, 290.
15   Bailey, *Standing in the Sun*, 385–6.
16   Serres, Michel, *Hermes – Literature, Science, Philosophy* (Baltimore: Johns Hopkins University Press, 1982), 56–7.
17   Ibid., 57.
18   Marx, Karl, and Friedrich Engels, *The Communist Manifesto* (New York: Pocket Books, 1964), 63.
19   Bailey, *Standing in the Sun*, 387.
20   Ruskin, *Works:* Vol XXVIII, 147.

embellished a more banal truth. According to Mrs Booth, towards the end of his life Turner often said 'I should like to see the sun again.' Not long before he died, 'he was found prostrate on the floor, having attempted to creep to the window, but in his feeble state had fallen in the attempt'. What is agreed is that on the morning he died the sun did break through clouds and filled his room with brilliant light and that he died 'without a groan'.[21] Bailey writes that 'The vortex had ceased to whirl. All was calm; the roar of the world had ended; and all his contradictions were resolved in silence.'[22]

Turner arrived shortly after the opening of Cremorne Gardens in the World's End. Occupying twelve acres between the King's Road and the river it was one of the great pleasure gardens of the era, a successor to Vauxhall Gardens and Ranelagh Gardens. It offered a number of attractions, including balloon flights, music, dancing, cafes and bars, a shooting gallery, a pagoda and promenades. The history of ballooning in Cremorne and in Chelsea more generally is fascinating. In his account of Chelsea Ballooning Reginald Blunt claims that 'CHELSEA, pre-eminent in so many directions, very narrowly missed being the scene of the first balloon ascent in England.' What is more to the point is that Chelsea was the scene of one of the first aviation accidents, when the French ballooner de Moret, in his haste to beat Vincent Lunardi to make the first ascent from English ground,

attempted to inflate his fire balloon on August 11th; but the fabric unluckily collapsed upon the furnace below and was partially destroyed. The crowd which had assembled chose to regard the whole affair as a fraud, and proceeded to wreck the remaining paraphernalia; and, as a result, the Royal Hospital authorities cancelled the permission which had been granted to Lunardi, who then arranged to make his attempt from the Artillery Ground at Moorfields.[23]

Ballooning took place in the World's End as early as 1837 in Baron de Berenger's 'Stadium for Manly Sports and Exercises', the immediate precursor to the pleasure gardens (its presence there still advertised in the name of Stadium Street). Charles Green famously ascended with a 'lady and a leopard' from the Stadium in that year. In the Gardens themselves numerous perilous ascents took place including one in which 'the

[21] Bailey, *Standing in the Sun*, 397.
[22] Ibid.
[23] Blunt, *Red Anchor Pieces*, 164.

huge Montgolfier [balloon] struck the Cremorne buildings as it rose, amid shrieks of alarm, and finally came to grief at Walthamstow, ripped open by a tree. Cremorne crowds always demanded thrills, and the management did its best to provide them.'[24] In 1865 there was the 'trial of an early dirigible, 200 feet long and 50 in diameter, with hand-driven propellers and a very large rudder; and Delamarne, its inventor, seems to have been able to Manipulate its course to a certain limited extent'.[25] Sir Henry Vivian gave an amazing account of a balloon journey from Cremorne in 1861, which prefigures the views that German bombers would have of the city nearly a century later.

On leaving the gardens we just cleared 'the minarets of the eastern city'; and now lay stretched out before us one of the most wonderful sights I had ever seen. Every street, square, and park of the vast metropolis could be distinctly traced by the lines of gaslight; it was as if a mass of burning sparks had fallen in regular forms and shapes. The river we could easily distinguish by a broad dark line crossed here and there by double lines of lights (where each bridge spanned it). We made out distinctly the King's Road, Eaton Square, Belgrave Square, Hyde Park, the Green Park, Regent's Park, Euston Square Station and the King's Cross Station, the parks being dark patches surrounded with lines of light, and the railway stations bright blazing spots. Altogether the looking down on this mighty city, spread out below us like some gigantic fire map, was most extraordinary and striking.[26]

This journey, as with many others, nearly ended in disaster, just avoiding landing in the sea off the Suffolk coast. The danger of ballooning was one of the factors that led to the closure of the Gardens in the late 1870s, along with the mismanagement of its proprietor and manager, John Baum. According to Blunt, in 1874 a ballooner known as De Groot, the 'Flying Man', fell 300 feet into Sydney Street. The now lightened balloon, containing his fellow ballooner Simmonds, drifted all the way to Essex, coming down on the Great Eastern Railway at Springfield, and just missing a passing train. This catastrophe, in Blunt's words, 'marked the beginning of the end for Cremorne, which had already, under Baum's weak management, become flagrantly and obtrusively disreputable'.[27]

[24] Ibid., 167.
[25] Ibid., 167–8.
[26] Ibid., 171–2.
[27] Ibid., 169.

The proximate cause of the end of the Cremorne was a libel case brought by Baum against Alfred Brandon, minister of the Chelsea Baptist Chapel. Brandon had published a pamphlet in 1876 entitled *The Trial of John Fox, or Fox John, or the Horrors of Cremorne*, signing it anonymously 'A. B. Chelsea'. It took the form of a crude attack in verse on the Cremorne. Baum felt obliged to sue Brandon, and in May 1877, he won a farthing's damages, a nominal victory in one sense but, in reality, the end of the Cremorne. This all took place at the exact same moment as the beginnings of another libel case, that between James McNeill Whistler and John Ruskin, which also ended with the award of a farthing's damages, and which also involved the Cremorne, more on which below.

Despite Baum's victory Brandon's witnesses had presented damaging evidence of the immorality of the Gardens. As this suggests, what the Garden, and the surrounding area, were most famous for was prostitution. In his book on his World's End childhood in the 1930s and 1940s Donald Wheal puts it fairly bluntly; 'Within a few years the World's End had become the greatest brothel not just in London but in Europe, probably even the western world'.[28] It was this, he suggests, that 'impeded the movement of Upper Chelsea into its western corner because the upper-middle classes, even the bohemian artists, were unwilling to live in an area of universal ill-repute'.[29] I discover from Wheal that Lamont Road, the street where I was brought up, was notorious for its brothels in the mid-19th century, with almost as many such establishments as family houses.[30] Disappointingly our own house was not among those mentioned in the report of local objectors to the Gardens. The Cremorne's reputation was salacious enough to have a pornographic magazine named after it. The *Cremorne* magazine, described by Ronald Pearsall as having 'obscene and incredibly incompetent illustrations', was produced in 1882 (though, for some reason, dated as if from 1851), in an edition of 300 at a guinea a copy.[31] That part of Chelsea may also have been made less desirable by the presence of the St George's Union Workhouse on the Fulham Road, the southern end of which looked over Gertrude Street,

[28] Wheal, Donald, *World's End: A Memoir of a Blitz Childhood* (London: Arrow Books, 2006), 125.
[29] Ibid., 133.
[30] Ibid., 127.
[31] Pearsall, Ronald, *The Worm in the Bud: The World of Victorian Sexuality* (Harmondsworth: Penguin, 1971), 464.

part of the Ten Acres Estate. That the World's End should have been so well known for prostitution seems apt. For many of those forced to make their living as prostitutes it may have seemed the end of their world, the last resort.

William Acton's report *Prostitution: Considered in Its Moral, Social and Sanitary Aspects*, first published in 1857, contains a rather lyrical description of visiting Cremorne Gardens to inspect the prevalence of prostitution. He aims to 'state some impressions of travel on a pleasant July evening from Charing-cross to Chelsea. As calico and merry respectability talked off eastward by penny steamers, the setting sun brought westward Hansoms freighted with demure immorality in silk and fine linen.'[32] In the evening the Gardens are 'for the gratification of the dancing public only', which he describes as 'some thousand souls – perhaps seven hundred of them men of the upper and middle class, the remainder prostitutes more or less *prononcées*'. For Acton, the sight is one of 'disillusion' for the middle-aged man, as he 'attempts to fathom former faith and ancient joys, and perhaps even vainly to fancy he might by some possibility begin again'. But, since it was

impossible to enjoy the place after the manner of youth, it was necessary, I suppose, to chew the cud of sweet and bitter fancies; and then so little pleasure came, that the Britannic solidity waxed solider than ever even in a garden full of music and dancing, and so an almost mute procession, not of joyous revellers, but thoughtful, careworn men and women, paced round and round and round the platform as on a horizontal treadmill.[33]

Acton describes any attempt to find 'noise, disorder, debauchery, and bad manners' as a 'Hopeless task!' There was 'barely vivacity, much less boisterous disorder' among the crowd, and almost no soliciting by women, '*with some exceptions*'. It was 'open to the male visitors to invite attention and solicit acquaintance', even though no 'gentlemanly proposition of the kind rebuffed, no courteous offer of refreshment, possibly declined'[34]. Acton also observes that, for the women, 'pretty and quiet dressing was almost universal, and painted cheeks a rarity'. However, he did also note a number

[32] Acton, William, *Prostitution, Considered in Its Moral, Social and Sanitary Aspects in London and Other Large Cities and Garrison Towns, with Proposals for the Control and Prevention of Its Attendant Evils* (London: Cass, 1972), 17.

[33] Ibid.

[34] Ibid., 18.

of physical characteristics, including 'many an etiolated eye and blanched chlorotic complexion, due to want of sun and air and general defibrinization [sic], but not more noticeable than in Mayfair'. Here and there he observed 'a deplorable hectic flush', and 'a great prevalence of sunken eyes, drawn features, and thin lips, resulting from that absorption of cellular tissue which leaves mere threads of muscle stretched upon the skull'. Acton attributes these to 'the dancing mania, which has been the only remarkable change of late years in their mode of life, superadded in many instances to the action of early privations, and perhaps hard work in domestic service and millinery factories, upon naturally delicate or defective organizations'.[35]

Cremorne Gardens features in *The Report of the Select Committee of the House of Lords on the Protection of Young Girls*, which was published in 1882, and which dealt with, among other things, so-called 'white slave trading', or what would be now called sex trafficking'. The Report's appendix gives an account of the case of Jane M----n and Fanny G----r, who both lived in Chelsea, almost certainly the World's End. Fanny recounts meeting Jane on 26 October 1976, at about six o'clock, at 'the corner of Langton-street, opposite Cremorne Gardens'. Jane was with a woman named Mrs Dummer, who asked the girls if they would like to go aboard and be actresses. She then took both girls to meet a man named Klyberg in Soho, who gave them money to obtain birth certificates in their older sisters' names from Somerset House.[36] Klyberg was a notorious white slave trader. The next day they were taken by train and boat to Holland, and, when there, informed that they would be working as prostitutes, which, in their testimony, they claim to have been indignant about. The Select Committee report helped make the case for the passing of the Criminal Law Amendment Act of 1885. The main catalyst for the Act's passing was journalist W. T. Stead's notorious article 'The Maiden Tribute of Modern Babylon', published in the *Pall Mall Gazette* in July 1885, recounting Stead's purchase of thirteen-year-old Eliza Armstrong from her parents. The Act was mainly intended to protect young girls from sexual exploitation, but it also included a clause added as an amendment proposed by the MP Henry Labouchere, which made the vague charge of

[35] Ibid., 18–19.
[36] *Report from the Select Committee of the House of Lords on the Law Relating to the Protection of Young Girls: Together with the Proceedings of the Committee, Minutes of Evidence and Appendix: 9 August 1882*. London: House of Commons, 1882, 134–5.

'gross indecency' between men illegal, rather than buggery, as had been the case before. A decade or so later, Oscar Wilde would be found guilty of gross indecency and sentenced to two years hard labour, the maximum the Act allowed. Unsurprisingly perhaps, given its reputation for prostitution, the World's End was where at least one of the young men with whom Wilde was accused of committing gross indecency, lived. In the trial Wilde denies knowing either the location of 50 Park Walk or 7 Camera Square, where Charles 'Charlie' Parker lodged, both of which were in the World's End. When he was an undergraduate my father met the aged Lord Alfred Douglas, a fact that seems to fold time, and bring what might seem distant strangely close.

Even after the Gardens closed, having had their licence refused, in 1877, the World's End maintained a reputation for prostitution that continued right until the mid-20th century. Wheal describes the continuation of the 'area's honourable tradition' during his childhood in the 1930s, in which 'Many a "Piccadilly Girl" came from World's End [...] perhaps it was the simplicity of the journey. Tuppence on the 22 bus took you, in little more than fifteen minutes, from the World's End pub to the Eros statue in the middle of Piccadilly'.[37] There were even traces of this tradition during my childhood in the 1960s, even as Victorian terraces such as Lamont Road were being rapidly gentrified. Opposite us, on the King's Road, the heir to a Hampshire baronetcy lived, with his wife and children in a house next to that in which two prostitutes lived.

Wheal points out that the closure of the Gardens was devastating for the area, given how many local people it employed or otherwise enabled to earn a living: gardeners, sweepers, entertainers, dancers, waiters, waitresses, cooks, cleaners, grooms, stable boys and, of course, prostitutes. The Gardens had 'generated unaccustomed wealth for what was, as late as 1835, a country district of farmland and nursery orchards'.[38] With its disappearance the houses on both sides of the King's Road, including the 'grander houses in Lamont Road and Hobury Street' were 'turned over to multiple occupancy',[39] which remained the case until the middle of the 20th century. Even when the rest of the borough was colonised by aristocrats and bohemians, the World's End remained obdurately poor, a last redoubt of working class Chelsea. It

[37] Wheal, *World's End*, 4–5.
[38] Ibid., 130.
[39] Ibid., 134.

was only in the late 1950s and 1960s, when my parents and others like them moved there that this changed at all, and much of the ethos of the older World's End remains evident.

Though Turner's apocalypticism and the fact that he lived in a place named the World's End is, of course, coincidental, the area did seem to attract like-minded figures. For example, in 1849, the painter John Martin, then 59, and his family moved into part of Lindsey House, a hundred yards east of Turner and decidedly in the World's End. Martin is best known for his extraordinary, and extraordinarily kitsch, representations of biblical and other scenes, often apocalyptic in nature, and almost always luridly dramatic. At the time of moving to Chelsea, Martin was working on his final great works, sometimes regarded as his masterpieces, the so-called 'Judgement Triptych', based, like Turner's 'Angel Standing in the Sun', on The Book of Revelations. (Fascinatingly, Martin had, at one point in his career, turned away from painting to devote himself to engineering projects, including a scheme to solve London's sewage problems with a riverside embankment. This anticipated Sir Joseph Bazalgette's successful schemes to do the same thing by over thirty years. Among the sections of the Thames on which the Embankment was built was the Chelsea riverside where Martin would reside at the end of his life.)

Turner's sojourn in Chelsea led to the young American James McNeill Whistler coming to live there. He was a provocative artist despite the apparent innocuousness of his subject matter. Whistler had lived in London, on and off, since 1859, and moved to Chelsea in 1862, to 7 Lindsey Row, also part of Lindsey House. It was here that he painted a number of pictures of the River. He was also known to frequent the Cremorne Gardens, and may have picked up women there.

In Chelsea, Whistler met the Greaves brothers, Walter and Henry, who were part of a World's End dynasty of Chelsea boatmen. Their father, Charles, had often been hired by Turner to row him to Battersea. With the Greaves brothers Whistler explored 'the jumble of old inns, stables, wharves and warehouses, and rickety houses held up by ancient pride, which clustered round the dark tower of the old church'.[40] In his account of Whistler's troubled

---

[40] Pocock, Tom, *Chelsea Reach: The Brutal Friendship of Whistler and Walter Greaves* (London: Hodder & Stoughton, 1970), 58.

and troubling relationship with the Greaves brothers, Tom Pocock imagines Whistler's early experiences of the River at Chelsea, and how it would inspire him to paint river scenes. He suggests that Whistler may have seen it from the 'deck of one of the paddle-wheel steamboats which plied between the piers of London and its riverside suburbs' or perhaps when 'he walked along the King's Road, where villas stood in thickets of lilac and laburnum among the shops, saddlers and inns, towards the old village of Chelsea and, like Carlyle, experienced a first view of the river with theatrical intensity'. Pocock continues

One evening, certainly, he must have stood at the western railing of wooden Battersea Bridge and watched the broad sweep of water beginning its southward turn between Battersea, Wandsworth, and Putney on the south bank and Chelsea, Fulham and Hammersmith on the north. From here, from his own rooftop and waterside church at Battersea, Turner had watched and painted the light. Now Whistler experienced and absorbed its subtle changes of mood between the fading of the strong, vivid Canaletto colours of late afternoon – sunlight on blue water and red brick houses – through sunset to twilight, dusk and dark. The magical transformation of the scene – not only of river, fine houses and ancient trees – but of the factories which had begun to cluster along the Battersea shore, had inspired him.[41]

Recalling such a sight enabled Whistler to forgo his usually sardonic wit for a moment and become briefly almost sentimental in describing the experience. 'When the evening mist clothes the riverside with poetry as with a veil and the poor buildings lose themselves in the dim sky and the tall chimneys become campanili and the warehouses are palaces in the night and the whole city hangs before us in the heavens...'[42] It was this that drew him to 'the unfashionable end of Chelsea, where Turner had tried to live incognito; tough, and the nearest London equivalent to the riverside streets of the *Quartier Latin*' in order to establish his own bohemia.[43] Also drawing him to this area was the 'blue river light... the misty, mysterious blue that he had just seen for the first time in oriental art – the prints of Hokusai... and blue and white china – that had just been recognised and embraced by the *avant garde* in Paris and which he was to help introduce to London'.[44]

[41] Ibid.
[42] Ibid.
[43] Ibid., 53.
[44] Ibid., 56.

It seems so appropriate that Whistler should live in a place that later became well-known as a centre for the counterculture. Indeed he is partly responsible for both making Chelsea and the World's End such a centre, and for the counterculture itself. His *fin-de-siecle* dandyism and aestheticism directly prefigure the alternative ethos of the 1960s. It is very easy to imagine him buying clothes in 1960s and 1970s World's End boutiques such as Granny Takes a Trip or Hung on You, or perhaps even Sex. Whistler was possibly the model for the murdered artist Basil Hallward in his sometimes friend and then enemy Oscar Wilde's novel *The Picture of Dorian Gray*. In the novel Lord Henry Wootton murmurs '*fin de siecle*' after a witty but world-weary exchange with his hostess, to which she replies '*fin de globe*'.[45] This is a connection that Thomas Pynchon understands, between the aestheticism of 19th century Chelsea and the murderous wars and psychedelic countercultures of the 20th century. *Gravity's Rainbow* starts with an account of a group of American servicemen billeted in Chelsea, near the River.

Bloat is one of the co-tenants of the place, a maisonette erected last century, not far from the Chelsea Embankment, by Corydon Throsp, an acquaintance of the Rosettis' who wore hair smocks and liked to cultivate pharmaceutical plants up on the roof (a tradition young Osbie Feel has lately revived)...[46]

After a mysterious and unexplained trip to Valparaiso in Chile, Whistler returned with a new idea for painting what he called 'Moonlights' and then 'Nocturnes', invoking music as he had done in calling other pictures 'Symphonies'. The first four of these were exhibited in 1872 in the Dudley Gallery to a mixed reception, with admiration from some critics and confusion and rejection from others. Though some of his Nocturnes were largely appreciated, his more daring experiments in this vein ran against strong resistance. His 'Black and Gold, the Falling Rocket' in particular, along with its companion piece 'Blue and Gold, No 3', were described by critics as 'wilful eccentricities', 'smears and smudges', 'deliberate caprices'. The *Daily News* went so far as to question Whistler's sanity or whether he was just poking fun.

Such responses were mild compared to the painting's most famous critical reception. In the 1870s The Royal Academy was the main public venue

---

[45] Wilde, Oscar, *The Picture of Dorian Gray* (London, New York: Oxford University Press, 1998), 179.

[46] Pynchon, Thomas, *Gravity's Rainbow* (New York: Viking Press, 1973), 5.

for the display of contemporary art. However, the work at the RA was fairly conventional and the Grosvenor Gallery was founded by some rich patrons, principally Sir Coutts Lindsay, in 1877 to show works that were too radical for the RA. It was while visiting the Grosvenor Gallery to see an exhibition of work by Burne-Jones that Ruskin came across 'Nocturne in Black and Gold: The Falling Rocket'. Incensed by what he saw, he wrote a coruscating notice in *Fors Clavigera*.

For Mr. Whistler's own sake, no less than for the protection of the purchaser, Sir Coutts Lindsay ought not to have admitted works into the gallery in which the ill-educated conceit of the artist so nearly approached the aspect of wilful imposture. I have seen, and heard, much of Cockney impudence before now; but never expected to hear a coxcomb ask two hundred guineas for flinging a pot of paint in the public's face.[47]

Whistler sued Ruskin for libel, which became one of the most notorious court cases of the time. The jury decided in Whistler's favour, but awarded him a farthing in damages, which led to his bankruptcy. This wasn't just about personal reputation but was a battle for the soul of art, with Ruskin defending its social responsibilities and value, and Whistler believing in 'art for art's sake'. As Whistler famously declared, 'Art should be independent of all claptrap – should stand alone [...] and appeal to the artistic sense of eye or ear, without confounding this with emotions entirely foreign to it, as devotion, pity, love, patriotism and the like.'[48]

In some senses the trial can be understood to be the beginnings of artistic Modernism. It can also be seen as the point at which art bifurcated, producing two different paths, that which led from aestheticism and art for art's sake to avant-garde autonomy and the other that cleaved to the Ruskinian path of social engagement.

The influence of 'art for art's sake' continued into the mid-20th century. A young art student at Harrow School of Art in the 1960s, recalled that 'The men who taught us were the last gasp of that generation. Things were changing; the introduction of the Dip AD was looking to a future of professionalism in the arts they weren't going to be a part of. They were glorious amateurs,

---

[47] Ruskin, *Works*, Vol. XXIX, 160.

[48] Whistler, James McNeill, *The Gentle Art of Making Enemies* (London: William Heinemann, 1890), 68.

the "art for art's sake" crowd which was on the verge of disappearing.[49] The student's name was Malcolm McLaren, and he would eventually rival Whistler in making the World's End notorious by taking the idea of 'art for art's sake' to its logical, nihilistic conclusion.

Walter Benjamin, in his essay 'The Work of Art in the Age of Its Technological Reproducibility', declared that with 'the advent of truly revolutionary means of production', such as photography, art responds with 'the doctrine of *l'art pour l'art*, that is, with a theology of art. This in turn gave rise to a negative theology, in the form of an idea of "pure" art, which rejects not only any social function of art, but any definition in terms of representational content.' For Benjamin, one result of art for art's sake is the aestheticisation of war as proclaimed and celebrated by Fascism. He quotes Luigi Marinetti's manifesto about the inhuman beauty of war.[50] Futurism inspired the first English avant-garde movement, Vorticism. It was started by Wyndham Lewis, and its name was given to it by the American poet Ezra Pound. Though short-lived, Vorticism did make possible the production of the extraordinary two volumes of *BLAST*, the movement's journal/manifesto. Pound was a great admirer of Whistler, whose work he saw prefiguring his own attempts to radicalise poetic form, particularly in terms of 'Imagism'. This was the name he gave to a form of poetry that had been first developed by T. E. Hulme as a reaction against the vapidities of Georgian verse. Pound coined the term in response to a poem by his ex-fiancée Hilda Doolittle. On the manuscript of the poem he wrote 'H D Imagiste', a description she spent much of her later career trying to avoid.

BLAST declared that 'The Turner Vortex rushed at Europe with a wave of light'.[51] Whistler's comparatively innocuous fireworks explosions are also forerunners of the terrifying fireworks of two world wars, sometimes blazing in the very spot where he painted his nocturnes. As Tom Paton puts it, writing about the *Luftwaffe* raids on London in 1944, and how they are anticipated by the Cremorne fireworks painted by Whistler,

though shorter than the night-long throbbing of bombers' engines of that first autumn, winter and spring, were made in the face of powerful defences, so that the

[49] Gorman, Paul, *The Life and Times of Malcom McLaren: The Biography* (New York: Little Brown, 2020), chap 4, Kindle location 1039.
[50] Benjamin, Walter, *Selected Writings. Vol. 3* (Cambridge, MA: Belknap Press, 2002), 121–2.
[51] Lewis, Wyndham. *Blast* No. 1: *Review of the Great English Vortex*, p. 11, June 20, 1914, 147.

explosions of bombs and the glare of fires were often lost in the noise and light of the defending guns, rockets and searchlights which, over Chelsea, presented a display of pyrotechnics such as the most ambitious impresario at Cremorne can never have imagined in his most fevered moments.[52]

Frances Faviell's description of the air raid of 29 December 1942 on the City of London also invokes the shade of Turner.

The terrifying glow in the sky could be seen all up the river, and it was so light in Chelsea that one could almost see to read in the streets [...] The sky was a bright orange-red – as it is soon after sunrise – indeed it gave the feeling of a sunny dawn in the night. We went up on to our flat roof, which was pretty high and gave a splendid view over London, and it was awful – although beautiful, a brilliant blood-red – the kind of sky in which Turner would have delighted. All I could think of were the words of the round, 'London's burning, London's burning. Fire, fire. Fetch water, fetch water, or all will be lost'...[53]

The Clash evoked this round for their other great London song, 'London's Burning'.

---

[52] Faviell, Frances, *A Chelsea Concerto* (London: Dean Street Press, 2016), chap 18, Kindle.
[53] Ibid.

3

The Sun Shone on the Nothing New

Recently walking through Paulton Square, just off the King's Road, near my parent's house, I noticed a blue plaque on one of the houses, proclaiming that Samuel Beckett had lived there in 1934, in number 48. I had not known that he was, albeit briefly, a Chelsea resident. The plaque only went up in 2016, so perhaps I can be forgiven for my ignorance, though I have read at least one life of Beckett and this detail escaped me then. In the 1930s Paulton Square was, just, in the respectable part of Chelsea, east of Beaufort Street, in SW3.

The blue plaque committee have honoured Beckett's grander London address but he subsequently moved to Gertrude Street, which runs parallel to our street. At that time, as Donald Wheal's memoir of his World's End childhood attests, the area was still working class, and, in his account, fairly rough.[1] Beckett had come to London in early 1934 to undertake psychoanalysis with Wilfred Bion. Paulton Square was not ideal, but it was close to his friend William McGreevy, then living down the road in Cheyne Gardens. After a stay in Dublin in August, he returned to Chelsea but moved to 34 Gertrude Street, in the house of Mr and Mrs Frost, both retired servants. He stayed there for a year, before terminating his analysis and returning to Dublin.

Beckett's first novel, *Murphy*, is partly set in the World's End, though he calls it by the name once used for much of that part of the borough, West Brompton. The second chapter describes the meeting of Murphy with his inamorata, the prostitute Celia, as she describes it to her grandfather, which takes place in the World's End.

She had turned out of Edith Grove into Cremorne Road, intending to refresh herself with a smell of the Reach and then return by Lot's Road, when chancing to glance to

---

[1] Wheal, Donald, *World's End: A Memoir of a Blitz Childhood* (London: Arrow Books, 2006).

her right she saw, motionless in the mouth of Stadium Street, considering alternately the sky and a sheet of paper, a man. Murphy.[2]

I know these streets well. They all still exist, unlike much of that part of Chelsea, and I have often walked there, as Beckett surely did. To get to these places from Gertrude Street, Beckett would have passed through the Ten Acres. Though they would certainly be less well looked after then as now, they would still be familiar to him. Though he would probably not have known it, if he went down Hobury Street, he would have passed the site of what is now the Ten Acres' only blue plaque, that on number seven, celebrating the novelist George Meredith's residence there. No date is given on the plaque for his time there, and nowadays you might be forgiven for thinking he had chosen to live there when he was well known. But in 1858, when he was there, the area was verging on being a slum. Meredith had come to Hobury Street with his son, after the collapse of his marriage. In his life of Meredith, Siegfried Sassoon describes him 'living in lodgings'.[3] I wonder if he was drawn there by the presence of the Moravian burial ground nearby. He spent nearly two years in the Moravian School in Neuwied, near Cologne, in Germany, starting when he was fourteen. According to Sassoon, the 'moral training of the Moravians was a fine thing for him'.[4] The failure of Meredith's marriage led to, among other works, his poetic masterpiece *Modern Love*. For some at least Meredith is a precursor to literary modernism. He was admired by Oscar Wilde, Henry James, D. H. Lawrence, and Virginia Woolf.[5] According to Woolf, Meredith was a 'great innovator' and 'much of our inability to frame any definite opinion of his work comes from the fact that it is experimental'.[6] In Gillian Beer's words, 'Meredith's closest kinship is with James Joyce.'[7]

The connection between Beckett, Joyce and Meredith is actually madly overdetermined. Beckett's first piece of fiction to be published, 'Assumption', is one of his attempts to deal with the influence of Joyce on his thinking. It was published in Maria McDonald and Eugene Jolas' *transition* [sic] magazine in 1929, in the same issue as Joyce's 'Fragments from *Work in Progress*', one

[2] Beckett, Samuel, *Murphy* (London: Calder, 1963), 13.
[3] Sassoon, Siegfried, *Meredith*. London: Constable, 1948, 22.
[4] Ibid., 4.
[5] Beer, Gillian, *Meredith: A Change of Masks: A Study of the Novels* (London: Athlone, 1970), 193.
[6] Woolf, Virginia, *The Essays of Virginia Woolf, vol. 6* (London: Hogarth Press, 1986), 551.
[7] Beer, *Change of Masks*, 193.

of the early instalments of what would become *Finnegans Wake*, as well as Beckett's essay on Joyce and the Wake, 'Dante… Bruno. Vico… Joyce'. It is a kind of detournement in five paragraphs of Joyce's *The Portrait of the Artist as a Young Man*, in particular the scene in which Stephen Dedalus visits a prostitute. The protagonist of Beckett's story masters his turmoil at the prostitute's arrival as follows: 'He thought of George Meredith and recovered something of his calm.'[8] As P. J. Murphy points out, the paragraph that contains that sentence also has an allusion to Meredith's novel *The Egoist*, and the story echoes some of the Victorian novelist's ideas about comedy.[9] Murphy also suggests that the reference to *The Egoist* is an oblique reference to Joyce himself, in that *The Portrait of the Artist as a Young Man* was first published in Harriet Shaw Weaver's literary journal *The Egoist*.[10] Given that Meredith came to the World's End to recover from the trauma that animated much of his fiction, it can be suggested, facetiously perhaps, that the area is the very birthplace of literary modernism. Or at least that the road to Beckett's Modernism goes, quite literally in the World's End, by way of Meredith's experimentation.

In a witty article entitled 'World's End: West Brompton, Turdy and other Godforsaken Holes', Keir Elam makes great play on *Murphy*'s being based partly in the area, and suggests how much the World's End district, 'true to its name', was 'charted by the venues of illness and death', including St Stephen's Hospital (which he would have been able to see from his digs in Gertrude Street), the Royal Brompton Heart Hospital, the Royal Marsden Hospital, and 'midway between the Brompton Cemetery and the Moravian Burial Ground'. (The Royal Marsden Hospital, which specialised in cancer treatment, was where the famous 'Brompton Cocktail', a mixture of morphine, gin and cocaine, given to relieve the most extreme pain in dying patients, was developed.) Elam suggests that it 'is not altogether surprising, therefore, if London, and specifically West Brompton, are associated in Beckett's work from this period with pathology, psychopathology, physical suffering and

---

[8] Beckett, Samuel, *The Complete Short Prose* (New York: Grove Press, 1995), 6.
[9] Murphy, P. J. 'Portraits of the Artist as a Young Critic: Beckett's "Dante… Bruno. Vico. Joyce" and the Rewriting of Joyce in "Assumption"', *Journal of Beckett Studies*, 9, no. 1 (1999): 27–52, 43. *JSTOR*, www.jstor.org/stable/26468346, accessed 20 May 2021.
[10] Ibid., 44.

death'.[11] He describes the short journey made by Celia at the beginning of the book, quoted above, as the 'most cartomanically precise and symbolically loaded localization of place in Beckett, as Celia's intended return trip in search of water, before she is turned to salt near Lot's Road, describes a geographically as well as allegorically impeccable pilgrimage to the very End of the World's End'.[12]

Clearly, as Elam points out, Beckett makes Celia traverse the precise location of Cremorne Gardens. Elam picks up on the name of the World's End Passage, a road that still exists, through or out of which he explored Beckett's obsession with the anal and the excremental. Finally, he proposes that the name of the World's End stands as a metonym of Beckett's bleak nihilism: 'This is the World's End: at once Place and Passage, space and body, discourse and stage, and since its end is its beginning, there is no way out of there, except back to hell.'[13]

Though the roads mentioned above are still there, much has changed in the World's End since Beckett lived there. Perhaps this gives the lie to the novel's marvellously Beckettian opening sentence: 'The sun shone, having no alternative, on the nothing new.'[14] It seems that, to the contrary, everything keeps changing. Or perhaps the nothing new that the sun shines on is that very change, as the only constant. *Murphy* is, of course, a profoundly bleak and nihilistic novel. The only solution for Murphy is annihilation. His gas boiler explodes and sets fire to his bedroom, killing him.[15] After the War, Beckett's work would become ever more apocalyptic, as a response to the Holocaust and to Hiroshima, Nagasaki and the Cold War.

Murphy was published in 1938, a year after another novel set in the World's End, Pamela Hansford Johnson's *World's End*, which gives a sense of the area as a dusty, sad place, in which the main characters are forced to live because of their constrained circumstances. In *England's Dreaming*, his history of Punk, Jon Savage quotes Evelyn Waugh's review of *World's*

---

[11] Buning, Marius, Matthijs Engelberts, and Sjef Houppermans, *Samuel Beckett: Crossroads and Borderlines = L'oeuvre Carrefour/l'oeuvre Limite. Samuel Beckett Today/aujourd'hui*; 6 (Amsterdam: Rodopi, 1997), 165.

[12] Ibid., 166.

[13] Ibid.

[14] Ibid., 177.

[15] Beckett, *Murphy*, 172–3.

End in the short-lived periodical *Night and Day.* Waugh describes the characters as 'economically, politically, socially, theologically, in a mess'.[16] Presumably, Savage sees this state as prefiguring that of the early Punks in the World's End. The plot concerns Arnold Brand and his wife, Doris. She has a job in a shop in Chelsea, and he is sporadically employed. The humiliation of his mostly unemployed status leads him to have an affair with a neighbour. His wife dies in childbirth and, in the end, he goes to fight in the Spanish Civil War.

Perhaps because the down-at-heel nature of the area was familiar enough to readers, there are not many descriptions of the World's End in *World's End.* However, in his wartime diaries, Charles Ritchie, the Canadian diplomat, and lover of the novelist Elizabeth Bowen, often visited friends in the World's End. In one entry he captures the depressed quality of the area.

9 July 1939. Sunday

Took a solitary walk by the river at World's End – swans making scanty meals in the mud flats craning their necks after filthy crusts and paddling about on their clumsy snow-shoes. In Chelsea Old Church elderly women with wispy hair were squatting on their haunches to read the inscriptions at the base of the monuments.

The dreariness of these slum streets on a Sunday afternoon is something almost supernatural. The pubs are still closed, but here and there a small magazine and sweet shop is open, the overcrowded little interiors give some colour for the eye – bright, shiny, flesh colours of nudes on the backs of magazines – the yellows and red of candies in glass jars.

At World's End a Salvation Army band was practising in a drizzle of rain – trumpet notes and the tumpity-tumpity tune – the women of the Army in their bonnets seemed a piece of Victorian London.[17]

There is one passage in *World's End* that offers a rather lyrical view of the river and what could be seen from it, which is particularly interesting because of its description of the newly built Battersea Power Station. It would be the location of the view seen from Turner's house, by Whistler in Cremorne Gardens, and by Beckett's Celia, if she walked in the opposite direction to that of Stadium Street.

---

[16]   Savage, Jon, *England's Dreaming: Sex Pistols and Punk Rock* (London: Faber & Faber, 1992), 4.

[17]   Ritchie, Charles, *Siren Years: Undiplomatic Diaries, 1937–1945* (London: Macmillan, 1974), 36.

It was past eleven, and the pavements were phosphorescent with recent rain. Crossing the right-angle of the King's Road, Brand turned into Milman Street and on to the embankment, where he went down the steps by Battersea Bridge to the small esplanade. The sky was massed with brown cloud, animal shapes on the drift. It was high tide. Under the bridge and far away where the faint factories rose on the fainter gloom, the lights dropped down into the flow, shimmering ribbons of yellow and red. A barge swept up the satin river, feathering cold waves, rattling the tethered boats one against the other. A lamp glowed high in the four chimneys. Far away to the left, on the south side of the river, was the new power station, brilliant and false as the floodlit fort and kraal at the Aldershot Tattoo. The white plumes floated into saffron, into cinnamon, into invisibility. Along the embankment the lessening lamps stretched in a semicircle, each one a minor moon.[18]

What is perhaps most interesting is, that despite being published in 1937, it gives a vivid sense of the inevitability of war as it was experienced in the late 1930s. All through the book the approach of war is discussed, feared, dismissed, but always somewhere in background. One of Doris' fellow shopgirls, whose boyfriend is a territorial, a member of the volunteer reserve force of the Army, claims that

'E says we may get it at any time, and it won't be like the last war, neither. 'E says they can shell London from the coast of France and we'd all be wiped out in a few hours. My boy says 'e could just do with a drop of war. Says it's coming sooner or later, anyway, and the quicker we get it the better. 'E makes me sick. I tell 'im I'll stop going with 'im if 'e talks like that.[19]

That the War is coming is presaged by the outbreak of the Spanish Civil War, for which, from 'the drawers labelled 1914–18 came the old reports of raped nuns, of children violated'.[20] There is also the more immediate presence of Fascism in London itself. At one point a 'bonny girl in a black shirt came into the shop. Molly, who was a Jewess, made a point of serving her.'[21] Ma Hogben, the Brand's landlady talks of a 'big meeting at the Albert 'All yesterday. Them Fascist fellows wanting to go for the Jews again'. Brand's drinking companion, the alcoholic musician and would-be Communist Party member McDonald even goes to that meeting, and gets beaten up and thrown out

---

[18]   Johnson, Pamela Hansford, *World's End. A Novel* (London: Chapman & Hall, 1937), 83–4.
[19]   Ibid., 61.
[20]   Ibid., 185.
[21]   Ibid., 65.

for barracking the speakers and their 'Anti-Semitic rant'.[22] Later in the book Brand witnesses a Fascist meeting in the World's End itself.

One night there was a meeting at World's End, where a boy with aqueous almond eyes screamed against the Jews. 'When we're in power there won't be a dirty Jew left in England. We'll kick 'em back where they came from and England'll be a place fit for the English. Who subsidizes the Red traitors? The Jews. Who sweats the workers? The Jews. Tell me this, where were the Jews in 1914?'

'Where were you?' a voice inquired. 'In nappies?'[23]

After Doris' death during her labour, Brand finds he is no longer able to stomach his normal day-to-day existence and job, and resolves to join his Communist friend MacDonald in the International Brigade in Spain. As he takes his leave of his landlady Ma Hogben, she holds out the paper. '"Mr 'Ogben always used to say we'd get given gasmasks. 'Ere's a Blackburn factory making fifty thousand a week, it says, to be stored up for us".' Brand tries to reassure her. '"It may not come, Ma," he told her, trying to joke. "Aren't I doing my best to prevent it?"'[24]. Even though it was written and published before the outbreak of the War, the book captures the sense of impending catastrophe and apocalypse.

The First World War saw the first concerted attacks on civilian targets by the Germans, with the Zeppelin and Gotha raids. As V. S. Pritchett put it in his book on London,

One sprightly morning in the early summer of 1916 ten or twenty small German bombers appeared over London, looking like gnats.... They dropped a few bombs, killed some horses in Billingsgate and turned Cloth Fair, Cheapside, and Aldersgate into rivers of broken glass... On this Morning Great Britain ceased to be an island. London, for centuries invulnerable behind its nasty seas and fogs, was at last exposed to attack from Europe.[25]

Paul Saint-Amour argues that this produced a sense of tense anticipation during the interwar period and a sense that the inevitable next war would result in far more cataclysmic attacks on civilians.[26]

[22] Ibid., 115–17.
[23] Ibid., 181.
[24] Ibid., 314.
[25] Pritchett, V. S., and Evelyn Hofer, *London Perceived* (London: Chatto & Windus, 1962), 166.
[26] Saint-Amour, Paul K., *Tense Future: Modernism, Total War, Encyclopedic Form* (London, Oxford: Oxford University Press, 2015).

Writing in the 1930s and clearly anticipating the war to come, Virginia Woolf describes a Zeppelin Raid in 1917 in her late novel *The Years*. She describes with beautiful delicacy the tensions of listening to an air raid happening above the heads of the novel's protagonists, who have retreated to a basement room to finish their supper. They chart the proximity of the Zeppelins by the relative loudness of the defence guns. Woolf recounts the anxious waiting as the raid gets closer, then retreats. She captures the terror of nothing happening, of 'profound silence', followed by 'a violent crack of sound, like the split of lightning the sky'.[27]

The experience of the Zeppelin raids in the First War, as well as that of the bombing of civilians in the Spanish Civil War and elsewhere, led to highly pessimistic expectations for the next war. In his book on the 'bombing war' Richard Overy quotes the philosopher Cyril Joad, writing in 1937.

Within a few days of the outbreak of the next war it seems reasonable to suppose that the gas and electric light systems will have broken down, that there will be no ventilation in the tube tunnels, that the drainage system will have been thrown out of gear and sewage will infect the streets, that large parts of London will be in flames, that the streets will be contaminated with gas, and that hordes of fugitives will spread outwards from the city, without petrol for their cars or food for their stomachs, pouring like locusts over the country in the hope of escaping the terror from the air.[28]

Similarly, Lewis Mumford, writing in 1938, predicted the effects of such bombing.

The sirens sound. School-children, factory hands, housewives, office workers, one and all don their gas masks. Whirring planes overhead lay down a blanket of protective smoke. Cellars open to receive their refugees. Red Cross stations to succor the stricken and the wounded are opened at improvised shelters: underground vaults yawn to receive the gold and securities of the banks: masked men in asbestos suits attempt to gather up the fallen incendiary bombs. Presently the anti-aircraft guns sputter. Fear vomits: poison crawls through the pores, Whether the attack is arranged or real, it produces similar psychological effects. Plainly, terrors more devastating and demoralizing than any known in the ancient jungle or cave have been re-introduced into modern urban existence. Panting, choking, spluttering, cringing, hating, the dweller in Megalopolis dies, by anticipation, a thousand deaths. Fear is thus fixed into routine: the constant anxiety over war produces by itself a collective

---

27 Woolf, Virginia, *The Years* (New York: Harcourt, Brace & Co, 1937), 288–91.
28 Overy, Richard, *The Bombing War: Europe 1939–1945* (London: Allen Lane, 2013), 27.

psychosis comparable to that which active warfare might develop. Waves of fear and hatred rise in the metropolis and spread by means of the newspaper and the news-reel and the radio program to the most distant provinces.[29]

As Joad and Mumford foresaw, and against Brand's hopes in Johnson's novel, the War did come, and with it the Blitz. Though the overwhelming terror anticipated by Joad and Mumford never quite occurred, the experience of bombing was clearly traumatising. The idea that the British exhibited an exceptional 'Blitz Spirit' is a convenient national myth that gets exploited egregiously every time this country suffers a crisis (most recently Brexit and Covid). Rose Gamble, who lived with her family in the Guinness Buildings in the World's End, described the fear engendered by the increasing inevitability of war when Jewish refugee girls came to her school. She had watched newsreels about atrocities against Jews in Germany, but it seemed nothing for her personally to worry about. However, '[S]eeing Elsa and Gudrun – who had been driven from their homes – every day at school made me realise what terrible and wicked things were happening.'[30] This sense of foreboding was made worse by Oswald Mosley's rallies and the clashes between Blackshirts and communists that were taking place. Her mother tried to reassure her that the 'coppers will soon sort all them rowdies out', but

I did worry though, more than that, I became really frightened. Dodie and I went to the pictures one Saturday afternoon, and for sixpence each we sat through two films, a cartoon, the organist and a newsreel. In addition to all this, they screened a recruitment film for the Territorial. It was called 'The Gap', and it showed what would happen if the gap in our anti-aircraft defences were not filled by urgently needed volunteers. I sat and watched an aeroplane bombing a row of defenceless little houses over and over again. The walls and windows crumbled in the blasts and roofs fell into the rooms. Nothing could be done to stop the aeroplane, and I just could not believe it. It couldn't be as dreadful as that![31]

Despite her mother's assurances that 'they', 'God... an' the newspapers, an' the Gover'ment' would make sure that the War would not happen, it did, and, in doing so, 'swept away life as we had known it and it disappeared for ever'.[32] She describes the first bombs to land in the World's End.

[29] Mumford, Lewis, *The Culture of Cities* (New York: Harcourt, Brace & Jovanovich, 1970), 275.
[30] Gamble, Rose, *Chelsea Child* (London: BBC Books, 1982), 191.
[31] Ibid.
[32] Ibid., 192.

Joey had only just arrived home on leave on the night the buildings were bombed. Mum was making him a cup of cocoa when the whistling crunch of the bombs fell in a line across the four blocks. Many of our neighbours were killed, but Dad staggered through the smoke and dust into the glare of the burning gas main in his long underpants, clutching two bits of salvage – the canary in its cage and a bottle of beer.[33]

Echoing her description of a Zeppelin raid in *The Years*, Virginia Woolf describes an air raid in her essay 'Thoughts on Peace in an Air Raid'. The essay starts 'The Germans were over this house last night and the night before that. Here they are again. It is a queer experience, lying in the dark and listening to the zoom of a hornet which may at any moment sting you to death.'[34] Later on, 'The drone of the planes is now like the sawing of a branch overhead. Round and round it goes, sawing and sawing at a branch directly above the house.'[35] Then, '[A] bomb drops. All the windows rattle. The anti-aircraft guns are getting active. Up there on the hill under a net tagged with strips of green and brown stuff to imitate the hues of autumn leaves, guns are concealed. Now they fire all at once.'[36] She continues:

The sound of sawing overhead has increased. All the searchlights are erect. They point at a spot exactly above this roof. At any moment a bomb may fall on this very room. One, two, three, four five, six... the seconds pass. The bomb did not fall. But during those seconds of suspense all thinking stopped. All feeling, save one dull dread, ceased. A nail fixed the whole being to one hard board. The emotion of fear and of hate is therefore sterile, unfertile. Directly that fear passes, the mind reaches out and instinctively revives itself by trying to create. Since the room is dark it can create only from memory. It reaches out to the memory of other Augusts – in Bayreuth, listening to Wagner; in Rome, walking over the Campagna; in London. Friends' voices come back. Scraps of poetry return. Each of those thoughts, even in memory, was far more positive, reviving, healing the creative than the dull dread made of fear and hate.[37]

Finally,

The searchlights, wavering across the flat, have picked up the plane now. From this window one can see a little silver insect turning and twisting in the light. The guns go pop

[33] Ibid.
[34] Woolf, Virginia, *Collected Essays. Vol. 6* (London: Hogarth Press, 1966), 242.
[35] Ibid., 243.
[36] Ibid.
[37] Ibid.

pop pop. Then they cease... At least the guns have stopped firing. All the searchlights have been extinguished. The natural darkness of a summer's night returns.[38]

The attritional anxiety engendered by the air raids in the Blitz is captured in Charles Ritchie's wartime diaries. For example here is his entry for 26 August 1940.

There go the sirens again! I do not know what will be left of our nerves after a winter of this. First the wail announcing impending doom. Then the city holds its breath as the last dying sound of the siren fades and we wait. Of course everyone is calm enough on the surface, but one gets jumpy at sudden noises. At first raids were exciting and frightening. Now they are getting unpleasant, risky and tiring.[39]

On 13 September he records his feelings about

A week of air raids. Our ears have grown sharp for the sounds of danger – the humming menace that sweeps from the sky, the long whistle like an indrawn breath as the bomb falls. We are as continually alive to danger as animals in the jungle.[40]

He then alludes to T. S. Eliot's Prufrock.

During a raid the silent empty streets wait for the shock like 'a patient etherised upon a table'. The taxis race along carrying their fares to the shelters. A few pedestrians caught out in the streets make their way with as much restraint as possible to the nearest shelter, keeping an eye open for protection – for friendly archways. They try to saunter but long to run.[41]

In his entry for 6 March 1941, Ritchie reflects on a conversation with the chauffeur of some friends, who was astonished by 'the way those old houses fall down so easy'. He recounts the destruction of a big aristocratic house where his mother had worked, and which, despite seeming 'such a fine well-built old house' was now 'just a pile of rubble'.[42]

Although his tone was practical I thought I could catch an undernote of dismay queerly mixed with relief. That great gloomy house may have hung on in his memory since childhood. It must have seemed as permanent as a natural feature of the landscape

[38] Ibid.
[39] Ritchie, *Siren Years*, 63.
[40] Ibid., 65.
[41] Ibid.
[42] Ibid., 93.

and clothed in dim prestige. Now brutally it vanishes. This sudden destruction of the accustomed must shake people out of the grooves of their lives. This overnight disappearance of the brick and mortar framework of existence must send a shock deep into the imagination. These high explosions and incendiaries are like the falling stars and blazing comets – noted of old as foretelling great changes in the affairs of man.[43]

Ritchie gives a vivid account of an air raid he witnessed in the World's End in October 1940. He was in the area visiting his old Oxford friend Frank Ziegler and his wife, Margery, in their house in Blantyre Street.

They are still living in this dangerous outpost near Lot's Road Power Station. It is the only street in World's End which has not yet been bombed. Their house, like the others, is a little square box of bricks of the type that falls down when a bomb comes anywhere near it. On this occasion the bomb fell in the next street. We all rushed out and I found myself helping to remove the people from the remains of three bombed houses. There was a large crater where one house had been, and in the centre of the crater were Margery and a doctor, trying by the aid of a torch to see who was injured and how badly. People were being pulled and pushed up the sides of the crater, to be taken off to the nearest pub to wait for the ambulance to come. These were the 'shock' cases – an old man who let them make an injection in his tattooed arm without question or even tension of his muscles – an old distraught mother gasping for breath and trying to collect what had happened to her – a tall scraggy daughter, her cheeks blackened with smoke powder and her hair wisping wildly about her head…. By now the sky was an ugly 'fire pink' glow from a row of houses burning noisily in a street nearby.[44]

Despite the proximity of the Lots Road Power Station, the Ziegler's house clearly survived. Ritchie describes spending an evening there in May 1941.

I shall remember that funny little converted box of a house and [Margery Ziegler's] window-boxes of dust-laden pink carnations and blue front door and the little drawing-room full of flowers and the slum neighbours going to and from the pub with caps pulled down over their eyes, and the river at the end of the street. She loves the house and has stayed in it all through the blitz, although it is only a box of bricks, and it is just luck that it has not already collapsed about her ears with all the land-mines that have fallen around it – for it is almost under the shadow of Lots Road Power Station. One of the principal German objectives. If there is an air raid I always think first of her sleeping on a mattress down in the passage below the level of the area railings, quite sure that she is not going to leave her own house to live anywhere else.[45]

43 Ibid.
44 Ibid., 74–5.
45 Ibid., 104.

The raid described by Ritchie may be the same mentioned by Frances Faviell in *Chelsea Concerto* – her book on the Blitz in Chelsea – on 16 October

when seven bombs fell on Chelsea, severing a water main and flooding all the basements between Milmans Street and Seaton Street, so that when the poor shelterers emerged in the early hours of the morning they were met by wardens and police whose job it was to evacuate them all from their flooded homes to Rest Centres.[46]

In her account she gives a sense of how that part of Chelsea was then regarded.

Riley Street was completely demolished at this time, but as everyone had been evacuated from it the bomb was really a blessing, for this street had long been an eyesore and a terrible slum. I had once lived in a small cottage in Apollo Place, into which Riley Street runs, and had been astounded at the cleanliness of the children after having been shown the homes from which they came.[47]

Chelsea suffered a great deal of destruction in the Blitz. Faviell records that

Chelsea has a proud record of her citizens in the days of the Germans' Blitz on London. They acquitted themselves magnificently in the Battle of the Bombs, emerging at the end of the war with a splendid list of decorations and awards for their gallantry under fire. The little borough was the third most heavily bombed in London. Of her war-time population no less than 2,099 were bomb casualties, 534 of these being fatal. This meant roughly that one in every fourteen persons in Chelsea was killed or injured. Her citizens, many of them distinguished in the world of art and letters, many of them ordinary, unpretentious workers at everyday jobs, joined together in a unanimously determined effort and worked magnificently in Civil Defence to battle with the bombs.[48]

Faviell recounts the terrifying strangeness of the bombing, such as she experienced during a raid in which

instead of darkness following the sunset it remained light – a curious yellow-orange light almost like sunrise. We went up on the roof and saw a terrifying sight far off down the river. A monstrous fire was obviously blazing and its gloriously reflected flames in the river cast the glare upwards and right over London. It was absolutely terrifying! As

---

[46] Faviell, Frances, *A Chelsea Concerto* (London: Dean Street Press, 2016), chap 13, Kindle.
[47] Ibid.
[48] Ibid.

it got later the bombs began whistling down everywhere – and more and more planes came droning over dropping them.[49]

She describes the 'continuous loud whistling whooshing sounds followed by dull, ominous, heavy thuds which shook the houses and then came several loud, reverberating explosions which shook the very ground of the streets'.[50] Faviell's book contains vivid and horrifying descriptions of the aftermath of bombing, such as the painstaking rescue of a twelve-year old girl from the basement of a bomb-wrecked house, taking seven and a half perilous hours. The girl had already been buried alive for four days and nights and was the sole survivor of the blast, her mother and brother both having been killed. Faviell also recounts the grim sights of dismembered bodies after raids, and her own experiences in having to put the pieces together again in preparation for burial.[51]

Another small book about the Blitz in Chelsea, A. S. G. Butler's *Recording Ruin*, is something of a forgotten masterpiece, and a fascinating eyewitness account of the effects of the bombing, particularly vivid, having been written at the time. Butler, an architect who worked with Edwin Lutyens, was in his fifties when the war broke out. He had served with distinction in the First World War, and sought to contribute to the war effort in the second by becoming a ruin-recorder, making inventories of bomb-damaged houses, mostly in Chelsea. What he describes as the 'average house of the district', 'about eighty years old, neat and ladylike in front, plain and sometimes squalid at the back' is pretty much the kind of house in which I was bought up. These houses are what constitute 'the heart of the place [...] in and around King's Road, from Sloane Square to the World's End'.[52]

Especially towards the latter, where life still hums in and out of the little shops, and through the shabby, inconvenient, blitzed and tattered houses – all much alike from Wellington Square to Tadema Road. Three storeys and a basement; the bulge at the back; a strip of garden; a slate roof with leaking valley in the middle; often a pillared porch, steep steps and some crumbling stucco enrichments. Most of Chelsea lives in these, quite patiently. I've been through hundreds – almost thousands. A few have gone. Quite a lot are wrecked and hardly any have escaped unwounded.[53]

---

[49] Ibid., chap 11, Kindle.
[50] Ibid.
[51] Ibid., chap 12, Kindle.
[52] Butler, A. S. G., *Recording Ruin* (London: Constable & Co., 1942), 144.
[53] Ibid.

He gives an account of the devastation wrought by bombing on one such house.

The floor and most of the furniture were entirely covered with broken glass and pow-dered plaster, mixed. Bits of glass were sticking in the back wall of the room. One of them jagged my sleeve. The marble surrounding the fire was lying on a heap of soot from the chimney; and the overmantel had thrown its vases under the sofa oppo-site. All the middle of the ceiling had come down, including the usual heavy plaster ornament and covered gas bracket. They were in a heap on the table, mixed with harmonium music and cake. The thin partition-wall next the hall had burst open and knocked two fat stuffed birds off a shelf. The windows were voids with ragged edges and a lot of the recent rain had blown through them, soaking the armchair which had since frozen stiff. Perhaps the dreariest things of all were the torn blinds, hanging in shreds with dried mud from the road on them.[54]

He continues to recount the damage to the rest of the house, with the 'kit-chen and other back rooms [...] merely squalid. A horrid mixture of glass and broken chairs, old pots, unwashed dishes, and a clock lying face downwards on a bowler hat'.[55] Another house 'deeply impressed' itself on his memory for a more disturbing reason. He could not work out why, despite the com-paratively light damage, the house was in a 'state of appalling devastation', 'as if a madman had rampaged through all the rooms'. All the cupboards and drawers had been wrenched open, and their contents strewn all over, the books flung from the bookcases, and ornaments smashed. Butler later discovers that the house had been looted. 'That, I thought, is quite the foulest thing in all this defiling barbarism.'[56] The most disturbing description in the book is that of a corpse glimpsed at the back of a bombed house, awaiting collection.

There – lying on the wrecked paving – was a woman's body, wrapped in a blanket and tied with string, pending removal. I could not see her face. Only her feet and ankles showed at the end of the bundle – neat and pretty ankles with silk stockings and nice shoes. But the feet to me seemed somehow the wrong way round... and I clutched a door and kicked it hard and felt – not physically sick nor horrified – but a sharp sensa-tion of despair.[57]

---

[54] Ibid., 16–17.
[55] Ibid., 17.
[56] Ibid., 145–6.
[57] Ibid., 64–5.

Donald Wheal's book on growing up in the World's End in the 1930s and during the War gives a vivid sense of its excitement and its sheer terror. On the one hand, he describes the freedom with which his gang and he explored the bombed houses in the area, saying 'we climbed tumbledown garden walls and ducked under shattered back doors to enter a dusty, cracked and broken windowed wonderland'.[58]

We found rooms with lop-sided antelope heads mounted on the walls. We found military portraits and racks of ancient gramophone records, piles of books, comfortable, though battered, cane armchairs, hammered brass Arab tables... old secretaries... old letters tied in bundles with silk ribbon... browning photographs... Each Saturday we were presented with an *embarrass de richesses*.[59]

Much to the envy of Wheal and his gang, a rival group are rumoured to have found a 'Chinese den with silk robes and magnificent curved swords (I think we were thinking of Japanese swords), and Chinese writing on scrolls and pipes'.[60] Wheal describes the intricate 'offices' his gang would assemble in one of the fifty or more flats in the abandoned Ashburnham Mansions, offering an almost utopian vision of freedom from adult constraints and limits, though also coming close to the looting that so appalled Butler.

Wheal is damning about the few Chelsea bohemians and artists he encounters during the War. He suggests that they were initially reluctant to join the war effort, and were slow to sense or understand the nature of real political danger, and were most concerned, 'in a heightened state of anguish about possible damage to their way of life' and 'often absurdly prepared to believe their modest efforts with the paintbrush justified their withdrawal from the war'. Wheal reserves particular scorn for 'Richard, surname no longer remembered', who was 'insufferably rude' to Wheal's father when the latter worked in the boiler room at Whitelands, up the King's Road.[61] Wheal does concede that Chelsea artists did go to the war, but claims there were exceptions, such as Richard. Whatever the truth of his assertions, it is clear that working class and bohemian Chelsea did not mix. In this regard, it is instructive to juxtapose Wheal's memoirs of the Blitz with Joan Wyndham's

---

[58] Wheal, Donald, *World's End: A Memoir of a Blitz Childhood* (London: Arrow Books, 2006), 239.
[59] Ibid., 240.
[60] Ibid.
[61] Ibid., 224.

wartime diaries, published in 1985 as *Love Lessons*. Wyndham, seventeen when the war started, moved with her mother from Berkshire to Milborne Grove, just off the Fulham Road, very near to the borders of the World's End. The world of would-be artists and actors she encounters is markedly different to that of Wheal's working-class Chelsea, despite their occupying more or less the same geography.

Wyndham captures the fear engendered by the bombing as the Blitz started. On the first night of the Blitz, her fear that each moment may be her last leads to her losing her virginity to the handsome Richard. (It's tempting to speculate whether this is the same Richard encountered by Wheal.) Other episodes also involve a mixture of fear and thrill. A couple of days later, her diary describes the experience of a 'loud crash followed by an explosion that shook the room', which makes her feel 'both thrilled and stimulated'.

As soon as the all-clear went we strode off to find the crater. It was in Bramerton Street, a whole house destroyed, the air full of smoke and dust, and all the inhabitants of that part of Chelsea beetling around the barricades like insects disturbed, pansies and lesbians and all.[62]

The reason for this now rather offensive invocation of 'pansies and lesbians' would be obvious to sophisticated Chelsea residents at the time. Bramerton Street was the location of the Gateways Club, mentioned earlier. At the time it was not specifically a lesbian club but welcomed outsiders of all sorts. Wyndham also admits to the crushing fear of the bombing. On Tuesday 15 October she writes that

This is certainly hell and no mistake. Hardly a minute's pause between each load of bombs and each one sounding as if it's going to hit our house. Gosh, it's awful; this is the heaviest bombing we've had since the war began, the absolute poetry of destruction. I sit in my shelter in my navy-blue siren suit, reciting Rupert Brooke 'If I should die think only this of me/That some corner of the Fulham Road-'.[63]

Donald Wheal describes the sheer terror of German bombing, finishing the book with a description of the bombing raid on what the Germans called the *Kesselhaus und Maschinenhalle* – the Power Station, in Lots Road, under which Ritchie's friends, the Zieglers lived – on 23 February 1944. That night,

[62] Wyndham, Joan, *Love Lessons: A Wartime Diary* (London: Heinemann, 1985), 149.
[63] Ibid., 171–2.

he recalls, the air raid warning was sounded at 10.07. After about twenty minutes, it seemed as if the raid was passing. However, outside their flat the presence of white and green flares encircling the World's End would have told them that a targeted attack on the power station was underway. At one point everyone in the flat stops to listen to 'the uneven rasp of bomber engines in the brief gasps between AA shells'. This is the point at which they knew that 'these particular bombers were for us'. All over there are 'people stiffened as the first 2,000lb high-explosive bomb screamed down and exploded in Upcerne Road, between us and Lots Road power station. Seven of my mother's girlhood neighbours were killed outright.'[64]

Wheal describes the waiting for the bomb to explode, maybe only a couple of seconds, though 'I can feel that wait today' and then the actual explosion, the effort of trying to breathe when the shock waves have sucked every millimetre of breath from your lungs', and the sheer panic it brings, especially with the knowledge that one more such explosion 'will detach breath from lungs for ever. And bring hundreds of tons of brick and rubble down on your head.'[65] After the explosion Wheal's father takes the family to Whitelands, the block of flats where he worked, and which had replaced the school which had briefly been Mosley's headquarters. What confronts them is hellish and apocalyptic.

In the middle of the King's Road a gas flame rose high above the buildings, seventy or eighty foot high, from a boiling, water-filled bomb crater. Beyond it we recognised the line of the King's Road, where perhaps twenty houses were piled rubble or burning ruins.[66]

For Chelsea resident Cyril Connolly, the bombing of the borough was a particular tragedy. In an article for *Horizon* in 1943, he suggests that it 'is sad on a spring evening to walk through the bombed streets of Chelsea'. For Connolly, this is in not true of other districts of London, such as Bayswater, or Kensington

which seem to have been created for destruction, where squares and terraces for half a century have invited dilapidation, where fear and hypocrisy have accumulated

[64] Wheal, *World's End*, 321.
[65] Ibid.
[66] Ibid., 327.

through interminable Sunday afternoons until one feels, so evil is the atmosphere of unreality and suspense, that had it not been for the bombers, the houses would have been ignited one day of their own accord by spontaneous combustion. Behind the stucco porches and the lace curtains the half-life of decaying Victorian families guttered like marsh-gas.[67]

By contrast, 'Chelsea in the milky green evening light, where the church where Henry James lies buried is a pile of red rubble, where tall eighteenth-century houses with their insides blown out gape like ruined triumphal arches, is a more tragic spectacle.'[68] For Connolly, Chelsea is a vanished paradise in which 'there existed a fine appreciation of books and pictures, and many quiet work-rooms for the people who made them'.[69] Chelsea was one of the 'last strongholds of the cultivated haute bourgeoisie in which leisure, however ill-earned, has seldom been more agreeably and intelligently made use of'. He concludes on an elegiac note: 'Now when the sun shines on these sandy ruins and on the brown and blue men working there one expects to see goats, and a goatherd in a burnous – *sirenes in delubris voluptatis*" – pattering among them.'[70]

Interestingly, there are few novels written at that time that tries to use the resources of poetic modernism to capture the strangeness of the war. One exception is James Hanley's *No Directions*, published by Faber in 1943, and set in Chelsea, near the River. It is a very strange, and nearly unreadable work, though fascinating in its attempt to capture the madness of the Blitz. It is set in a rooming house and involves a series of surreal descriptions of the lives of its residents, who include the artist Clem, his wife, Lena, who has 'cancer of the heart', Richard, who tries to keep a sense of order in the madness, and the outsider, Mr Johns, the drunken sailor, who is given shelter in the house by another resident. The book also features an introduction by Henry Miller, who is effusive in his praise, describing it as 'one long roar of oceanic trash drowned in a green jungle of cracked ice, dementia, hysteria, vomit, flames and hallucination'. Miller describes the plot and style of the book as a reflection of the situation it reflects upon.

---

[67] Connolly, Cyril, *The Condemned Playground. Essays: 1927–1944* (London: Routledge, 1945), 272.
[68] Ibid.
[69] Ibid.
[70] Ibid., 274.

Everything happens in a house in London during an air raid. It is a mad-house, an exact replica of the outer mad-house which is the world, only this mad-house is in the mind, and only a cataclysm can put an end to the crazy clock-work. The style which Hanley employs to register this fantastic *dégringolade* is superbly suited to his needs. One feels that the author is not merely in the seemingly meaningless suite of events which are piled on one another pell-mell but in the débris and bric-a-brac of the mind itself. It is the language of utter disorder and demoralisation, maintained as rigidly and consistently through-out as is Kafka's in the nightmare he inhabits.[71]

Some of the descriptions in the book are extraordinarily vivid and poetic. At one point, when walking to the River, Lena sees a barrage balloon descend to the ground.

She looked, she saw a balloon coming down, slow, elephantine movements; lost, isolated movement in a still world, you had to watch. It was like something out of another time, you thought of an undiscovered sphere, a new kind of mammal. Coming, lower, lower. She was at the corner of a short stretch, she knew it would descend here, she had to see this touch ground, she knew not why. But it must touch ground. She looked up; she saw its shape. She hoped that round a corner, out of a hole, down a street, across a road, she might see a face, and she saw this.

Lower, so reaching roof level, lower and suspended between houses, then touching ground. Something enormously swollen, a bugaboo. She watched it settle, shiver, it was still. Gigantic rubber ears, they looked like ears.[72]

This is Clem witnessing a raid.

Every level of air hurling as he ran, and wherever he ran he saw that great shuddering sailor, dark against the river of light, against a reeling wall, looming up as from some great hole in the earth, the great shuddering sailor. He stopped dead, looked up, light was scattering light, a steeple careered crazily through space, under his feet a river in tumult, flowing wild. Great engines roaring past, and faces, faces, faces. He ran up some steps, he reached a roof, he leaned against the iron railings and he watched, he felt tremble under him, the city rocked with outrageous power. A life lived to see this. A great wall collapsing, a door hurling in the air like a demented sail, caught in a wind deluge, a falling girder. He could feel the pressure of the earth under him, he let go the railings and ran across the flat roof to the other side, he clung with one hand to an iron gate, it collapsed at a touch. And always the light sweeping past, as though blown by the great wind, a life lived to see this, a grey city rocking. Not what you felt, you couldn't

[71] Hanley, James, *No Directions* (London: Nicholson & Watson, 1946), v.
[72] Ibid., 61–2.

even think, mind's doors closed up. It was what you saw. He stared entranced at the blazing sky. All that light, a sea, an ocean of light, from what vast reservoir had it flooded up, this drenching light, blazing red, and suddenly to his left a falling green, cataracts of light, red, and yellow and green, this riot of colour shouted at you.

'God!' he said, 'it's magnificent, it's—'[73]

The poet Hilda Doolittle, known as H. D., chose to remain in London during the war, living with her partner, Bryher, in their flat in Chelsea. It was then that she wrote both her reminiscences of her childhood, *The Gift*, and her poetic response to the war, *Trilogy*. According to Diane Collecut, while Bryher 'was tramping the shattered City to piece together remnants of Shakespeare's London, Mrs Aldington was making pilgrimages to Chelsea, to trace the remains of the Moravians that had settled there, as in her native Pennsylvania, in the eighteenth century'.[74] It was also a journey to recover memories of her mother, Helen Doolittle. The dedication reads.

To
HELEN
Who has
brought me home
for Bethlehem Pennsylvania 1741
from Chelsea London 1941
L'amitié passe même le tombeau

The Gift is H. D.'s responses to the terror of the Blitz and the bombing raids on London. She was writing about the end of the world, as it must have seen, partly in the World's End. As Charlotte Mandel puts it, in her review, the book 'exploded into her consciousness during nightly bomb raids that sounded apocalyptic destruction and fire from the sky'.[75] It was written partly for H. D. to be able to master her intense fear of death during the bombing, by enabling her to find refuge in memories of her childhood in Bethlehem and her Moravian heritage. She had felt this fear before the War, remembering her experiences in the First World War in London. This had led her to undertake

---

[73] Ibid., 135.
[74] Bradshaw, David, and Kevin J. H. Dettmar, (eds), *A Companion to Modernist Literature and Culture. Blackwell Companions to Literature and Culture* (Malden, MA: Blackwell, 2006), 358.
[75] Mandell, Charlotte, 'The Gift: A Review', *English Literature in Transition 1880–1920*, 42, no. 3 (September 1999): 344–8.

analysis with Sigmund Freud, which helped her recover a connection with her mother. *The Gift* is riven with apocalyptic fears of burning to death and of debilitating accidents. Furthermore, the war itself keeps intruding, exploding into the text. The book even starts with a memory of a girl burning to death in a hooped crinoline skirt that has been set fire by a candle. Images of death by burning are found throughout the text. The young H. D. or rather Hilda is fascinated and terrified by the prospect of a shooting star falling to earth and burning them to death. At times the war itself bursts through or into the text as if she could not stop it, like the bombs of which she is so terrified. The chapter entitled 'Because One Is Happy' starts with an account of a time-bomb that 'had neatly nosed its way under the pavement edge, less than two minutes' walk from my door'.[76] This leads to a consideration of the very nature of terror in the light of the possibility of imminent death.

The silt of time is dynamited to powder, along with the walls of the house on the corner; while one's own walls still shake with the reverberation, there is that solemn pause; time is wiped away. In three minutes or in three seconds, we gain what no amount of critical research or analytical probing could give us, knowledge of the reactions of man in danger, of men in danger, of all men and all women; we shrink, we become time-less and are impersonalized because in fact we are all really one of thousands and thousands who are equally facing a fact, the possibility, at any given second, of complete physical annihilation.[77]

During the bombing there are no national boundaries for H. D. She does not think that 'it is a German who dropped that bomb'. It is, rather, like 'something out of our Doré Bible, the burning of this or that city, the locusts and plagues of Egypt, the End of the World, the Day (in fact) of Judgment'.[78] She describes the way her body is frozen, paralyzed with fear, as the noise of passing enemy planes becomes intolerably loud. And yet in the very midst of this terror 'exaltation rises like sap in a tree. I am happy. I am happier than I have ever been, it seems to me, in my whole life.' 'We were able' she writes 'night after night, to pass out of the unrealities and the chaos of night battle, and see clear.'[79] The only regret she felt at such moments was that she might

[76] Doolittle, H. (H. D.), *The Gift: The Complete Text* (Gainesville: University of Florida Press, 1998), 109.
[77] Ibid.
[78] Ibid.
[79] Ibid., 110–11.

be annihilated before she had time to bear witness to this joy, and to the fact that 'when things become unbearable, a door swings open or a window'. The door that is opened for H. D. is the one that leads her back to her Moravian past in Bethlehem Bin the last decade or so of the 19th century, which she recounts in *The Gift*.

At the heart of the book is the chapter entitled 'The Secret', in which the young Hilda has what almost amounts to a séance with her grandmother, Mamalie. The secret of the chapter's title is the 'Hidden Church' of revolutionary mystics in the Moravian church, who banded together with Indian (in H. D.'s terms) medicine men to promote world peace and mystical harmony. In her book on H. D. and Freud, Dianne Chisholm suggests that for 'the middle-aged poet, struggling to survive World War II, the erotic revival of this memory acts as a latent transfusion of "visionary power," transforming mortal fear into mystic, orgasmic joy and the prophetic will to live/write for tomorrow'.[80]

For all H. D.'s capacity to find such joy in the midst of the experience of bombing, the reality of a bombed city was depressingly banal. Muriel Spark describes the appearance of British cities in 1945 at the beginning of her novel *The Girls of Slender Means*.

The streets of the cities were lined with buildings in bad repair or in no repair at all, bomb-sites piled with stony rubble, houses like giant teeth in which decay had been drilled out, leaving only the cavity. Some bomb-ripped buildings looked like the ruins of ancient castles until, at a closer view, the wallpapers of various quite normal rooms would be visible, room above room, exposed, as on a stage, with one wall missing; sometimes a lavatory chain would dangle over nothing from a fourth or fifth-floor ceiling; most of the staircases survived, like a new art-form, leading up and up to an unspecified destination that made unusual demands on the mind's eye.[81]

At the same time, some found the devastation of London oddly beautiful, or, rather, found beauty in that devastation. Bryher, for example, offered a lyrical description of the ruins of Aldermanbury, the area in which she spent much time researching Shakespeare's London.

Nobody now can see Aldermanbury as it once was, a sea of flowers in a city of desolation. It may seem strange to write this about the wreckage left by bombs and fire but

---

[80] Chisholm, Dianne, *H.D.'s Freudian Poetics: Psychoanalysis in Translation* (Ithaca, NY: Cornell University Press, 1992), 120.
[81] Spark, Muriel, *The Girls of Slender Means* (London: Macmillan, 1963), 1.

the area between St. Mary's Church and the Cathedral in that summer of 1943 was one of the most beautiful places I have seen. Yet I knew many of the great landscapes of the world, the Alps in their summer and their winter glory, the wide tawny desert, the curving Mediterranean bays. All these were part of a memory but this suddenly quiet island rising from the avalanche of ruins was their equal. The stones had tumbled from the walls exactly as they had as Paestum but their dusty surface was a blaze of color. Here was a clump of marigolds, there was some viper's bugloss, but it was the willow herb that had taken possession of the place, spreading its purple banner across the dust. All was silence but it was sunny and as far as this could be a consolation, in that time of frustration and unhappiness, if all the other virtues were in retreat, beauty stayed.[82]

One of the revelations of Bryher's wartime memoirs was that H. D. and she knew Walter Benjamin. I had thought he was almost unknown in the Anglosphere during his lifetime. In *Days of Mars* she describes seeking consolation from the sight of a forlorn Hyde Park, full of guns and searchlights, by going into a bookshop, and looking at Arthur Koestler's recently published book *Scum of the Earth*. It is in this manner that she finds out about Benjamin's death at the Spanish border. She reminisces about meeting him in Paris the previous year, and failing to argue strongly enough that he should leave for New York immediately.[83] Perhaps her epiphany in Aldermanbury had been informed by Benjamin's own fascination with ruins, which he saw as allegories of the tragedy of modernity and, indeed, allegories of allegory itself. Ruins appear throughout Benjamin's work from his earliest publications through to the image of the Angel of History seeing history as a continuous catastrophe of wreckage piled at his feet. Perhaps Bryher knew Benjamin's aphorism, that 'Redemption looks to the small fissure in the ongoing catastrophe'.[84]

In *Days of Mars*, Bryher remarks that

I often wonder today when I read about the rejection of order by the young if this is not due to memories inherited from parents who were adolescent during the war and suffered so much from austerity and restraint? 'Your rebellion goes back to the Forties,' I think, as they stroll noisily down the streets in their dirty clothes, 'it does not belong to the Sixties at all'.[85]

---

[82] Bryher, *Days of Mars: A Memoir 1940–1946* (New York: Harcourt, Brace, Jovanovich, 1972), 103.

[83] Ibid., 22–4.

[84] Walter Benjamin, 'Central Park', *New German Critique*, 34 (Winter, 1985): 50.

[85] Bryher, *Days of Mars*, 5–6.

4

After the Rain

Technically, the Second World War ended in 1945, sixteen years before I was born. It ended in the sense that hostilities ceased and the long, slow business of rebuilding a shattered world started at that point. However, at another level it continued, at least as a kind of spectre haunting this country, that has never properly gone away. It's a bit like those extraordinary 'photographs' that were created by the atomic blasts at Hiroshima and Nagasaki, in which the images of vaporised objects, and sometimes, bodies, were captured on the surface of walls, projected there by the sheer power of the blasts. The War imprinted itself on the psychic background of our lives. So powerful and ubiquitous were the images of London in the Blitz for me as a child, I still see a kind of overlay of devastation floating over the city as it now is, a form of double vision. I am old enough to remember the bombsites that were still present in London right up until the 1970s. Despite the many conflicts that have been waged since, in Britain at least, it is still called simply the War. People will still say that 'such and such has been the case since the War'. Even eighty years later the War still haunts us as was seen in the debate around Brexit and the egregious invocations of the so-called 'Blitz Spirit'.

As a response to the War, the surrealist poet David Gascoyne attempted to write a poem that saw the bombsite as a kind of religious space. 'The Bomb-Site Anchorite' was intended to be a verse narrative of three pages or more, but Gascoyne abandoned it after writing only a small fragment. What he wanted to write about was

an encounter with a survivor of the last War obsessed with what might be termed post-Auschwitz theology, a character strictly speaking invented in order to give utterance to my own meditations on whether it is possible any longer to envisage the divine in the second half of the 20th century.[1]

He imagined someone who had become a hermit 'amidst the ruins of a post-war bombarded city'. 'What I had seen of London after the Blitz was enough to fill my dreams with scenes of derelict streets and districts of shattered buildings for years after the late 1940s.' Gascoyne imagined the anchorite in question to have set up a shelter 'to live in and ponder on eschatology and outside it to have built an altar made of rubble – "to the Unknown God"'.[2]

Perhaps the best and most extraordinary literary representation of postwar London is Rose Macaulay's penultimate novel *The World My Wilderness*, published in 1950. The title comes from one of the two epigraphs, four lines of verse attributed to anon, but actually by Macaulay herself. The other is from T. S. Eliot's *The Wasteland*, and it is clear that Macaulay regards the ruins of London after the war as something like that poem's eponymous waste. It is the story of Barbary, a near-feral girl of seventeen, bought up neglectfully by her beautiful Anglo-Irish mother, Helen, in wartime France. During the War, Barbary has run wild and become deeply involved with the Maquis, the mountain resistance, an involvement that has ended up with her being implicated in the murder of her collaborationist stepfather. Helen sends Barbary back to England to live with Barbary's father. Barbary refuses any attempt to make her genteel and, instead, hangs around the ruins of the City of London with her equally feral cousin Raoul, and various spivs and deserters living in the ruins. What makes *The World My Wilderness* so particularly fascinating is that Barbary is a harbinger of the coming counter-culture of beatniks and hippies, *avant la lettre*. Barbary's dirty clothing and lack of normal manners is a continual affront to her highly respectable step-mother. But it is not as if she is being deliberately insolent or provocative. It is, rather, that such concerns are for her meaningless in the light of the kind of things she has seen and experienced. Barbary is actually the same age as the first generation of postwar countercultural figures, such as, for example, Henrietta Moraes, the bohemian, artists' model and muse in the 1950s and 1960s, who was fifteen when the War ended. Macaulay provides some beautifully vivid descriptions of a bombed City of London.

---

[1] Gascoyne, David, *Selected Poems* (London: Enitharmon, 1994), 251.
[2] Ibid.

The maze of little streets threading through the wilderness, the broken walls, the great pits with their dense forests of bracken and bramble, golden ragwort and colts-foot, fennel and foxglove and vetch, all the wild rambling shrubs that spring from ruin, the vaults and cellars and deep caves, the wrecked guild halls that had belonged to saddlers, merchant tailors, haberdashers, waxchandlers, barbers, brewers, coopers and coachmakers, all the ancient city fraternities, the broken office stairways that spiralled steeply past empty doorways and rubbled closets into the sky, empty shells of churches with their towers still strangely spiring above the wilderness, their empty window arches where green boughs pushed in, their broken pavement floors – St. Vedast's, St. Alban's, St. Anne's and St. Agnes', St. Giles Cripplegate, its tower high above the rest, the ghosts of churches burnt in an earlier fire, St. Olave's and St. John Zachary's, haunting the green-flowered churchyards that bore their names, the ghosts of taverns where merchants and clerks had drunk, of restaurants where they had eaten – all this scarred and haunted green and stone and brambled wilderness lying under the August sun, a-hum with insects and astir with secret, darting, burrowing life, receive the returned traveller into its dwellings with a wrecked, indifferent calm. Here, its cliffs and chasms and caves seemed say, you do not wish to get away, for this is the maquis that lies about the margins of the wrecked world, and here your feet are set; here you find the irremediable barbarism that comes up from the depth of the earth, and that you have known elsewhere. 'Where are the roots that clutch, what branches grow, out of this stony rubbish? Son of man, you cannot say or guess...'[3]

The book is riven with apocalyptic and religious overtones. While playing in St Giles, one of the City's ruined and deserted churches, Barbary starts to chant the *Dies Irae* from the charred remains of a hymn book, and then mimics a ritual of repentance.[4] Raoul and she cover the walls of the old offices they occupy with 'paintings of the Last Judgment and souls in hell'. A more ambitious '*jugement dernier*' is made for the altar end of church as well.[5] Once, when Barbary is chanting the *Dies Irae* and Raoul is holding a black kitten towards the altar of the church, a clergyman whose mind has been destroyed by the bombing interrupts them and starts to preach. '"We are in hell now," he said, staring apprehensively about him. "Hell is where I am, Lucifer and all his legion are in me. Fire creeps on me from all sides; I am trapped in the prison of my sins..."' He continues to proclaim that he has shut himself off from God while the 'flames press on' and that he is 'Trapped, trapped, trapped; there's no hope'. Finally, he finishes with 'For this is hell, hell,

---

[3] Macaulay, Rose, *The World Is My Wilderness* (London: Collins, 1968), 128–9.

[4] Ibid., 65.

[5] Ibid., 128–9.

hell', before his voice breaks and, shuddering, he falls to his knees, 'his face in his scarred hands'. For Barbary this is terrifying in that it confirms her belief in the existence of hell and the absence of any deliverance. Eventually, another clergyman arrives and gently leads the disturbed priest away, explaining that his church had been bombed in 1940, and that he had been trapped in the wreckage of two days; 'he could scarcely move, and the flames raged round him. [...] He thinks he's in hell and can't get out.'[6]

For Jeff Nuttall 'VE Night took place in one world and VJ Night in another'. He describes the first victory as a 'brown, smelly, fallible, lovable place, an old-fashioned, earthy, stable place'. The second victory, achieved by atomic weapons, by contrast, took place in a world 'in which an evil had been precipitated whose scope was immeasurable, the act being, in itself, not an event, but a continuum, not an occasion but the beginning of a condition'.[7] We had 'espoused an evil as great as the Nazi genocide, we had espoused the instrument for the termination of our benevolent institution, society, and our certain identity, human'.[8]

We had driven honour away a few short months after finding it. Neither could we survive the next war, for the next wasn't going to be remotely like the one we had 'shown we could take'. The next war would certainly be more terrible than anything we had known, was probably more terrible than we could calculate, was possibly going to terminate the entire species.[9]

For Peter Wyden, in his account of the development of the atomic bomb and its first use, 'Hiroshima was an event of such magnitude that it divided history into two periods, before the bomb, and after it – "Day One" of a new age, in which *all* life would be at risk.'[10] According to Nuttall, one result of this was that for the young 'membership of the H-bomb society automatically cancelled out anything' anyone of authority might say. The generations had divided, with those who had not reached puberty at the time of the bomb finding that they 'were incapable of conceiving a life with a future'.[11]

A few months before the War, James Joyce had published *Finnegans Wake*, his six hundred-page novel, regarded by many as almost entirely

6 Ibid., 167–8.
7 Nuttall, Jeff, *Bomb Culture* (London: McGibbon and Kee, 1968), 18.
8 Ibid., 19.
9 Ibid.
10 Wyden, Peter, *Day One: Before Hiroshima and After* (New York: Simon and Schuster, 1984).
11 Nuttall, *Bomb Culture*, 20.

unreadable. Others have argued that his experimentation with language anticipated the world after the War and the Atomic Bomb, with phrases such as 'blown to Adams' as well as this passage.

The abnihilisation of the etym by the grisning of the grosning of the grinder of the grunder of the first lord of Hurtreford expolodotonates through Parsuralia with an ivanmorinthorrorumble fragoromboassity amidwhiches general uttermosts confussion are perceivable moletons skaping with muliculus while coventry plumpkins fairlygosmotherthemselves in the Landaunelegants of Pinkadindy. Similar scenatas are projectilised from Hullulullu, Bawlawayo, empyreal Raum and mordern Atems. They were precisely the twelves of clocks, noon minutes, none seconds. At someseat of Oldanelang's Konguerrig, by dawnybreak in Aira.[12]

As Sean Braune puts it 'the explosion that ("expolodotonates") over Hiroshima and the paranoia regarding nuclear threat so prevalent at the time of Joyce's writing'.[13] Joyce's 'abnihilisation of the etym' is also a reflection on how the world after Day One will be transformed through emerging media such as television.

In the heliotropical noughttime following a fade of trans-formed Tuff and, pending its viseversion, a metenergic reglow of beaming Batt, the hairdhoard bombard-ment screen, if taste-fully taut guranium satin, tends to teleframe and step up to the charge of a light barricade. Down the photoslope in syncopanc pulses, with the bitts bugtwug their teffs, the missledhropes, glitter aglatteraglutt, borne by their carnier waive. Spraygun rakes and splits them from a double focus: grenadite, damny-mite, alextronite, nichilite: and the scanning firespot of the sgunners traverses the rutilanced illustred sunksundered lines. Shlosshf A gaspel truce leaks out over the caeseine coatings. Amid a fluorescence of spectracular mephiticism there caoculates through the inconoscope stealdily a still, the figure of a fellow- chap in the wohly ghast, Popey O' Donos hough, the jesuneral of the russuates.[14]

If, as some have supposed, the Wake is an account of a dream, then perhaps it prefigures the nightmare of life after Hiroshima. Writing very shortly after that event the psychoanalyst Edward Glover suggested that

the actual and potential destructiveness of the atomic bomb plays straight into the hands of the Unconscious. The most cursory study of dream-life and of the

[12] Joyce, James, *Finnegans Wake* (London: Faber, 1964), 353.
[13] Braune, Sean, "From Lucretian Atomic Theory to Joycean Etymic Theory." *Journal of Modern Literature*, 33, no. 4 (2010): 167–181.
[14] Joyce, *Wake*, 349.

phantasies of the insane shows that ideas of world-destruction (more accurately destruction of what the world symbolizes) are latent in the unconscious mind. And since the atomic bomb is less a weapon of war than a weapon of extermination it is well adapted to the more bloodthirsty phantasies with which man is secretly pre-occupied during phases of acute frustration. Nagasaki destroyed by the magic of science is the nearest man has yet approached to the realization of dreams that even during the safe immobility of sleep are accustomed to develop into nightmares of anxiety. The first promise of the atomic age is that it can make some of our nightmares come true. *The capacity so painfully acquired by normal men to distinguish between sleep, delusion, hallucination and the objective reality of waking life has for the first time in human history been seriously weakened.*[15]

J. G. Ballard was sufficiently taken by this passage that he uses some of it as an epigraph for a section of his short story 'The Terminal Beach'.[16]

I found a laconically English response to the atomic threat in a book by the now largely forgotten novelist and actor Rachel Ferguson. In her book on Kensington, *Royal Borough*, which mixes memoir and local history, amidst the accounts of fire watching in the War, theatrical productions, cat shows, and ghost stories, there is a section entitled 'If an atomic bomb falls on the Town Hall'.[17] In it she describes going to a 'couple of quite admirable lectures at the Town Hall by Captain Holmes, on the care and treatment of Atom bombs'.[18] She is reassured by 'our national and extraordinary adaptability and lack alike of retrospective rancour and anticipatory panic', while 'we concentrate upon maps and diagrams and statistics, straight, as it were, from the horse's mouth'.[19] Her trust in Captain Holmes's bookkeeping and the sight of 'fellow Wardens' from the War to volunteer, along with all the other attendees, for 'atomic service'. This means making 'an orderly rush, or mass convergence, upon the Town Hall, if it is atomically struck'.[20]

But – how many rushers would there be left? For, taking Point Zero (the spot where the bomb exploded) as the Town Hall, Captain Holmes then revealed that the atom bomb has a possible malignancy potential (or scope of havoc) of a maximum of two

---

[15] Glover, Edward, *War, Sadism and Pacifism: Further Essays on Group Psychology and War* (London: Allen and Unwin, 1946), 274.

[16] Ballard, J. G., *The Terminal Beach* (Harmondsworth: Penguin Books, 1974), 138.

[17] Ferguson, Rachel, *Royal Borough* (London: Jonathan Cape, 1950).

[18] Ibid., 300.

[19] Ibid., 301.

[20] Ibid.

miles. This at once rules out Roma and myself as ministering angels, in that, as we live well within a quarter of a mile of the Town Hall, we might have instantly become charred ruins ourselves, together with all those present living nearer Point Zero than Piccadilly on one side and Chiswick on the other.[21]

Ferguson, however, is reassured by the 'impressive, workable and comforting' arrangements with other boroughs to come to the rescue, with the prospect of Captain Holmes in command, and even the idea that, 'even in Hiroshima by no means all the populace were killed, and that, as with the relatively archaic H.E. [high explosive] bomb, there were types of building that escaped destruction'. She even suggests that there was no need 'to seriously fear starvation, in that it was demonstrated that the atomic bomb does not destroy or poison root vegetables'.[22]

Ferguson was right to be pessimistic about the chances of surviving nuclear war. Already by 1948 the government's Joint Intelligence Committee report on the effects of such a war, which they saw being possible by 1957, in relation to Soviet capabilities, being as follows.

It is estimated that in London a crater 450 yards in diameter and 40 to 50 yards deep would be produced. Damage to underground services will be severe... Total collapse of all buildings including multi-storey framed structures is to be expected up to a distance of about 600 yards from ground-zero... and heavy internal damage, probably resulting in fires, up to at least 1,500 yards... Suburban houses of the type common in England... would be destroyed or would require demolition... to a distance of about 1,400 yards from ground zero would be rendered uninhabitable... to about 2,000... Severe flash burns will occur on the unprotected parts of the bodies of people in the open at distance up to 2,000 or 3,000 yards from ground-zero. ... Gamma radiation from an airburst will cause death to people caught in the open to a distance of about 1,400 yards from ground-zero.[23]

In the mid-1950s the secret committee headed by the civil servant Sir William Strath produced what became known as the Strath Report, which was profoundly pessimistic and chilling. The committee's prognosis was that half the population would be killed, radiation would kill millions more, and agriculture, communications and industry would all be destroyed, and martial law would

[21] Ibid.
[22] Ibid., 301–2.
[23] Hennessy, Peter, *Winds of Change: Britain in the Early Sixties* (London, New York: Allen Lane, 2019), 159.

almost certainly have to be put in place. A number of decisions were taken as a consequence of the report and other discussions of the possibility of nuclear war; one was the necessity of maintaining a force of nuclear weapons to deter the Soviets from attacking; another was that it would be impossible to produce nuclear shelters for the general populace, but that plans for the government and the Queen to escape to special bunkers should be put in place. One of the most extraordinary discussions arose from the need for the prime minister to be able to order a counter-attack having decided we were being attacked, especially when he was on the move[24].

By this time the American president was already being accompanied by an officer bearing the codes needed to launch retaliatory missiles. The British solution was to install a radio in the prime minister's cars, 'which would permit messages to relayed in plain language through the Automobile Association's radio network'.[25] The radios would be used to get the prime minister to a telephone. At the time public telephones required that the caller used a number of pennies to make a phone call. In a memorandum from Bryan Saunders, a civil servant responsible for the Government Car Pool, that it might be necessary to 'see that our drivers are supplied with four pennies – I should hate to think of you trying to get change for a sixpence from a bus conductor while those four minutes are ticking by'.[26] Tim Bligh, Macmillan's Permanent Private Secretary, replied that

a shortage of pennies should not present the difficulties which you envisage. While it may be desirable, when motoring, to carry a few pennies in one's pocket, occasions do arise when by some misfortune or miscalculation they have been expended or one is penniless. In such cases, however, it is a simple matter to have the cost of any telephone call transferred by dialling 100 and requesting reversal of the charge, and this does not take any appreciable extra time.[27]

In 1963 the government published a pamphlet entitled *Advising the Householder on Protection against Nuclear Attack*. This is described, rather disingenuously, as a 'training manual for the civil defence, the police and fire services', though it is clearly aimed directly at the general public. It is a terrifying document, despite the charming coloured drawings. The Introduction

[24] Ibid.
[25] Ibid.
[26] Ibid., 193.
[27] Ibid.

states baldly that in 'areas close to the explosions most people would be killed instantly and nearly all buildings would be completely destroyed'.[28] This is reiterated in the next section on 'Basic Facts', which explains what happens when an H-Bomb explodes'. It is worth quoting in full.

The explosion of an H-bomb would cause total destruction for several miles around; the size of the area would depend on the size of the bomb and the height at which it was exploded. Outside this area survival would be possible but there would be three dangers:

HEAT BLAST FALL-OUT

An H-bomb explosion creates a huge white- hot fireball which lasts for about 20 seconds and gives off tremendous heat. The heat is so intense that it can kill people in the open up to several miles away. It could also burn exposed skin very much further away. Striking through unprotected windows it could set houses alight many miles away.

Blast would follow the heat waves like a hurricane. Buildings would be destroyed or severely damaged for several miles from the explosion, and there would be lighter damage for many miles beyond. There would be a further large area where, although houses suffered no structural damage, windows would be broken and there- would be danger from flying glass.

Fall-out is the dust that is sucked up from the ground by the explosion and made radio-active in the rising fireball. It rises high in the air and is carried down-wind, falling slowly to earth over an area which may be hundreds of miles long and tens of miles wide. Within this area everything in the open would be covered with a film of radio-active fall-out dust. Fall-out would start to reach the ground in the heavily damaged areas near the explosion in about half an hour- Further away it would take longer, and about one hundred miles away the fall-out might not come down for four to six hours.

Fall-out dust gives off radiation rather like X-rays. The radiation cannot be seen or felt, heard or smelled. It can be detected only by the special instruments with which the civil defence, the police and fire services would be equipped. Exposure to radiation, that being too close to fall-out dust far too long, can cause sickness or death, The radiation rapidly becomes less intense with time and after two days fall-out is about one hundred times less harmful than at first...

... but even then

it is still dangerous.[29]

---

[28] Home Office, and Central Office of Information, *Advising the Householder on Protection against Nuclear Attack* (H.M.S.O., 1963), 4.
[29] Ibid., 5–6.

The rest of the pamphlet gives details of the obviously futile measures one might take to mitigate the effects of a nuclear attack, such as building a fallout room, preparing essential supplies and so on. It also describes 'What to do if it happens', along with an account of the warning system – red alert, a rising and falling note on the siren meant imminent danger of attack, while grey alert, an uninterrupted note of steady pitch meant fall-out expected in an hour, and black alert, a gong, or whistle sounding a Morse D, dash dot dot, meant imminent danger of fall out. A period note is struck with the advice about what to wear to go outside after an attack to undertake tasks such as firefighting: 'If you have to go outside put on gumboots or stout shoes, a hat or headscarf, coat done up to the neck, and gloves.'[30]

The terror of nuclear annihilation is beautifully captured in a very sober double-page spread I recently saw, which dated from 1950. It was in *The Picture Post*, the British liberal, antifascist magazine of photojournalism in an issue engaging with the implications of the prospect of the development of the hydrogen bomb. The image shows London seen from some God's-eye view looking across from its southern edge. In the middle of city is the familiar shape of the H-Bomb mushroom cloud. Beneath it the caption reads 'THIS IS WHAT WOULD HAPPEN IF A HYDROGEN BOMB WERE DROPPED ON THE BRITISH HOUSES OF PARLIAMENT'. The image is particularly strange in that, apart from the actual blast, London looks, as yet, unaffected, indeed domestically familiar.

At various points on the image locations are named, including those that are comparatively far, Chelmsford, Colchester, Clacton-on-Sea, Brentwood, Burnham-on-Crouch, Southend and Tilbury, and then those closer such as Erith Marshes, W. Middlesex Reservoirs and Greenwich, and finally places with which, as a child, I was familiar, Kew Gardens, Clapham Common and, right in the centre, Regents Park and Hyde Park. Radiating out from the epicentre of the blast are four concentric circles marked by dotted white lines. The outermost of these bears the legend 'Within 80 miles buildings would be destroyed by one hydrogen bomb', the next 'Within 16 miles stone would be liquefied by one hydrogen bomb', the third, 'Within 8 miles destruction by one hydrogen bomb would be complete', and the innermost 'This circle of 2½ miles radius represents the limit of destruction of one uranium bomb' (the

---

[30] Ibid., 20.

term uranium bomb refers to the type of nuclear weapon also known as an atom bomb, such as those dropped on Hiroshima and Nagasaki).

Our house in the World's End was just outside the innermost circle. Next to the big image there is a smaller one showing the outline of the south-east of England, with the names of various cities and towns. Overlaying this are three concentric circles, the innermost, the darkest being, according to the caption the area in which everything would be destroyed. The outer circle, which reaches as far as towns such as Peterborough and Salisbury is presumably the range of lesser damage. The caption continues that a 'bomb 55 times as big as that planned would have a spread of 1,500 miles. It could be carried by sea and blow up the whole continent of Australia.' I only saw these images recently, but I internalised the idea they encapsulated from an early age, that something as solid, as Victorian, as London, with its parks and commons, its reservoirs and docks, could be utterly destroyed, liquified, in a few seconds, and that this destruction would radiate out from a central point, as represented in these kind of malign nuclear mandalas. One of the responses to this prospect was the setting up of the so-called 'Four Minute Warning'. This was reckoned to be the time between the launching of missiles by an hostile power, and their detonation. It was the stuff of childhood and adolescent nightmares. The Warning would have taken the form of sirens, as well as announcements on the television and radio.

One of the few early fictional imaginings of the atomic destruction of London is found in Roald Dahl's almost entirely unknown first adult novel *Some Time Never*, published in 1948. It is mostly unknown because Dahl more or less repudiated it and refused even to acknowledge its existence. It's an adult reworking of Dahl's highly successful 1943 children's book, *The Gremlins*. As such, it is a strange mixture, partly a highly realistic account of Second World War aerial combat, as experienced by three flyers, Peternip, Progboot and Stuffy, and of the experience of nuclear devastation, and partly a twee fable about the eponymous gremlins, an imaginary race of malicious beings dedicated to the destruction of human beings. The parts that do not concern the gremlins are rather brilliant; the description of what it is like to fly fighter planes in combat is extraordinary, and obviously authentic, given Dahl's own wartime experiences. The best bit is the account of a nuclear attack from the point of view of various protagonists. It was clearly Dahl's attempt to face his own terror and to write through it. The first description is from the point of view of Peternip, who had been a fighter pilot and, at this point in the plot, is a music critic who deals with his postwar melancholy by going to classical concerts. As the attack takes place he has just left one such concert and is talking to another critic about the playing.

'It makes you feel good somehow,' Peternip said, 'somehow it makes you feel good to know ...

Suddenly the whole sky became a blaze of light and Peternip felt a momentary scorching heat upon his head... and then blindness... a fearful searing pain and he knew he was lying down upon the road but that was all he knew except the agony, a brilliant piercing agony which enveloped his whole body... took control of his mind and he began to shriek and he knew he was shrieking but he couldn't hear his voice... he clasped his hands tighter and he had a vague impression of the skin coming away like damp paper from the flesh... and then he lost consciousness and he died.

That was at about three o'clock on a summer afternoon.[31]

The book then moves to Peternip's fellow ex-flyer, Progboot, who is now a civilian test pilot. He is described as 'leaning against the wing of a jet plane on an aerodrome about twenty miles outside Manchester'. He is also in the middle of a conversation with a designer when he suddenly proclaims 'What was that!' He and his interlocutor look up at the sky which 'was lit for a moment by a brilliant white flash away to the south. There was just this momentary shining whiteness which flashed so brightly that the whole countryside around changed colour and then it was gone and the sunshine afterwards seemed pale.' Both Progboot and the designer know that this is possibly an atomic strike. 'My God, it couldn't possibly be...' says Progboot. 'No' the designer replies, 'It couldn't'. Others come out and stand around in groups looking up at the sky with 'startled, puzzled, rather frightened faces, talking about the flash'. Any doubt about what it was is dispelled when

from the other direction, from the sky over Manchester, there came a brighter and a closer flash, so bright and white and fierce that for Progboot everything went white, then black, then white again and in a few seconds the heat and blast arrived and he was thrown to the ground, quite gently, as by a strong wind, and he felt the wave of hotness on his face and then the pain and the sudden sickly smell of burning flesh

---

[31] Dahl, Roald, *Sometime Never: A Fable for Supermen* (New York: C. Scribners Sons, 1948), 144–5.

and he was sitting on the ground, blind but fully conscious of the fearful pain around his face.[32]

For me, the most personally affecting part of the narrative is the experience of the third flying companion, Stuffy, not least because it takes place in Central London. At the time of the attack Stuffy is on a tube train on the way to meet Peternip after the concert the latter has been attending. He is still underground when the explosion which, even 'deep down in the Underground, comes with the sound of "a twelve inch gun close by", followed by loud rushing noise from the Underground tunnel and a wave of warm air', which sweeps over the platform and is 'like a wind that had passed over scorching deserts and which now brought with it in its passage the faint flavour of hot and distant places'.[33] As it sweeps over the platform it leaves behind a 'curious smell of burning stone and a dry warmness in the air'. Stuffy and another man manage to get to the surface, where they witness a scene of utter devastation 'at half past four on a summer's afternoon', which leaves Stuffy unable to stand, speechless and cold with fear.

Every building on every side as far as the eye could see had collapsed, and now, where once had stood the proud solid stone buildings of Regent Street, Piccadilly, Haymarket and Leicester Square, there remained only large heaps of scattered masonry with here and there a jagged piece of wall still standing.[34]

Furthermore, there is no sunlight and the sky is 'shrouded over with a brownish haze', the air 'thick with dust' and 'an atmosphere of emptiness, of twilight and of night approaching'. All along the streets are the wreckage of cars and buses, with the paint scorched off their sides, and are now 'black, colourless, rather small sad tangled things'. Even worse is the sight of the 'bodies of men and women... twisted in grotesque attitudes of sudden death', as well as pieces of bodies, arms, legs, strewn across the pavements. Stuffy sees the body of a man whose exposed skin is 'scorched to a dark blackish red' and the face somehow 'melted away leaving a flat dark red pulpy-looking mess'. Stuffy realises that there is no blood anywhere and works out that the bodies have been 'broiled alive', cooked as a steak is, so that the 'blood would

[32] Ibid., 146.
[33] Ibid., 148–9.
[34] Ibid., 153.

instantly be sealed inside'.[35] The most vivid description is of a double-decker bus in the middle of the road.

As he went past it he saw though the open glassless windows that the bus was full of people, all sitting in their places, silent, immobile, as though they were waiting for the bus to start again. But their faces were scorched and seared and half melted and all of them had had their hats blown off their heads so that they sat there bald-headed, scorch-skinned, grotesque, but very upright in their seats. Up in front, the black-faced driver was still sitting with his hands resting on the wheel, looking straight in front of him through the empty sockets of his eyes.[36]

Given that this takes place in Piccadilly Circus, the bus could easily be a number 22 or 19, possibly on the way to Chelsea and the World's End. For that reason this passage gives me a particular horrified frisson, in the way that it connects the iconic figure of my childhood, the Routemaster Bus, with nuclear annihilation.

In the 1968 film *If...*there is a brilliant rendition of the kind of adolescent despair engendered by the threat of nuclear annihilation. Set in an unnamed and, to some extent, generic old English public school, it's the story of Mick, Wallace, and Johnny, three nonconformist pupils who know, absolutely, that everything about the school – its vacuous appeals to tradition, its tepid Anglicanism, and its jingoistic militarism – is ridiculous and conceals a cruel and repressive system of domination and submission. The headmaster is a remote figure, talking glib nonsense about the modern world to the senior pupils. The heroes' housemaster is entirely ineffectual, and their house, College, is run by a cadre of the senior boys, who are called Whips. The staff are either cruel or strange. The teaching is, at best, eccentric. The junior boys are called Scum and are, in effect, servants for the senior boys, and, in some cases, are preyed upon sexually.

The plot follows the three friends as they try to resist the school's attempts to make them conform. Mick demonstrates his rebelliousness from the beginning by coming back to school with a moustache, which is against the rules. A bit later Mick and Johnny steal a motorbike from a showroom in the town and ride to a café, where Mick picks up the girl who serves them. They all becomes increasingly rebellious. Wallace starts a clearly loving

[35] Ibid., 155.
[36] Ibid., 158.

relationship with a younger pupil, who, earlier, had been passed around the Whips as a kind of sexual plaything. The Whips try to make an example of the three, especially Mick, with a brutal caning. Finally the three boys, the younger boy and the girl stage a violent insurrection on Founder's Day with a cache of automatic weapons they have discovered in the school. Because of its ending, *If...* was highly controversial at the time. It was released not long after the events in Paris in May 1968, when students and workers came together to rise up against the government, so a positive representation of violence of the sort shown in the film was problematic. It was given an X certificate.

Several scenes are set in one of the boy's studies, probably Mick's. It's a shabby room, with a bed and some broken-down chairs. At the beginning of the film there are a few images, clearly taken from magazines, on the walls. In the first scene set in the study Mick shows Johnny an image of an African guerrilla, and they agree it is, in their words, fantastic, and Mick cuts it out and sticks it on the wall. Every subsequent scene in the study shows the walls ever more covered with images, until the whole study has become a massive collage of pictures of nude women, soldiers, wild animals, primitive masks, and faces.

In *If...* at no point are any of the boys seen working in the study. They use it, rather, as an enclave away from the repressive culture of the school. In the study they drink vodka, read magazines and cut out pictures, and talk about death and the coming holocaust. At one point Mick looks wistfully into the distance and proclaims, 'The whole world will end very soon – black, brittle bodies peeling into ash', at which point Wallace, bathetically and solipstically, declares that 'I'm going bald. Must be something they put in the soup. I'll look senile before I even leave this dump.'

The study is a haven inside the school, which is itself already a kind of enclave away from the wider world. The boys in the study know this, and have filled the walls with images of the chaotic world beyond those walls. Ostensibly, there is no order in the arrangement of images, none that makes sense at least, so the accumulation of images is a kind of nonsense. (I wonder if the film's director, Lindsay Anderson, was thinking of the walls of playwright Joe Orton and his partner Kenneth Halliwell's room in Islington, famously covered in collaged images. There is, incidentally, a World's End connection here. Not long before he murdered Orton, Halliwell exhibited some of his collages on a gallery on the King's Road called Anno Domini.

According to Orton's diaries, Halliwell was dubious whether 'anybody will go and see the pictures stuck away at the wrong end of the King's Road'.[37]) But the boys also know that what they put on the walls is what is real, and the school, with all its anachronistic traditions and legacies, its structures and rules, and even the headmaster's vapid bromides about modernity, are entirely false and nonsensical in the light of what is happening outside its walls.

In that sense, *If...* is also about the painful birth of a new world in the ruins of the old. The modern public school is a 19th-century invention, even if many of the most famous are much older. It was in that century that the ethos of such schools developed in relation to the needs of imperial Britain. Public schools are very adept at modernising, or at least appearing to modernise, but they remain, to this day, Victorian institutions. I think Anderson makes the school in *If...* appear old-fashioned even by the standards of the 1960s, to highlight the difference between it and the images on the study wall. It's almost as if, by assembling this chaos of loosely connected and resonating images, the boys are imagining the World Wide Web and the world of frenzied networked connectivity, itself a product of the Cold War. Perhaps they can intuit this world just beginning to come into being. It is a world in which every single one of the 19th-century values the school adheres to will be rendered meaningless. It is the world after Auschwitz and Hiroshima, in which the idea of a set of stable truths, traditions and high values to be passed on from one generation to another seems grotesque.

The boys are prefiguring what Evan Calder Williams calls 'salvage punk', which he sees as originating in the 'scattered corpse-scape' of the First World War, when 'Kurt Schwitters draws forth Merz from Commerz, pulling the innate venom of fragmented things from the bad sheen of commercial life'. The next stage involves the 1960s going 'Kaputt',

Then the long '70s roar into view, in all their gritty urgency and Satanic deformations of hippie non-thought, with real militancy losing a pitched battle to the triumphs of counter-revolution. In Italy, the Red Brigades shoot Moro and leave him in the trunk of a Renault. In New Hampshire, the end of the Bretton Woods system undoes the filaments of currency as certainty and shape. In England, 1969, *The Bed Sitting Room*

---

[37] Orton, Joe, and John Lahr, *The Orton Diaries: Including the Correspondence of Edna Welthorpe and Others* (London: Methuen, 1986), 123.

and Monty Python think the end of it all as little more than the relentless repurposing of the same old shit.[38]

Atomic fear seeped into everything, even children's books. My mother bought me a copy of *The Compleet Molesworth* by Ronald Searle and Geoffrey Willans, sometime in the 1960s, which I loved. I came across a second-hand paperback copy recently and it bought back not just memories of reading it the first time, but also how much of an artefact of its time it was. Even though it is clearly intended as a parodic representation of an old-fashioned public school, it is also a product of the Cold War. One of the books is called *Whizz for Atoms*, and includes a chapter entitled 'How to Survive in the Atommic [sic] Age'.[39] All the books are full of space ships and the apparatus of Dan Dare-style fifties science fiction. What it also has is something missing from previous fictional accounts of schooldays, a powerful, if comically expressed, sense of the futility of education and the stupidity of those in charge.

The Molesworth books are clearly informed strongly by the war experiences of both Searle, a POW in a Japanese camp, and Willans, who served in the Royal Navy and fought in the Battle of Crete. As Paul Fussell pointed out in *Wartime: Understanding and Behaviour in the Second World War*, his furious deconstruction of its myths, the most cogent literary engagements with the Second World War and its implications were either experimental or humorous, or both. Molesworth is clearly humorous but also, arguably, experimental in the use of schoolboy slang and misspellings as a kind of experiment with language and a refusal of dominant modes of orthodox expression. At some level, Molesworth is as dark a fiction as that of Beckett or of Bacon's paintings. This is also true of Searle's other creation, the girls' school St Trinian's. Extraordinarily Searle, having got bored of the St Trinian's series, despite their success, killed off all the characters in a nuclear explosion in the final book of the series, *Souls in Torment*.[40]

In *Wartime*, Fussell notes the almost total absence of any sense of nobility of war, or even of any real attempt to engage with it in poetic or literary terms.

[38] Williams, Evan Calder, *Combined and Uneven Apocalypse* (Ropley, Hants: Zero Books, 2010), 15.
[39] Willans, Geoffrey, and Ronald Searle, *The Compleet Molesworth* (London: Max Parrish, 1958).
[40] Searle, Ronald, *Souls in Torment* (London: Perpetua, 1953).

He suggests that the ideological vacuum of the Second World War can only be properly responded to through what Susan Sontag named as the 'aesthetics of silence', which she sees in the work of Pinter, Beckett, Ponge, Bergman and Robbe-Grillet, or through a 'sparseness of technique that Tom Wolfe ascribes to Ronald Searle's POW drawings'. Even more devastating was that the 'war was so serious it was ridiculous',[41] a fact realised by novelists such as Kurt Vonnegut and Thomas Pynchon. It took Vonnegut twenty-three years to find the means to recount his witnessing of the fire-bombing of Dresden. Eventually, he found it in the dark comedy of *Slaughterhouse-Five*. So it goes.

This 'nuclear whimsy' pervaded postwar culture. John Bird's 1959 Cambridge Footlights revue, *The Last Laugh*, was 'an entertainment around the theme of nuclear destruction' and 'opened with the news of an atomic bomb falling on Britain and closed with a song called "Goodbye World"'. Produced by William Donaldson and featuring Eleanor Bron and Peter Cook, it was not a success but all involved would later go on to greater fame with *Beyond the Fringe* and other such productions.

There was also a kind of 'nuclear camp' as exemplified in this response to the bomb from Chelsea resident Quentin Crisp. In *The Naked Civil Servant*, his memoirs, he describes how he did not take the drawbacks of his work as an artist's model seriously, as he expected them, and the whole world, to end at any moment, an eventuality he apparently welcomes.

When the war threw me over, I took up with the atom bomb. We were to be married in the spring of 1963. Take heart, I said to myself, all may yet be lost. *Time* magazine, which cannot be contradicted except by its own subsequent issues, promised that something called the 'missile gap' would then be at its widest. They said that when this happened, the enemy would strike. They and I were unduly optimistic.

He continues by invoking the 1879 novel *The Egoist* by one-time World's End resident George Meredith.

That was years ago. If the bomb comes now it will be too late. I shall embrace radio-activity only in the resigned spirit in which Laetitia agreed to marry the Egoist – partly to round off the story and partly to save the bomb's good name.[42]

---

41 Fussell, Paul, *Wartime: Understanding and Behaviour in the Second World War* (New York: Oxford University Press, 1989), 136.

42 Crisp, Quentin, *The Naked Civil Servant* (London: Flamingo, 1996), 216.

The idea that apparently lightly comic productions such as Molesworth reflect the darker existential questions of its time is less absurd than it might appear. In *Bomb Culture* Jeff Nuttall explicitly claims the absurdist Goon Show, which ran on the radio from 1951 to 1960, as a response to the fear of nuclear war.

The origin of the Goon Show and its curious humour lay, I believe, in British National Service. National Service in the time of the H-Bomb, when all defence was geared to massive nuclear retaliation anyway, was an imposed absurdity which English teenage conscripts sustained by forming their own sense of humour, a combination of corny music-hall comedy, the humour of English comic papers like *Dandy* and *Beano*, hatred of war and the officer classes [...] and a wild nihilistic element which derived from the absurdity of the army itself.[43]

Spike Milligan even managed to render the horrors of the War farcical and comic in his series of autobiographical reminiscences, starting with *Hitler: My Part in His Downfall*. I am intrigued that the *Beano* is cited. As a child, I was an avid and regular reader. It turns out that it was a deliberately subversive publication, particularly with the work of anarchist, anti-war campaigner and CND member Leo Baxendale, who was responsible for, among other characters, the Bash Street Kids.

That the Goons are, in some sense, a response to the H-Bomb, finds confirmation in *The Bed-Sitting Room* by Goons member Spike Milligan and John Antrobus. This is a surreal and absurdist work, first performed in 1962, and set in the aftermath of the Second World War, 'the Nuclear Misunderstanding', which lasted all of two minutes and twenty eight seconds, including the signing of the peace treaty. In 1969 Richard Lester made it into a film, not entirely successfully, though it is visually arresting and imaginative. Filmed mostly in what must be an industrial waste site, to represent post-apocalyptic London, it is full of brilliant touches, such as roads full of the shells of cars, all rust red as if scorched. The title comes from the mutation suffered by one of the survivors, Lord Fortnam, who believes that he will turn into a bedsitting room, which indeed he does. Other characters also mutate into wardrobes and parrots. A father, mother and daughter, played by Arthur Lowe, Mona Washbourne and Rita Tushingham, live in a carriage on the Circle Line, with the train still travelling between ruined and

---

[43] Nuttall, *Bomb Culture*, 116.

deserted stations. Tushingham's character, Penelope, is being wooed by Alan, played by Richard Warwick, who was Wallace in *If...*. Whimsical though the film mainly is, the plot revolves around Penelope's capacity to give birth, and thus help continue the human race. Her first child is a monstrous mutation, though the second is normal, thus allowing for a small degree of optimism. Evan Calder Williams sees it as exemplary of 'salvage-thought at its best', and a 'staggering vision of waste and remnant, of frozen necrotic relations, and of what we keep doing to keep ourselves busy after the end of the world'.[44]

A few months after my birth, my parents took me to stay with my grandmother and her second husband in New York. We were there during the Cuban Missile Crisis, and either my grandmother or my father did look for the nearest fallout shelter, even though they certainly realised that using it in the event of a nuclear attack would have been pointless. New York, though quite a distance from Cuba, was within range of the SS5 ICBMs the Soviets had stationed on the island. My mother remembers endless broadcasts about the location of fallout shelters. At one point someone – my grandmother? My father? – suggested that they should find their nearest shelter.

In his book *The Fate of the Earth*, Jonathan Schell describes what would happen if a one megaton bomb, roughly the size of the Soviet Union's warheads in the early 1960s, with eighty times the explosive power of the Hiroshima bomb, was detonated above the Empire State Building. It 'would gut or flatten almost every building between Battery Park and 125th Street, or within a radius of four and four tenths miles, or in an area of sixty one square miles'. Within that area 'any buildings that had not been flattened would be collapsed, and the people and furniture inside would be swept down into the street'.[45]

At 'a distance of two miles or so from ground zero, winds would reach a hundred and eighty miles an hour. Meanwhile the fireball would be growing until it was more than a mile wide, and rocketing upwards to height of over six miles'. Anyone close to the fireball would be 'charred and killed instantly'. Within a radius of nine miles anyone would receive third degree burns. Within the 'dazzling white light' of the fireball itself 'searing heat would ignite everything flammable and start to melt windows, cars, buses, lampposts and

44 Williams, *Combined and Uneven Apocalypse*, 116.
45 Schell, Jonathan, *The Fate of the Earth* (New York: Knopf, 1982), 47.

everything else made of metal or glass. People in the street would immediately catch fire, and would shortly be reduced to heavily charred corpses'.[46]

Schell continues to enumerate the short- and long-term effects of this comparatively small bomb detonated in an airburst, before deepening the horror by describing the effects of such a bomb being detonated at ground level, those of the twenty megaton bomb likely to be used in the early 1980s, and finally the effect of multiple attacks of such bombs on the United States. He ends this section of the book with his famous pronouncement that the result of such an attack would be the United States being reduced to a 'republic of insects and grass' (the only life forms likely to survive comparatively unharmed).[47]

Writing in the 1970s about the 1950s revival then taking place, and looking back to how that period actually felt, the art critic Kim Levin pointed out how the period saw not just the 'red-blooded, clean-cut All-American boy and the hefty, blond cheerleader', but also the 'drifter, the mystic, the wandering madman', who were, in the words of Allen Ginsberg 'listening to the crack of doom on the hydrogen jukebox'. As she puts it 'the '50s were waiting for the end of the world'.

The incomprehensible idea of the Bomb had sunk into people's souls. Hiroshima and Nagasaki had become public knowledge; bigger and better bombs – made from the invisible atom, form vaporous hydrogen – were being tested. The trauma permeated the decade. Behind the good times and happy days loomed the indelible newsreel image of an incredible growing mushrooming phallic cloud over the water at Bikini, irrational and horrifying. Or the image of a flower, disintegrating, shrivelling into oblivion. Or the human shadow burnt onto the wall. The crumbling wall. Searing light, blinding heat, total annihilation. Nothingness was possible.[48]

However, in the end this particular apocalypse didn't happen. One of the strangest ideas in Quantum Physics is Hugh Everett's many-worlds interpretation, connected closely with his work on the effects of nuclear war, and which, put simply, suggests that everything that might happen has, and there are an enormous or perhaps infinite number of parallel universes, each the

---

[46] Ibid., 48.
[47] Ibid., 65.
[48] Levin, Kim, *Beyond Modernism: Essays on Art from the '70s and '80s* (New York: Harper and Row, 1988), 36.

result of a different outcome at each moment in time[49]. It is something like Jorge Luis Borges' garden of the forking paths, taken to its logical conclusion. Everett himself, convinced, perhaps, of his 'quantum immortality' drank and smoked himself to death from a heart attack at the age of fifty-one.

I have no idea whether Everett's idea is at all plausible, though I know some scientists continue to take it seriously. It does offer an interesting way to think about time. Presumably, there is fork, or a number of forks, in the garden in which the Soviets did not withdraw their missiles from Cuba and the Third World War did break out, with New York and other cities on the Eastern seaboard being destroyed, and my parents and myself obliterated. (It is perhaps appropriate to invoke Everett's ideas in this context. After graduating from Princeton he accepted a post at the Weapons System Evaluation Group at the Pentagon, looking at the effects of nuclear fallout in the event of nuclear war.)

But, in this forking path, or set of such paths, that did not happen. The Soviets withdrew the missiles, the world breathed again and we returned to London after six weeks in New York. And yet, in another sense, perhaps the Bomb did go off, not literally, but culturally perhaps, a slow chain reaction that would take from the early 1960s to the mid-1970s, that exploded in the form of the permissive and psychedelic cultural tendencies of that period. As Peter Hennessy puts it in his history of Britain in the early 1960s.

One of the many reasons for being eternally thankful that the Cuban missile crisis did not trigger a global war that shattered the world in late October or early November 1962 is that Cliff Richard did not take the palm for the highest form of pop music that Britain was to attain. If the five megatons of Russian nuclear weapons British intelligence thought likely to strike Liverpool had fallen, or the nine megatons deemed possible on London and surrounding areas had dropped, there would have been no Beatles and no Rolling Stones...[50]

---

[49] Byrne, Peter, *The Many Worlds of Hugh Everett III Multiple Universes, Mutual Assured Destruction, and the Meltdown of a Nuclear Family* (New York, London: Oxford University Press, 2010).

[50] Hennessy, *Winds of Change*, 319.

5

The London Pale

Until the late 1960s, the old World's End, as described in a number of memoirs of working class life there, still existed much as it had since the late 19th century. Between the King's Road and the river were streets of terrace houses similar to that of my parents, albeit slightly smaller. At the centre of the World's End was a traffic island, with public lavatories. In his account of life in the area after the War, Peter Painter describes the 'ever-changing flow of human tides and currents', which 'as it passed through the old World's End a great whirlpool of energy was created as it swirled around the traffic island at its heart'.[1] Painter believes that 'it was this swirling energy that [...] gave the old World's End so much of the character that marked it out from the rest of West London'.[2] Donald Wheal also recalls this from the 1930s, and it being ruled by La-di-dah, a flat-capped epileptic, toothless newspaper seller, whose nickname derived from his pronunciation of 'News, Star, Standard'.[3] He must have been selling papers there for a long time. He is surely the same news seller Rose Gamble remembers from the 1930s World's End, whom she called 'old Deaffy, poor scruffy, little old Deaffy who sold newspapers at the World's End, whom I had laughed at with the other kids when he hurled himself to the ground in an epileptic fit'. Gamble compares his 'starved, half-mad eyes staring from under his bandaged head' to the famous self-portrait by Van Gogh[4].

Alf Goldberg writes of the 'speakers' corner' on the traffic island where he witnessed speakers such as Bertrand Russell and Sir Samuel

---

[1] Painter, Peter D., *The World's End: Chelsea Unplugged* (Morrisville, NC: Lulu, 2012), 5.
[2] Ibid.
[3] Wheal, Donald, *World's End: A Memoir of a Blitz Childhood* (London: Arrow Books, 2006), 2.
[4] Gamble, Rose, *Chelsea Child* (London: BBC Books, 1982), 185–6.

Hoare.[5] A more ominous presence in the area was Sir Oswald Mosley and his British Union of Fascists. Wheal also remembers the Blackshirts and Communists regularly clashing on the traffic island, which were less Cable Street battles and more street scuffles. He suggests that he must have seen Mosley speak there, though he cannot remember him (Mosley presumably coming down the King's Road from Whitelands House). From the island Blantyre Street and, parallel to it, the World's End Passage, ran diagonally across the whole of the southern part of the World's End. I can remember these streets, though only just. A composite photograph I found, in a book of photographs of old Chelsea collected by John Bignell, of the World's End looking south across the now demolished area does bring much of it back. The area west of Milman's Street was razed and redeveloped as the comparatively modest, low rise Cremorne Estate in 1967. In the early 1970s the streets east of Cremorne Road were pulled down and replaced with the imposing, brutalist World's End Estate, with its seven redbrick tower blocks.

My parents were among the first generation after the War to 'gentrify' areas such as the World's End. Gentrification, the process by which more affluent people move into poorer areas, is now largely damned. At the time, the late 1950s and early 1960s, it seemed less problematic, and what would turn out to be the evisceration of Chelsea as a working-class community unforeseeable. That said, the question of the gentrification of Chelsea actually has a long and controversial history. In his 1956 book on Chelsea, *From Five Fields to World's End*, Richard Edmonds alludes to stories from the *Daily Chronicle* from 1909, lamenting the fact that 'twenty thousand people were being moved from the borough so it could be improved'.[6]

'The entire face of historic Chelsea is undergoing a change, declared the *Chronicle*, and street after street of artisan dwellings had been and continues to be levelled as though swept down by an enemy's guns, and blocks of fashionable mansions are springing up in their place. Hundreds of small traders have seen their businesses swept away at a blow, while thousands of working people have been shipped off to all parts of London in search of other homes.

[5] Goldberg, Alf, and Barry McLoughlin, *World's End for Sir Oswald: Portraits of Working-class Life in Pre-war London* (Blackpool: Progressive, 2006), 15.
[6] Edmonds, Richard, *Chelsea. From the Five Fields to the World's End ... With Eighteen Drawings by Dennis Flanders* (London: Phene Press, 1956), 19.

More dramatically, in 1929, the prospect of the sale of fourteen acres of land between Elystan Street and Milner Street, led to the formation of an Eviction Defence Army by local residents, who used thick sticks, clappers, bells and whistles, to rush to points threatened by bailiffs, and delay the progress of the demolition. Edmonds suggests that, throughout the 20th century, the 'pattern has been the same'. Writing in the mid-1950s he suggests that

The artisans have gone out and the more well-to-do have come in. The pace of events, now fast now slow, has had its impact to such a degree that to-day nearly all of Chelsea east of Beaufort Street has achieved some degree of fashionability. West of Beaufort Street there are changes too, with much of North Stanley, notably Limerston Street, taking on a new look.[7]

The voluptuous actress Diana Dors lived in the World's End in the late 1940s in what one of her biographers describes as a 'shabby King's Road bedsit'.[8] It was there she became, in the words of the same biographer, 'the muse of the Chelsea set', including her then boyfriend Michael 'Dandy Kim' Caborn-Waterfield. She met him in the Cross Keys pub, described in an earlier chapter. He was a public-school educated roué and womaniser who caught Dors' attention by ignoring her. She also encountered the society osteo-path Stephen Ward at this time. After she left both Caborn-Waterfield and Chelsea she married Denis Hamilton, who abused her. She and Hamilton held sex parties in their house in Maidenhead. One of the main features in the house was a two-way mirror, which has its own curious history. It was bought by Hamilton's friend, the slum landlord Peter Rachman, who installed it in his house in Bryanston Mews West, where it was smashed by his mistress Mandy Rice-Davies. It later featured in the legal proceedings of the Profumo affair. It was brought up by prosecutors in Stephen Ward's trial to imply, falsely, that he was a pimp.

    One of the interesting trajectories of this particular phase of gentrification was how it crept westward from the centre of smart London in Mayfair and Knightsbridge to the Eastern end of Chelsea, and then further West, as more affordable houses were sought. A little later it would also go north to Notting Hill Gate and West to Fulham, and after that, unimaginable in the early 1960s, south of the River to Battersea and Clapham. In *The Last Curtsey*, her

[7] Ibid., 19.
[8] Bret, David, *Diana Dors: Hurricane in Mink* (London: JR, 2010), 26.

account of being a debutante, Fiona McCarthy describes the moment at which the postcode SW10, which was hers and ours, became acceptable to 'society'. As she puts it concerning her and her parent's move to Limerston Street in 1958,

The postcode SW10 was only just becoming viable in upper-class circles, where every nuance counted and the self-appointed arbiters could be ferocious in sorting the genuinely upper class from the socially spurious: a few years earlier the only acceptable postcodes were SW1, SW3 or (at a pinch) SW7. The term Chelsea was barely accurate for a street beyond the bend in the King's Road in what was technically World's End, a working class area then in the early stages of being gentrified.[9]

My parents bought the house from the estate agent Roy Brooks, who was famous for his witty and scabrous descriptions of the houses he was selling. His advertisements in the *Sunday Times* and the *Observer* were gems of wit and social observation. They were anthologised, and among those in the anthology is a house in Lamont Road itself.

FASHIONABLE CHELSEA, Lamont Road. Do not be misled by the trim exterior of this modest period res with its dirty broken windows; all is not well with the inside. The decor of the nine rooms, some of which hangs inelegantly from the walls, is revolting. Not entirely devoid of plumbing, there is a pathetic kitchen and one cold tap. No bathroom, of course, but Chelsea has excellent public baths. Rain sadly drips through the ceiling on to the oilcloth. The pock-marked basement floor indicates a thriving community of woodworm, otherwise there is not much wrong with the property. In the tiny back garden an Anderson squats waiting... Lse 40 yrs? G. R. £50. Sacrifice 6,750.[10]

Sadly, for me at least, this turns out not to have been our house, which was in far better condition. Thus it was at the moment that my parents moved there, just before my birth, that SW10 came recognised as within the pale of acceptable London. I found an almost comic confirmation of this when reading *The World in Winter*, an apocalyptic science-fiction novel written by John Christopher. It was published in 1962, so he must have been writing it at almost the exactly the same moment. In the novel freak weather conditions have led to a new ice age, and a concomitant social breakdown. Christopher

[9] McCarthy, Fiona, *The Last Curtsey* (London: Faber and Faber, 2007), 33.
[10] Brooks, Roy, *Mud, Straw and Insults: Confessions of an Honest Estate Agent* (London: John Murray, 2001), 7.

was also prescient in that the winter of 1962 to 1963 was one of the coldest on record, and was remembered as the 'Big Freeze'. Much of the novel concerns the attempts of the protagonists to escape to warmer environments such as Africa, where they are treated with the same contempt that immigrants endured in Britain at the time Christopher was writing.

At one point the centre of London, now known as the 'London Pale', is cordoned off as a safe refuge while the rest of the city is left to anarchy and despair. The exact limits of the Pale are defined as

From the chilly plush of Cheyne Walk [...] up the Earl's Court Road; then, in a long and nearly straight line, Holland Park Avenue, Bayswater Road, Oxford Street, and High Holborn. Up Clerkenwell and Old Street to take in the bulk of the City, down Bishopsgate and a small diversion along Leadenhall Street to take in the Mint and the Tower and a few wharves in the pool [...] with the river as its southern boundary.[11]

This is an almost perfect delineation of the London my parents would have recognised as being in the more implicit pale of social acceptability, with the World's End in, but only just. That Fulham and south of the River are both beyond it would have also seemed entirely right then. I laughed when, a little later in the novel, someone talks about 'a nasty attack from Fulham last night'.[12] In my childhood, Fulham was certainly beyond the pale, to the extent that I was offended when a recent article in *The Guardian* described the World's End as being in that borough.

The sense that, in the 1950s and 1960s, the River was the ultimate border can be seen in the shock generated by wealthy Nell Dunn and her husband, Eton and Oxford educated husband Jeremy Sandford's move from Chelsea to then entirely working-class Battersea. Dunn reflected on her experiences among the working class of South London in her short stories, published as *Up the Junction* (1963) and in her novel *Poor Cow* (1967), which was turned into a film, directed by Ken Loach, in the same year. Sandford made the groundbreaking drama *Cathy Come Home* (1966).

Though the redevelopments south of the King's Road mean that almost all that part of the World's End, as it existed from the late 19th to the mid-20th century, has disappeared, some of the original streets remain. Among these remnants is a small cul-de-sac just off the river end of Riley Street, named

[11] Christopher, John, *The World in Winter* (London: Penguin, 2016), 56.
[12] Ibid., 58 – 9.

Apollo Place. This short street of small houses has some claim to be a place of considerable importance in the history of the post-war avant-garde. It was in number 9 that Francis Bacon lived with David Sylvester in the early 1950s.[13] Later on in that decade John Minton moved in to number 9.

It seems extraordinary to me that the two greatest painters these islands have produced, Turner and Bacon, should have both lived in the World's End, albeit briefly in each case, with little more than fifty yards separating their respective houses. Also that, a few hundred yards to the north, one of the great writers, Samuel Beckett, should also have stayed. It is arguable that Bacon achieved in painting what Beckett did in literature. They both find a means within their respective artistic forms adequate to the horrors of the Holocaust and Hiroshima. In each case they clearly realised that the only way to engage with these fundamentally unrepresentable phenomena was not to try to represent them. Bacon's own response to the same situation can be found in his great work 'Three Figures at the Base of a Crucifixion' from 1945. Like Beckett's *Endgame*, this has nothing and yet everything to do with the concentration camps and all the other catastrophes of this period.

The most tragic resident of Apollo Place was John Minton. A talented painter and illustrator, he had been part of the Neo Romantic movement mentioned earlier. In the 1940s and early 1950s his work was fashionable and well received. He bridged the awkward gap between fine art and illustration, between Bacon and Ronald Searle. In the later part of the 1950s, Minton began to fall out of fashion, owing to the turn against illustration and towards abstraction and Bacon's purer form of representation. That, and his tortured relation to his sexuality and burgeoning alcoholism, led Minton to commit suicide in 1957.

Minton left the house in Apollo Place to Henrietta Moraes, one of the signature figures of 1950s Bohemia, and an habituée of the Colony Room and Gargoyle Club, the French Pub, and the other venues in which it flourished. In her memoirs she describes the house as 'like an Arabic house, with a little doorway, bare walls, railings and nothing else to be seen'. Despite being just round the corner, the sound of traffic on Cheyne Walk was not heard in the houses, only 'the sound of tugs and barges'.[14] During her stay there,

---

[13] Peppiatt, Michael, *Francis Bacon in the 1950s* (New Haven: Yale University Press, 2008), 30.
[14] Moraes, Henrietta, *Henrietta* (London: Hamish Hamilton, 1994), 51.

Moraes and others experienced a number of psychic events, including sightings of strange men, sounds of partying when none had been taking place, experiences of invisible energy, and of 'unidentifiable but terrifying presences'. Her friend Hussain saw 'a man sitting in an armchair' and 'the classic African phenomenon of a bucket of blood containing a decapitated head'.[15] Once, when Hussain and she were lying in bed, she opened her eyes and saw 'a dirty sulphurous yellow light hovering in the air on the other side of the room near the bedroom', which made her freeze in terror in the knowledge that it was 'deadly evil' and if it touched either Hussain or her they would die. She researched the history of Apollo Place and found out that 'the first African slaves to come to England had been brought up the Thames as far as Turner's house [...] This whole area had originally been the site on which the warehouses for the slave-trade traffic had stood.'[16]

While she was living in Apollo Place Moraes agreed to let the photographer John Deakin take some images of her for Francis Bacon to use in his paintings. When he arrived, Deakin told Moraes that 'He wants them naked and you lying on the bed and he's told me the exact positions you must get into.' After a while, she abandoned herself to the positions demanded, with her legs wide open and then began to have doubts. 'Deakin, I know you've got it wrong. Francis can't possibly want hundreds of shots of these most private parts in close-up. I just don't believe that is what he is interested in painting. It can't be so.'[17] Deakin, however, insisted that he was right and that is what Bacon had asked for. Sometime later, while having a drink with Bacon and Deakin in the Colony Room, Bacon revealed that Deakin had indeed got it wrong and reversed the shots. He wanted images of her taken from the reverse position with her head in the foreground. Deakin came back to Apollo Place and took more photographs, this time the right way round for Bacon. However, Moraes later found him selling copies of the first series to sailors in a Soho drinking club, at ten bob a shot. She demanded he buy her a drink as a recompense, and he indeed bought her several.

Bacon used the images taken by Deakin for a number of paintings, including 'Portrait of Henrietta Moraes' and 'Lying Figure with Hypodermic Syringe', both from 1963, 'Lying Figure', 'Lying Figure with Hypodermic

[15] Ibid., 68–9.
[16] Ibid., 70.
[17] Ibid., 71.

Syringe', and 'Henrietta Moraes', from 1966, and finally 'Lying Figure' from 1969. The inclusion of syringes in some of the paintings is not, of course, intended as an illustration of some drug dependency on the model's behalf. It is, rather, a pictorial device. As Bacon put it:

I've used the figures lying on beds with a hypodermic syringe as a form of nailing the image more strongly to reality or appearance. I don't put the syringe because of the drug that's being injected but because it's less stupid than putting a nail through the arm, which would be even more melodramatic.[18]

Nevertheless, that Moraes was dependent on drugs during much of her life, including methedrine and, later, heroin, adds a certain piquancy to those paintings.

It was while living at Apollo Place that Moraes met Allen Ginsberg and Gregory Corso, first in Paris with her husband, Dom Moraes, and then when they arrived in London. In Oxford she witnessed them reading at New College. Corso read his notorious poem 'BOMB', in praise of the hydrogen bomb, and was heckled by members of the CND in the audience. In the printed version, published by City Lights, the poem is arranged typographically in the form of a mushroom clouds. With the arrival of Ginsberg and Corso, as Moraes puts it, the 'first transatlantic beatniks had arrived'. The arrival of the beatniks, and their confrontation with the CND, signals the moment the earnest protest movements of the 1950s gave way to the more anarchic and wild counter-cultural responses to the horrors of the postwar era, the shift chronicled in Jeff Nuttall's *Bomb Culture*. Moraes did not stay long at Apollo Place. As Chris L. Smith puts it, rather archly, in his book *Bare Architecture: A Schizoanalysis*, 'Moraes would eventually be lost to the Apollo Place house as she was lost to most things. She was far too Dionysian for Apollo Place. Too much of the street to be homely. Too much of the milieu to be anything other than uncanny.'[19]

Moraes, originally a member of the small world of 1950s Bohemia, centred on Chelsea, Soho and Fitzrovia, took up with a younger crowd of aristocratic flower children in the 1960s. She travelled with Sir Mark Palmer's proto-New Age assemblage of horse-drawn caravans in the late 1960s and

[18] Smith, Chris L., *Bare Architecture: A Schizoanalysis* (London: Bloomsbury, 2017). 7
[19] Ibid., 120.

early 1970s, going from one aristocratic or rock star residence to another. Palmer even designed the horse-drawn hearse for her funeral in 1999. By the time she had joined this caravanserai she was no longer living in the World's End, but clearly she was always drawn there. In her memoirs she claims that she never liked north London, and found that even Notting Hill Gate seemed like a 'strange country'.[20] 'I loved the river, I always want to be near the river when I'm in London. I am drawn magnetically to it, and most powerfully to the stretch between the end of Chelsea Embankment to Turner's Reach and the King's Arms.'[21] One of the reasons she did return in the 1960s was to go the methedrine clinic in the World's End, to feed a habit that was clearly extremely deleterious to her health. She describes blacking out three times between the World's End and Park Walk, at which point she decides to give up the drug. After ten days recuperating she goes for a walk on the King's Road, wearing 'a moss-green velvet suit bought in Granny Takes a Trip'.[22] Moraes is buried in Brompton Cemetery, on the edge of the World's End.

The culture clash of the World's End is captured by a number of images I have found of the same view. The first is from Edmonds' book on Chelsea. Two of the drawings by Dennis Flanders are of great interest; one is of the then newly built Cremorne Estate, south of the King's Road, in the World's End; the other is the World's End pub and surroundings as it was shortly before my parents moved to the area, and before much of the area around it was torn down to build the World's End towers. In the drawing one can clearly see the Sunlight Laundry on the left, on the opposite side of the King's Road to the pub, and the Salvation Army hostel to the pub's right, behind which are visible the old terraces of that part of the King's Road. Also in the picture is a greengrocer's stall just in front of the pub. This is still clearly a working class area.

As such an area it was the part of Chelsea with the most evident allegiance to the local football team, Chelsea F.C. As a boy wandering around the World's End, I kept noticing a graffiti consisting of a single word, 'shed', on numerous walls in the area. This was my introduction to the strange occult magic of words; this enigmatic single syllable that seemed to have no discernible meaning or message to communicate, except, perhaps, its own existence. It was a kind of poetry, particularly in its eschewal of an article,

[20] Moraes, *Henrietta*, 38.
[21] Ibid., 38–9.
[22] Ibid., 91.

definite or indefinite. Not 'the shed' or even 'a shed', but just 'shed', stark, declarative and slightly threatening in its enigmatic mystery.

That I was ignorant of the word's actual meaning in this context showed how disconnected I was from the culture of the area in which I lived. 'Shed' turned out to refer to what was known as the Shed at the Chelsea Football Club's Stamford Bridge Stadium, which was about half a mile from where we lived (and on the other side of the railway line, thus technically in Fulham). The Shed was the terrace at the south end of the stadium. Built in 1930, and originally named the Fulham Road End, it was almost immediately always referred to as the Shed, owing to its tin roof. The Shed thus became the preferred location for the most die-hard and vocal fans. It was thus equivalent to Liverpool Football Club's the Kop, which was named after Spion Kop, a steep hill that was the site of a battle in the Boer War in 1900. The word 'shed' on the walls of the World's End was therefore not some signal of architectural appreciation but a statement of allegiance to Chelsea Football Club. I remember Chelsea fans in the King's Road in the 1960s as frightening, but it's also possible that I had been made more nervous than I should have been, which in turn is a reflection on how football fans were regarded.

The same view of the pub appears at the end of very curious and largely forgotten film, shot in 1955 and 1957, but not completed until 1959, entitled *Food for a Blush* (or *Food for a Blluuusssshhhhh!*, as the title is spelt onscreen). This strange, amateur half-hour film, directed by and starring two students from Chelsea School of Art, Nicholas Ferguson and Elizabeth Russell, is described on the BFI website as a 'surreal journey through bohemian Chelsea in the mid-50s'.[23] It's not a great film but does capture something of what the very beginnings of the 1960s counterculture must have felt and looked like. The plot, such as it is, involves Russell's disastrous marriage and abandonment by Ferguson as a handsome bohemian. The style is very staged and is obviously aiming at a kind of cinematic surrealism. I liked it for its glimpses of Chelsea and the King's Road in the mid to late 1950s, with shots showing the bend in the King's Road, and the boutique Bazaar.

Russell has been quoted as saying that the film is a 'picture of the post-Teddy-Boy-aimless-coffee-bar feel of the King's Road of 1955', adding that the sole remedy for this sense of ennui and melancholia 'is work, be it only

[23] Birchall, Danny, 'Food for a Blush', BFI Screenonline, www.screenonline.org.uk/film/id/452792/index.html, last accessed 4 February 2021.

to make a film about the somehow disappointing feel of being 20 in 1955'.[24] In his account of the decade following the War, Douglas Sutherland remarks about how 'London was full of lonely and bored people, drifting around without roots or purpose'.[25] For Michael Bracewell the film captures the 'atmosphere of endless waiting, of the search for a new language, of being trapped between adolescence and adulthood within the ruins of a city which still felt Victorian'. He goes on to suggest that is it both 'pre- and proto-Pop', and that there 'is a sense that the art school cast of *Food for a Blush* are in need of a new language, and indeed a whole new culture, through which to express both their identity and their frustrations'.[26] As Bracewell points out, by the time the film was actually released in 1959, such a language would exist, 'in the form of pop music and a burgeoning, mass-media popular culture'. He also alludes to the final shot, which is that of the same side of the World's End pub as in the Flanders illustration.

there is a prophetic subtext to the long, silent closing shot of the film, in which a group of unsmiling Teddy Boys lounge impassively to face the camera outside The World's End pub – occupying one of the ley lines of punk, which would be flourishing on precisely that stretch of the King's Road a little more than 20 years later.[27]

The third image is a photograph featured in *Day of the Peacock: Style for Men 1963–1973*, Geoffrey Aquilina Ross's book on the rise of dandyism between the early 1960s and early 1970s. The picture shows one of the founders of the boutique Granny Takes a Trip, John Pearse, with model Regine Boulanger. Both are dressed in what Ross calls 'Granny's finery', referring to the clothes sold in the boutique Granny Takes a Trip. Behind them is the pub with the words THE WORLD'S END just above Pearse's head. In front of the pub are a group of local men and youths, looking very different to the dandified Pearse. Directly behind Boulanger there is the greengrocer's cart also seen in Edmond's book, with the greengrocer himself in what I can tell, even in a black and white photograph, is a brown coat.[28]

[24] Ibid.
[25] Sutherland, Douglas, *Portrait of a Decade: London life 1945–1955* (London: Harrap, 1988), 68.
[26] Bracewell, Michael (2009), 'The Thrill of It All', www.frieze.com/article/thrill-it-all-0, last accessed 4 February 2021.
[27] Ibid.
[28] Ross, Geoffrey Aquilina, *Day of the Peacock: Style for Men 1963–1973* (London: V & A Publishing, 2011), 84.

Ross describes the location of Granny's as a 'dilapidated stretch' of the King's Road, 'awaiting gentrification known to all as the World's End, after a pub of that name that had serviced the locals since Victorian times'.[29] He continues that

In fashion terms this outpost was in unknown territory, about as far from the trendy boutiques around Sloane Square as it is possible to go. Diagonally across the road are an ailing Woolworth's store, another weary pub, a greengrocer and a housing estate. The shop's immediate neighbour was a sedate office of the Royal British Legion.

He describes 'the paint-peeling terraced houses' of the area, which I suppose must have included ours.[30]

The gentrification of the World's End is lamented in Michael Moorcock's novel *Mother London*. Two of the main characters are described as strolling through the area that has become

so upwardly mobile there was scarcely a house without the scaffolding, the knocked-through downstairs, the dormer window which indicated the new optimism, the optimism of appreciating capital, replacing the old optimism of ideals which had ceased to be in vogue by the late '70s.

One of the characters, Mr Kiss, remarks to the other, Dandy Banaji in 'resigned astonishment' that

I remember when World's End really deserved the name, don't you, Dandy? A church surrounded by rusty corrugated iron, a miserable chip shop, a fly-specked newsagent and a run-down pub. You could wind up here of a winter evening and the most entertainment was feeling the cold grease forming on your skin while you watched old newspapers blow across the overflow from a blocked drain.[31]

Dandy replies that 'I lived across there in sleazy Langton Street.... Now there's art galleries, Penguin Books, wine shops. And look at those warm red blocks and the bit of greenery. Council flats! I'd be proud to live here now. Christine Keeler does. But I suppose I couldn't afford it. Where are all these wealthy people coming from, old man? That's the mystery.'[32]

[29] Ibid., 85.
[30] Ibid.
[31] Moorcock, Michael, *Mother London* (London: Weidenfeld and Nicholson, 2016), 403.
[32] Ibid.

6

Slouching Towards Bethlehem

What my parents could not have realised, when they bought their house, is that Chelsea and the King's Road in particular was about to become one of the centres of a tumultuous cultural and stylistic upheaval. My Chelsea, in which I lived a normal life of going to school, shopping, visiting the library, friends, parties and so on, was, at the same time, the Chelsea of Swinging London, and of Punk. For a brief moment, between the late 1950s and late 1970s, the King's Road was one of those strange attractors or vortices of radical cultural change that emerge at different times. Others might include the Left Bank in 1920s Paris, and the Lower East Side in 1950s New York. Reading historical accounts of the Counterculture and Punk is a strange experience of double vision; it's almost as if they are describing an alternative universe, co-existing with mine, and with almost all the same landmarks and places, but subtly different. I found Sex Pistol Steve Jones' autobiography fascinating in this context, given that he is another West London boy, albeit from a very different background, despite which he and I share a number of landmarks in our respective lives.[1] On the face of it, at least my parents' house seemed at odds with the world by which it was surrounded. The paintings, bronzes, old master drawings, antiques and books seemed from an entirely different universe to that of the King' Road, though in fact it was a bit more complex than that.

Our house is five minutes from Edith Grove, where some harbingers of this upheaval had found shelter. Four rough beasts from Dartford and other points east had slouched towards no. 102 Edith Grove, where for a year and

---

[1] Jones, Steve, and Ben Thompson, *Lonely Boy: Tales from a Sex Pistol* (London: Windmill Books, 2016).

a half, around 1962 to 1963, they lived in considerable squalor. Three of them, Mick Jagger, Keith Richards and Brian Jones, would achieve unimaginable fame as founder members of the Rolling Stones (and in Jones' case an early death by drowning in a swimming pool). The fourth, James Phelge, did little in comparison, though his disgusting habits have accorded him a strangely legendary status. Stories are told of him greeting visitors naked save for his streaked y-fronts on his head. The Rolling Stones used the pseudonym Nanker Phelge for the writing credits for some early songs, after Phelge, and 'nankering', the name they gave to a particular revolting facial expression used by Jones.

In *The World's End: Chelsea Unplugged* Peter Painter describes the presence of the Stones in what was still a working class neighbourhood. According to Painter 'a rumour went around the World's End that The Beatles had moved into a flat just around the corner in Edith Grove'. This was just at the point when the band was becoming famous. It turned out that The Beatles were actually in the area to visit their friends, 'an unheard of bunch of fellow-rockers, called the Rolling Stones', who had moved into a 'shabby flat at number 102 Edith Grove', which 'was very much inside the boundary of the rough and tough World's End and, just like any other newcomers to our patch, they would have to face their own particular initiation'.[2] Painter describes the Stones 'running the cauldron of the streetwise kids who seeing this bunch of long-haired beatniks in their sloppy joes, would taunt them with shouts of, "Get your hair cut!" or, another favourite, "Soap and water!"'.[3]

Painter admits that the dirty appearance did 'little to deter the attention they got from many of the local girls'. One day Painter himself was taken to their 'dingy sanctuary' by his 'attractive sister Carol'.[4] 'All I remember of that day was that there were a lot of people there, and the place was a chaotic mess: dirty plates and glasses littered the floor and piles of cigarette ends covered almost every conceivable surface'.[5] The next time Painter tried to gain access to the flat, looking for Carol, he was told to 'Fuck off sonny!' by Brian Jones, eyes bloodshot, who slammed the door in his face. However, the Stones could often be seen in the local greasy spoon, sharing three

[2] Painter, Peter D., *The World's End: Chelsea Unplugged* (Lulu, 2012), 35.
[3] Ibid., 36.
[4] Ibid.
[5] Ibid.

breakfasts among the five of them. Such breakfasts were necessarily rushed as they had to 'face more taunts from the much sturdier local dustmen, rag-and-bone men and builders, whose territory they had dared to enter'.[6] Painter was also able to listen to the Stones rehearse in The Weatherby Arms, a local pub that has long since disappeared. In particular, he remembers them rehearsing one song over and over again at a particular session, which turned out to be their first single, 'Come On'. Painter suggests that this rehearsal was likely to be accompanied by shouts from the crowd of working men in the pub of '"What a bleeding racket! Don't you know any other songs! You call that singing" etc. etc.' With the help of the Beatles the Stones soon achieved success and 'Just as we were getting used to having the Stones around and had almost accepted them as World's Enders, their own, by now meteoric rise, would signal the time for them to leave us.'[7]

In his memoirs the Stones' manager Andrew Loog Oldham describes his first visit to what he called the 'scummy' Edith Grove flat in order to photograph the band. 'The worn dirty lino in the kitchen and the gas meter in the hall appalled me. There was no telephone and the place smelt like a never-ending fry up.'[8] However, the resulting photographs, taken on the Embankment, with the Stones wearing their own clothes, having forgotten their recently acquired stage apparel, was perfect for what Oldham wanted. 'That look, that "just out of bed and fuck you" look – the river, the bricks, the industrial location – was the beginning of the image that would define and divine them. Word got out: the results of the Embankment photo session were "disgusting. The Stones were unkempt, dirty and rude".'[9] The role the Edith Grove flat played in the formation of the Stones and their image is important enough for a replica of its interior to have been built for *Exhibitionism*, the Rolling Stones exhibition at the Saatchi Gallery in 2016.

The emergence and global success of bands such as the Beatles and the Stones, who took the American form of rock and pop music and made it their own and sold it back to the United States, now looks inevitable. Before this happened such a state of affairs would have seemed impossible. Writing in 1957 about Tommy Steele, the highly astute Colin MacInnes sees the

---

[6] Ibid.

[7] Ibid., 36–7.

[8] Oldham, Andrew Loog, *Stoned* (New York: Vintage, 2008), 218.

[9] Ibid.

future of British popular music more in terms of a return to the Music Hall.[10] What he did not, could not predict is the degree to which British rock music took over and dominated the world from the 1960s to the 1980s, partly by making the American idiom its own. Part of this was to do with the image that British rock musicians chose to project.

I was never aware of the presence of the Stones in Chelsea. I was far too young to be so when they were in Edith Grove or even when Mick Jagger and Marianne Faithfull moved to Cheyne Walk, just south of the King's Road, later in the decade. Keith also moved to the same street, but to a grander house a little further east. However, I was aware that the King's Road was a place that attracted and accepted eccentrics of various sorts. That is perhaps why Ian Fleming had the promiscuous alcoholic psychopath James Bond live in Wellington Square, off the eastern end of the King's Road. For many years I half suspected that I had dreamt of the presence of a pet lion in the World's End. However, it turns out that such a creature did exist, and his story circulates on the World Wide Web in various forms. Christian the lion was bought, apparently on impulse in Harrods, by two young Australian travellers in 1969, who lived with him in the World's End, at the Sophisti-Cat furniture store, for a while before returning him to Africa. Later on they are reunited with him and, from the video on the Web, it appears that he recognises them and embraces them. (To be honest I find the true story less alluring than the more mysterious memory I had, especially given the degree of sentimentalising it has invoked.)

More intriguing is the story of another Chelsea eccentric, Amanda Feilding, who, as a young woman, was filmed trepanning herself. Apparently always interested in mysticism and altered states of consciousness, Feilding had been influenced by a Dutch medical school drop-out and LSD advocate named Bart Huges, with whom she lived in the mid-1960s. Huges trepanned himself in 1965, and persuaded Eton and Oxford-educated Joseph Mellen, by then her partner, to do the same, which he did a year later, aided by Feilding. She trepanned herself in 1970, and filmed the process, which was later released as *Heartbeat in the Brain*. Feilding stood for Parliament in her local Chelsea constituency twice, in 1979 and 1983, gaining 49 and 139

---

[10] MacInnes, Colin, *England, Half English: The Life and Times of Colin MacInnes: A Polyphoto of the Fifties* (London: Faber and Faber, 2012), 55.

votes, respectively. In the 1960s Feilding and Mellon ran, and I guess lived above, the Pigeonhole Gallery, in Langton Street, at the end of Lamont Road.

Bore Hole by Mellen has been republished recently. First published in 1970, for a long time it was a cult work, not least because of its scarcity.[11] I read it, hoping for some insights into 1960s Chelsea, and mainly got the sense that Mellen was a bit of bore hole himself. His obsession with Huges' ideas and especially with the need to compensate for 'sugarlack' when tripping clearly bored many of his fellow psychedelic adventurers. The description of his own trepanning, which took several goes, is fairly repellent and no great advertisement for following his lead. It seems possible that the public advocacy of trepanning by Huges, Mellen and others may have influenced the scene in the greatest of London films, *Performance* where Chas (James Fox) shoots Turner (Mick Jagger) in the head, and the camera appears to follow the bullet through the brain, past an image of the Argentinian writer Jorge Luis Borges and out onto the street.

I also don't remember ever seeing Amanda Feilding in Chelsea, though there's every chance I passed her, possibly many times. I do remember the general countercultural ambience of which she was part; the brightly dressed avatars of 'swinging London', the hippies and the Chelsea Drugstore. I also remember my parents suggesting a walk up the King's Road with my godfather, who was over from New York, to see the Drugstore when it had just opened, and being confused about the word drug, because I knew that drugs were a bad thing. All this was part of the vast, mythic world of adults and life beyond childhood, too large to be fully grasped, and full of inarticulable promise.

In *Swan River*, his memoirs of his family, David Reynolds marks the moment when the counterculture started to colonise the road.

That year, 1965, the shops in the King's Road changed rapidly. Sainsbury's closed and Lord John opened, a development deplored by my mother's elderly relatives, with the exception of Auntie Toto and Uncle Godfrey who liked 'the colourful young people' and anyway bought their food in Oakeshott's and Harrods. Pat and I followed the progress of the boutiques closely; Michael's Man Boutique on the corner of Tryon Street became my favourite and Pat's was Granny Takes A Trip which was about a mile down the road on the bend before the World's End. If either of us wanted to buy a

---

[11] Mellen, Joe, *Bore Hole* (London: Strange Attractor Press, 2015).

shirt or a pair of trousers we would spend an afternoon walking from Sloane Square up to 'Granny's', examining the clothes in every shop before making a decision.[12]

Chelsea then hummed with the counterculture. Lindsey House features in the penultimate sequence in *Blow-Up*, which shows the main protagonist Thomas going to a party in Chelsea. A lot of pot is being smoked at the party. The director Michelangelo Antonioni paid beautiful people from the King's Road £30, a lot of money then, to be extras for the party scene, which meant simply to get stoned. According to Kieran Fogarty, quoted in Jonathan Green's *Days In The Life*, Antonioni threw in a couple of kilos of grass and told the extras to get on with it.[13] Filming took five days with participants stumbling in and out, and everyone waiting on the elusive model Veruschka. Fascinatingly, Gibbs' flat had been used earlier for a BBC programme about LSD, in which the producers supplied free psychedelics for the participants and filmed the results. In *Blow Up*, having failed to persuade his publisher to come with him to the park to see the dead body he thinks he has photographed, Thomas crashes out and then wakes on a vast bed to find the house deserted. The interior is pure aristo-pop, and, as such, anticipates Turner's extraordinary residence in *Performance*, which is hardly surprising as the flat belonged to designer Christopher Gibbs, who was responsible for the look of Turner's house.

Scott Walker of the American pop group the Walker Brothers had a flat near Stamford Bridge, where he was terrified by the noise of football supporters, which he mistook for the noise of his own rabid fans. On his visit to England, Bob Dylan played his first gig in The Troubadour on Old Brompton Road, in 1962, next to the Coleherne pub, already then gaining a reputation as a leather bar. In 1966 Guinness heir Tara Browne died at the intersection of Redcliffe Square and Redcliffe Gardens, more or less halfway between the Troubadour and my primary school. Browne is, of course, featured in the Beatles' song, 'A Day in the Life', though they change the circumstances of his death. He was taken to St Stephen's Hospital, on the Fulham Road, and just above the Ten Acres, the same place that Stephen Ward, the victim of the Profumo affair, was taken after his suicide bid.

---

[12] Reynolds, David, *Swan River* (London: Picador, 2002), 198.
[13] Green, Jonathan, *Days in the Life: Voices from the English Underground, 1961–1971* (London: Pimlico, 1998), 90.

The King's Road itself was a kind of 'pornotopia', or gave the impression of being one, for men at least. Pornotopia was named and defined by Stephen Marcus in *The Other Victorians*.

Pornotopia is literally a world of grace abounding to the chief of sinners. All men in it are always and infinitely potent; all women fecundate with lust and flow inexhaustibly with sap or juice or both. Everyone is always ready for anything, and everyone is infinitely generous with his substance. It is always summertime in pornotopia, and it is summertime of the emotions as well – no one is ever jealous, possessive, or really angry. All our aggressions are perfectly fused with our sexuality, and the only rage is the rage of lust, a happy fury indeed.[14]

The cockney journalist and columnist Frank Norman wrote one of his columns in the 1960s about the experience of walking down the King's Road in that period.

Of late I have taken to visiting Kings [sic] Road Chelsea, of a Saturday morning, to drink of course at the Markham Arms and ogle the stunning mini-skirted girls as they parade up and down without destination in the company of their narcissistic boy friends, with lank medusa hair, frilly shirts and gormless expressions. I feel old, ugly, fat and lonely. I long to speak to them but lack the courage. I am inhibited by my thoughts and their appearance. When I see a beautiful young girl wearing an ultra-brief mini-skirt I take it to be a sign of availability (how could she flaunt herself so and mean otherwise). But my grubby little thoughts are more often than not far from truth – they are merely keeping abreast of fashion. What chagrin life can bring at times.[15]

In his chapter on photography in Len Deighton's *London Dossier*, Adrian Flowers describes the presence of young women on the King's Road as the perfect foil for the male gaze, not least because they are no longer entirely human.

The swinging variety of bird is to be found concentrated in the King's Road, Chelsea, on a Saturday afternoon. They are perfect subject matter for the casual observer, suitably stationary, because of the traffic jam both in the road and on the pavement. Flocks of these creatures occur welded to the folded hoods of vintage and modern open cars. The lone variety drive their own smaller versions. Three-thirty p.m. is the peak display time on a sunny occasion. Everyone is there to be seen.[16]

[14] Marcus, Steven. *The Other Victorians: A Study of Sexuality and Pornography in Mid-nineteenth-century England* (London: Weidenfeld and Nicolson, 1966), 273.

[15] Norman, Frank, *Norman's London* (London: Secker and Warburg, 1969), 250.

[16] Deighton, Len, *The London Dossier* (Harmondsworth: Penguin Books, 1967), 152–3.

I was searching on YouTube for films of the King's Road in the 1960s and 1970s and I found a brilliantly cheesy bit of footage. It's only about a couple of minutes long, and cuts between shots of the crowded pavements seen from moving car, and of a man in close-up, (presumably) driving the car, and what can only be described as gawping at what he sees on those pavements. The shots of the crowd show many women wearing mini-skirts, the piece of clothing that epitomised the King's Road as a kind of pornotopia.

In Swan River David Reynolds describes his first glimpse of a girl in a miniskirt on the King's Road.

We took a bus back and sat upstairs on the right, smoking. The traffic moved slowly. Just after the bus passed Sydney Street we heard a man's voice say, 'Blimey! Look at that.' The people sitting on the left were all looking out of the windows. The bus was stationary. We stood up to see what was happening and everyone else on our side of the bus stood up as well. 'Chroist! Can you see that, Dave?' A tall girl with long blonde hair was walking past the Gaumont cinema wearing a white shirt and a light brown skirt. The skirt was at least a foot shorter than any skirt I – or, it seemed, anyone on the top of this bus – had ever seen.

Reynolds describes the effect on onlookers with people on the pavement 'standing back and staring, while on the 'bus people who didn't know each other were sharing their opinions', which ranged from appreciation of the spectacle through to disgust. A young woman informs the bus passengers that the girl is wearing 'Mary Quant's miniskirt. Just launched.'

I was seeing in the street now something I had only expected to see somewhere very private sometime in the distant future. The woman with curly hair turned round and put her hand beside her mouth. 'We'll all be wearing them next year.' She smiled.[17]

Though the mini-skirt was possibly first developed by André Courrèges in France in the early 1960s, they were made popular in England by Mary Quant. The beginnings of the King's Road as a fashion parade was started when Quant founded the first boutique, Bazaar, in 1955. Quant is a far more important figure than it might seem at first. She was not just a pioneer of the fashion of the period, including the mini-skirt. She can be seen to have artic-ulated and perpetuated a particular image of the feminine, one that had, and continues to have, problematic resonances. Quant 'invented the girl', and

---

[17]   Reynolds, Swan River, 199–200.

was responsible for the 'Lolita Look'. As she put it herself she catered for 'grownups wearing teenage fashion and looking like precocious little girls'.[18] The Quant girl can, or may wish, to be mistaken for a schoolgirl.

In her classic work on the cultural meaning of modern fashion, *Adorned in Dreams: Fashion and Modernity*, Elisabeth Wilson describes the Mary Quant look as more like the 'Madcap of the Upper Fifth than some pop group's collective mistress or a girl at the wrong end of a heroin needle'.[19] She points out that though the clothing of the permissive society was described as 'unisex', it was really childlike, and when girls, 'for all women were girls in those days', wore such clothes 'they were looking not like men or boys but children. It was, as the twenties at times had been, a paederastic period, although to the Christopher Robin look of the twenties the sixties preferred a decadent Lolita image.' She sees this look

personified by the newly famous models of the period, it was the decade of the rage doll, of the waif, of the pre-pubertal Twiggy who shot to fame before she reached the age of consent, the age of the Mary Quant schoolgirl in gym slip and black stockings and of Grace Coddington as Pierrot. The waif became even more decadent in the early 1970s when Ingrid Boulting incarnated her in the sleazy sinuosity of Biba's art nouveau and art deco pastiches.[20]

In an interview she gave for the *Guardian* Special Report on permissiveness, the interviewer asks Quant why 'fashion has virtually abolished the bust' given that at 'fashion shows the model girls appear to have bosoms as flat as two pancakes'. Quant suggests in response that the 'bosom is a mother hood symbol. In times of war solders far from home yearn back to the comforts of mother and all that, and their pin-up girls all have big bosoms. Marilyn Monroe, Jayne Mansfield, they could all be considered by-products of the war. Her questioner invokes fashion theorist James Laver's theory of the shifting focus to different erogenous zones, and asks 'what is the erogenous zone of our present fashion period'.

The crutch. This is a very balanced generation, and the crutch is the most natural erogenous zone. Clothes are designed to lead the eye to it. The way girls model clothes, the way they sit, sprawl, or stand is all doing the same thing. It's not 'come

[18] Quant, Mary, *Quant by Quant* (London: Cassell and Co, 1966), 83.
[19] Wilson, Elizabeth, *Adorned in Dreams: Fashion and Modernity* (London: Virago, 1985), 176.
[20] Ibid., 176–7.

hither', but it's provocative, saying 'I'm very sexy, I enjoy sex, I feel provocative, but you're going to have a job to get me. You've got to excite me. I can't be bought but if I want you I'll have you.'[21]

In the same year that Quant started Bazaar, one-time Chelsea resident Vladimir Nabokov published *Lolita*, his provocative classic account of illicit desire and love. In 1962 Stanley Kubrick released his film version of *Lolita*, though Sue Lyon, the actor playing the eponymous 'nymphet' was fourteen, rather than twelve. To a great degree this entirely misses the point of the book, as Nabokov pointed out. He wanted Lolita to be distinctly prepubescent, so as to emphasise the sheer strangeness of obsessive love. Yet, in his decision to cast a teenager as Lolita, Kubrick connected the sexualised figure of the young girl and its thanatotropism to the apocalyptic nihilism of the period. In 1964 he released *Dr Strangelove: Or How I Learnt to Stop Worrying and Love the Bomb*, his response to the possibility of nuclear holocaust. Peter Sellers plays multiple characters in both, suggesting that, even if their respective subjective matters are very different, they are somehow connected.

The end of the War saw the debut of the term teen-ager (with the dash). It probably was first used in 1941 in *Popular Science Monthly*, but the most famous early appearance of the word was in *Life Magazine* in 1944. That the time the article is published in 1944, as the Second World War is coming to an end, is not coincidental. At the end of his book on the emergence of the teenager, Jon Savage rather provocatively connects the idea of the teen-ager with the Atomic Bomb.

Nineteen forty-five was Year Zero, the start of a new era heralded by the revelations of Nazi inhumanity and the unleashing of the ultimate terror weapon. The mass production of arms and commodities had resulted in an acceleration of life. The A-bomb's apocalyptic revelation precipitated a new kind of global consciousness and a new kind of psychology. Faced with the prospect of instant vaporization, many humans began to focus totally on the present, if not the instant.[22]

Thus, according to Savage, the old world was dead the young were best placed to flourish in the new world, as a *tabula rasa*, a new start. According to Savage, the 'Teenager resolved the question posed by the war: what kind of

---

[21] Hoggart, Richard, *Permissive Society: The Guardian Inquiry* (London: Panther, 1969), 23.
[22] Savage, Jon, *Teenage: The Creation of Youth Culture* (London: Pimlico, 2008), 464.

mass society will we live in?' the answer was a 'future ordered around plea-sure and acquisition: the harnessing of mass production to disposal leisure items like magazines, cosmetics, and clothes...'. Thus the teenager was the 'ultimate psychic match for the times: living in the now, pleasure-seeking, product-hungry, embodying the new global society where social inclusion was to be granted through purchasing power'.[23]

In *The Fate of the Earth* Jonathan Schell suggests that the threat of nuclear extinction brings the very purpose of sexuality into doubt. He goes on to say that it is no coincidence that both pornography and nuclear destruction are described as 'obscene', as in the former we 'find desire stripped of any further human sentiment or attachment' and in the latter 'we find violence detached from any human goals, all of which would be engulfed in a holocaust'. Thus, according to Schell the 'entire world, cut adrift from its future and its past' has become what the Japanese call a 'floating world', a pleasure quarters.[24]

While browsing in a shop specialising in pop ephemera while researching for this book I came across a pulp paperback from the early 1970s about the Permissive Society, called, simply, *King's Road*, by someone named Mariella Novotny.[25] The cover features Novotny herself in a hat and a skirt and nothing much else, with one arm across her breasts while the other appears to be pulling her skirt down towards her genitals. Novotny's image typified the King's Road ideal of the sexy girl or dolly bird. Novotny's book is set partly on the King's Road, though most of the plot concerns Black Power activism and transgressive sexuality of various sorts. She describes the typical Saturday afternoon on the road and its erotic allure and frustration, as experienced by her protagonists C. B. and Tristessa.

The King's Road was in full swing. It reflected the best and the worst of young taste. An intriguing mixture of vivid beauty and vulgar exhibitionism. The regular crowd was interspersed with tourists and thrill seekers. They feasted their starved senses on the goods freely displayed. Dreamed of touching but knew they never could. If old age was not the bar then a conformist upbringing was. They had to be satisfied with sensual fantasies and wishful thinking. People like C. B. and Tricesta had no need to fantasise, they had no hang-ups with their bodies. Sexual self expression was part of

[23] Ibid., 465.
[24] Schell, Jonathan, *The Fate of the Earth* (New York: Knopf, 1982), 158.
[25] Novotny, Mariella, *King's Road* (London: New English Library, 1973), 53.

their life, automatically accepted. They needed no titillation, no pseudo stimulation. But the onlookers went home, nursing their erections, hurried for cover and masturbated, feeling guilty.[26]

Before my encounter with her book, I had never heard of Novotny. She turns out to be a much more interesting person than her brief literary career suggests. As mentioned earlier, Novotny was also the person doing the whipping at the notorious 'Man in the Mask Party', the orgy held in December 1961, which Mandy Rice-Davies and Christine Keeler attended with Stephen Ward, and which featured at Ward's trial, the establishment attempt to deal with the Profumo Affair. Novotny, whose name was kept out of the trial report by Lord Denning, was of Czech origin, and was reputedly a spy and had been expelled as a security risk from the United States, having, allegedly, slept with President Kennedy.[27] Novotny's extraordinary life involves not just the above, but rumours that she was involved in a Soviet plot to discredit Western leaders.[28] Later in her life she was also part of a British Intelligence plot to use brothels to compromise people of interest, including the head of a Caribbean island and a police operation to break up a massive fraud operation.[29] She has a strange literary legacy, having apparently inspired J. G. Ballard to name one of the characters Karen Novotny in his experimental work *The Atrocity Exhibition*.[30]

Girls involved in the Profumo affair, such as Christine Keeler and Mandy Rice-Davies, represented the new type of female desirability, as heralded by Quant, away from the curvaceous, large-breasted ideal of the 1950s. Stephen Ward's girls were all broadly of the same physical type; gamine, slim, with narrow hips and waist, the look later made popular by models such Jean Shrimpton. This had been something that Keeler's first employee, the club owner Percival Murray also saw as increasingly desirable. As Caroline Kennedy and Philip Knightley put it in their study of the framing of Ward

Murray saw in Christine a quality which has instant appeal for a certain type of man – she was a child-woman. Her photographs do not capture this quality. Keeler

[26] Ibid.
[27] Pizzichini, Lilian, *The Novotny Papers: 'A Bit Vulture, A Bit Eagle'* (Stroud: Amberley Books, 2021), 51–2.
[28] Ibid., 164–5.
[29] Ibid., 216ff.
[30] Ballard, J. G., *The Atrocity Exhibition* (London: Harper Perennial, 2006).

was very small but perfectly proportioned. Her dark, oval eyes set wide apart and her high cheekbones were, she said, part of her American Indian ancestry. She had little skill in applying make-up or wearing clothes and always managed to look slightly scruffy. She spoke quietly and with effort, as if always trying to remember lessons. She moved very sensuously and let men know that she was fully aware of the effect that this had on them. Overall – and this is the previously-unrevealed secret of her attraction – she appeared like a sexually-aware 12-year-old girl who has dressed up in her mother's clothes, put on her mother's make-up and is prepared to play at being a woman, no matter what that involves.[31]

Ward clearly understood this, given his habit of addressing Keeler as 'little baby'. In her own account of the Profumo affair, Keeler alleges that Ward was a spy, and was using her to find 'information on nuclear warhead stockpiles in Britain, Germany's armed forces, new missiles, aircraft and submarines and the strategic policy of the British government, especially in UK-US military co-operation'. In particular, she claims that the main question for Ward was 'when were nuclear warheads going to be positioned in West Germany'.

For people like me who lived through it all, it did feel as though the end of the world might be around the corner. We weren't nuts going around with sandwich boards announcing 'The End of the World is Nigh', just ordinary people terrified of a nuclear holocaust. It all seemed so possible. From about the age of twelve I had lived with advice on what to do in a sudden nuclear attack. I can still remember it because it was so silly: 'Duck into the nearest doorway, close your eyes very tightly and try to cover any exposed parts of the body.'[32]

All this coincided with the emergence of legitimate soft pornography, starting with Playboy in the United States in the early 1950s. British imitators emerged in the mid-1960s onwards, with porn impresario Paul Raymond's short-lived *King* in 1964, *Penthouse* in 1965, *Mayfair* a year later, and a revamped version of a smaller magazine, *Men Only*, in 1971, followed by *Club International* in 1972. Christine Keeler was *King*'s first pin-up. Later, in the early 1970s, Mariella Novotny wrote articles for *Club International*.

The porn mags promoted a literal male pornotopia. As Marcus Collins points out, this was an entire way of living, a 'model of masculinity which

---

[31] Kennedy, Caroline and Philip Knightley, *How the English Establishment Framed Stephen Ward* (Scotts Valley, CA: CreateSpace, 2013), 68–9.

[32] Keeler, Christine, *Secrets and Lies: The Trials of Christine Keeler* (London: John Blake, 2019), 77–8.

covered everything from what to wear to how to make love... repudiating the "burden of breadwinning" in favour of a more relaxed, expressive, indeed "emancipated" mode of living'.[33] In Collins' words the porn magazines presented 'a utopian vision of a sexualized society populated by the two sexes undergoing parallel emancipations'.[34] Even Mary Quant spoke approvingly of such porn in an interview for the *Guardian* Special Report on permissiveness. 'Pornography is great, if it's good' she declares, and, on being asked what is good pornography, replies that 'Good pornography is erotic but pleasing. Only ugliness is obscene. Yes, I am for pornography if it's good, against if it's ugly.'[35]

For Collins what distinguishes this wave of pornographic magazines from earlier such publications is how they were part of the 'permissive moment' in British society from the Obscene Publications Act of 1959 to the Divorce Act a decade later, with the Chatterley Trial, the Profumo Affair, the legalisation of homosexuality, and the rise of pop culture and the counter-culture in between. As such they enabled pornography to emerge out of the shadows and become part of a wider cultural moment, for better or worse.[36] The King's Road was a signal part of the fantasy, promulgated in soft porn, in which 'Britain was promoted relentlessly as a sexual Shangri-la', with 'the British "bird"' proclaimed as 'suddenly the most attractive, the most desirable, the most startling girl in the world'. The Chelsea Girl was the ideal, 'the zoom-away girl in the souped-up Mini' in *Mayfair*'s words, and 'sixties porn models were presented as ingenues drawn inexorably to the sexual magnet that was swinging London'.[37] Part of this involved presenting the models not as the anonymous figures of earlier pornography but fully rounded personalities with fabricated profiles. As Marcus points out, two personae were favoured; the 'redeemed tomboy', and the 'child-woman'.[38] To begin with at least soft pornography was presented as part of the general emancipation of society, and thus an ally of feminism.

[33] Collins, Marcus, 'The Pornography of Permissiveness: Men's Sexuality and Women's Emancipation in Mid Twentieth-Century Britain', *History Workshop Journal*, 47, no. 1 (1999): 105.
[34] Collins, 'Pornography', 117.
[35] Hoggart, *Permissive Society*, 21.
[36] Collins, 'Pornography', 102.
[37] Ibid., 104–5.
[38] Ibid., 110.

The Ice Age shows how, for many, the liberation offered by the 1960s was itself less idealistic than we might think. One of the characters describes how she didn't let her previous employer, in his sixties

go too far with her, because he was after all old enough to be her father, but she certainly didn't mind his dirty jokes and dirty postcards, his souvenirs from Copenhagen, his Sex Diary and his Danish playing cards, and she didn't mind him putting his hand down her blouse in the summer or up her skirt in the winter, for a quick feel. Why not? It didn't hurt her, she didn't mind a squeeze. This was the age of the mini-skirt, the swinging sixties, the days of liberation, and dirty old men like Stan felt that the golden age had arrived at last: they had waited long enough for it, had worked away for Ventex in the repressed provinces with repressed and ageing wives, through a world war and through years of austerity, and suddenly here it all was, the world of Penthouse and the Beatles, the world of large steaks and double cream on real gateaux, the world of girls and nightclubs and expense account champagne.[39]

For some, of course, the new permissiveness was far from utopian. There is an image by Chelsea photographer John Bignell that shows some beautiful young people sitting or standing outside Picasso's Café in the King's Road. On the right there is a girl wearing a curly wig, seen in profile. Her name was Claudie Delbarre, and she was eighteen years old, French, and an au pair, a model and possibly a prostitute. She lived in a bedsit in Walpole Street. She had been sent to *Penthouse Magazine* by the head of her model agency and was supposed to return for a second visit. Twenty-four hours or so after the photograph was taken, on 19 February 1967, she had been murdered. The man who killed her, Robert 'Bobby' Lipman, thirty-seven years old, and the son of an American property developer, was convicted of manslaughter, rather than murder, on the grounds that he was tripping on LSD, and did not know what he was doing.

Disturbingly perhaps, the Internet has other pictures of Delbarre. Looking at them feels voyeuristic, not least because they are poignant and she looks vulnerable rather than seductive. Two in particular stand out for me. One is captioned as follows: 'CLAUDIE DELBARRE an eighteen year old French au pair girl who was murdered in her Walpole Street room, stands by Picasso Café.' She is clearly actually in the World's End, in Limerston Street, and the turning into Lamont Road is visible. The other shows her on the other

[39] Drabble, Margaret, *The Ice Age: A Novel* (London: Weidenfeld and Nicolson, 1977), 57–8.

side of the King's Road, in Milman's Street. Behind her it is possible to see the block on the King's Road in which number 430 is found. At the time when the photograph was taken, 430 was occupied by Michael Rainey's Hung on You boutique, one of a number of such establishments to occupy that address. In the photographs she is posing in a very short minidress, and peep-toe kitten heel shoes. Perhaps these pictures were intended for the portfolio for *Penthouse*. As with any such pose, there is a considerable vulnerability, an exposure to the judgement of the male gaze. Perhaps she hoped that modelling would allow her to avoid having to undertake sex work. If the date on the website is to be believed, the photographs were taken ten days before the end of her world.

Delbarre's story captures both the allure and the sadness of Chelsea and the King's Road in the late 1960s. This found expression a decade or so later in Elvis Costello's song '(I Don't Want to Go to) Chelsea'. In his memoir *Unfaithful Music and Disappearing Ink* Costello describes how the song came out of spending weekends watching a 'late run of '60s films set in London', including *Morgan: A Suitable Case for Treatment*, Richard Lester's *The Knack... And How to Get It* and *Smashing Time*, 'about two northern girls making their name in the capital'.[40] This last film, which he describes as 'a pop satire about a dim, eager girl and her plain but more cynical friend and the reversal of roles that overtakes them in pursuit of music and fashion stardom' that stuck in Costello's mind. He describes how

Seven years earlier, at the world's end of the '60s, I'd gone with my Dad to a few of the more enduring clothing haunts of Chelsea on a rare outing together. The shops still had fashionably psychedelic names like I Was General Gordon's Favourite Pilchard and The Marshmallow Cricket Bat.[41]

At the time of writing the song Costello suggested that

Chelsea seemed even more of an unattainable neighborhood. It stood for both the groovy past and was reported in the papers as the hot-bed of the new punk ferment; apparently the work of dastardly haberdashers or people who had half grasped some French political manifesto from 1969.[42]

---

[40] Costello, Elvis, *Unfaithful Music & Disappearing Ink* (London, New York: Viking 2015), 145.
[41] Ibid., 146.
[42] Ibid.

The song itself with lyrics such as 'she's last year's model/They call her Natasha when she looks like Elsie/I don't want to go to Chelsea', seem to invoke both the supposed glamorous image and the more mundane reality of the Chelsea girl, who may or may not be a prostitute.

Perhaps Delbarre's dress came from the most famous countercultural boutique Granny Takes a Trip, a hundred yards from where each of the photographs was taken. In *The Look*, his important study of pop and rock style, Paul Gorman describes the beginnings of Granny's, in early January, 1966, when 'a trio of exotically dressed youths set about erecting a bizarre sign above an equally unusual retail outlet down the wrong end of the King's Road, the World's End'[43]. Apparently, Chelsea Football Club was playing at home that day, and fans hooted and jeered at the shop with its name in art-deco script and its interior, decked out 'as a psychedelic New Orleans bordello, mixing Aubrey Beardsley reproductions with *fin-de-siècle* opulence amid blow-ups of French postcards of naughty '90s minxes in silk stockings, a Wurlitzer jukebox, a horn gramophone, glass beaded curtains and marbellised wallpaper'.[44] For Raphael Samuel, Granny's was the very first English example of 'retrochic', and vintage chic. He cites Harriet Love's Vintage Chic Store, which opened in New York in 1965, as the first, with Granny's close behind.[45] The trio in question were aspiring artist Nigel Waymouth, his then-girlfriend, Sheila Cohen, an 'obsessive collector of vintage clothes', and John Pearse, an ex-mod and Savile Row apprentice tailor. What Granny represented was a reaction against the modernism and plasticity of contemporary culture, and a kind of camp nostalgia for Victorian and Edwardian frills, velvets and satins, and a fascination with aesthetic figures such as Aubrey Beardsley and Alphonse Mucha. Beardsley would be the subject of a major retrospective at the Victoria and Albert Museum later that year, as well as of a new biography by Stanley Weintraub. The shop soon attracted the rock aristocracy with the Beatles, Rolling Stones and Pink Floyd all wearing clothes bought from Granny's.[46]

[43] Gorman, Paul, *The Look: Adventures in Pop and Rock Fashion* (London: Sanctuary, 2001), 65.
[44] Ibid.
[45] Samuel, Raphael, *Theatres of Memory. Vol. 1, Past and Present in Contemporary Culture* (London: Verso, 1994), 89.
[46] Gorman, *The Look*, 65.

That the shop was in the World's End was, apparently, quite daring. Gorman suggests that 'the choice of location... could not have been more out of the way. Around the bend of World's End, it was not only across the town from the happening areas of Carnaby Street and the West End but it was also a good mile west of King's Road epicentre, where Mary Quant's Bazaar had established the Chelsea look half a dozen years earlier'. Pearse described the area as 'a complete khazi'.[47] Nevertheless, Granny's, which was featured in *Time* magazine's famous 'swinging London' article, was a prime mover in the sudden emergence into full visibility of the countercultural style, in which the normal suits and frocks worn by most people were replaced by the most exotic and androgynous clothing possible. *A Day in the Life*, Robert Greenfield's life of the beautiful and doomed couple Tommy and Pussy Weber, quotes Waymouth's take on the World's End.

'Historically,' Nigel Waymouth said, 'that part of Chelsea had always had a great deal of notoriety attached to it. In medieval times and in the eighteenth century, it was sort of a den of thieves and had a louche reputation. It was the dead end of the King's Road, and we revived it by doing something that dragged people down there. Saturday was the big day. That was the parade on the King's Road. Every hairdresser in the world was there. Our first customers at Granny Takes a Trip were local debutantes and gays. Then John and Paul and Mick and Keith and Anita Pallenberg came in, and we started selling to the Saturday crowd. And the word spread.[48]

Granny's was much more than a boutique. It was a major hub of the psychedelic counterculture, notorious for its druggy reputation as it was famous for its clothes. The front of the shop was a work of art in itself, frequently changing. Among its more well-known incarnations were a cartoon image of Jean Harlow, which covered the whole of the front, leaving only her mouth as a way of looking into the shop, the giant, blown-up photographs of Native American chiefs Low Dog and Kicking Bear, and a real car. This turns out to have been Pearse's own 1947 Dodge, which broke down on the way to the airport, at which point Waymouth suggested that instead of taking it to the breaker's yard, they should cut it in two and have the front half protruding out of the shop. Because the shop was set back from the pavement on the King's Road

---

[47]   Ibid.
[48]   Greenfield, Robert, *A Day in the Life: One Family, the Beautiful People, and the End of the '60s* (Cambridge, MA: Da Capo Press, 2009), 109.

with a raised area directly in front of it, such a daring display was possible. You can still see the site today, now occupied by a shop offering 'Bespoke Italian Chandeliers and Artistic Features'.

In his book about the burgeoning youth culture, *The Young Meteors*, published in 1967, Jonathan Aitken describes visiting Granny's. He suggests that as one continues 'up the King's Road towards the World's End, one reaches a gay conglomeration of boutiques which so often change their styles, clientele and location (seven new boutiques opened here between November 1966 and January 1967), that it would be unwise to attempt to mention them all in detail'.[49] He does, however, mention the Gloryhole boutique at 342a King's Road, where 'owner Gerald McCann holds court in a pear-shaped den with puce wallpaper' (I doubt anyone would get away with that name nowadays), Sue Locke's shop at 414 King's Road and that at 430 King's Road, where 'ex-naval officer Bill Fuller, aged 33, and his girlfriend Carol Derry, 26, (daughter of the famous test pilot John Derry) sell "the cheapest clothes in London this side of Biba's", and have an unusual line in imported French designs'.[50] This last must be the first boutique to occupy what will become one of the most famous addresses in British fashion, more on which later. Aitken reserves his most fulsome description for Granny's.

A few yards further along amidst a row of peeling tenements [by which he means the very houses in the Ten Acres, one of which was my family home], one comes to what is undoubtedly the weirdest boutique in London. A matchbox size building adjacent to the British Legion Headquarters, it is painted bright purple, carries above the door the slogan 'One should either be a work of art or wear a work of art' and is inscribed, in massive computer-type lettering, with its title 'Granny Takes a Trip'.[51]

Aitken points out that the 'name has obvious LSD connotations', though the owners deny it, claiming it reflects the idea that 'if a grandmother saw a young person wearing the clothes on sale in this boutique she would go back on a mental trip that would take her mind back fifty years to the past'. Aitken concedes that this is plausible, describing the shop as 'an establishment run by bizarre eccentrics for bizarre eccentrics'. He lists the 'second-hand garments of a bygone age' including

[49] Aitken, Jonathan, *The Young Meteors* (London: Secker and Warburg, 1967), 23.
[50] Ibid., 23–4.
[51] Ibid., 24.

Charleston dresses of the 1920s, Victorian bustles from the 1880s, Boer War helmets, African fezes, Arab head-dresses, Chicago gangster suits from the pro-hibition era, military uniforms, blown-up photographs, of Edwardian chorus girls at £2 each, antique swords, glass walking sticks, Victorian feather boas, an antique gramophone...[52]

There is also a 'mass of with-it accoutrements, such as mini-skirts... op art shirts, gold-rimmed sunglasses, floral ties, velveteen breeches, yellow suede jackets, pink PVC dresses and so on ad halluciatonem'[53]. Aitken quotes Nigel Waymouth on the appeal of the shop.

Our shop, in pop jargon, would be described as very camp. Camp is kind of taking the mickey out of sex by being theatrical. Sort of playing out fantasies in real life. It's a romantic dream world we're catering for. Lots of young people wearing old and for-eign clothes, at least around the house – it's all part of this camp thing.[54]

The idea of camp as a pop-cultural reference was extremely new. Susan Sontag's 'Notes on Camp' had only been published in 1964, three years earlier.[55]

Nigel Waymouth was also one half of Haphash and the Coloured Coat, along with Michael English, perhaps the most influential under-ground graphic designers, in England at least. They designed posters for clubs such as UFO and Middle Earth, record sleeves, events including the 14 Hour Technicolour Dream at Alexandra Palace. Along with Pearse they also recorded an album under the name Haphash and the Coloured Coat. Entitled 'Featuring the Human Host and the Heavy Metal Kids', it is reputedly an influence on German Cosmische Rock pioneers Aamon Dull. A second album was recorded without English, but with, among others, Mike Batt, best known for the theme tune for The Wombles. The term 'heavy metal', later applied to a particular genre of hard rock in the 1970s, as well as 'Heavy Metal Kid', were both coined by William Burroughs in *The Soft Machine*.[56]

[52] Ibid.
[53] Ibid.
[54] Ibid., 24–5.
[55] Sontag, Susan, "Notes on 'Camp'". *Partisan Review* 31, no. 4 (Fall 1964): 515–530.
[56] Burroughs, William S., *The Soft Machine: the Restored Text* (London, New York: Penguin, 2014), 149.

The image of Jean Harlow on the front of Granny's was the work of the design collective BEV, an acronym taken from the names of its constituent members, Douglas Binder, Dudley Edwards and David Vaughan. They had all studied together at Bradford School of Art, where they had been inspired by the bright colours of Asian immigrants' houses. In London they set up a business painting murals, furniture, cars and anything that could be decorated in bright, psychedelic colours. Their most famous productions were a massive mural on both sides of the Lord John boutique in Carnaby Street, Paul McCartney's piano and their own AC Cobra American sports car, which featured in a Kinks shoot. They painted murals in various Beatles' houses, as well as in the Kinky boutique in the King's Road.

Like many such collectives they worked in a variety of media, and, among other things, organised the Million Volt Light and Sound Rave, a multimedia extravaganza held at the Roundhouse in late January and early February 1967, featuring, among others, the short-lived electronic music collective Unit Delta Plus, consisting of Delia Darbyshire, Brian Hodgson and Peter Zinovieff. Because they were involved with McCartney at the time, they asked him if he would contribute something. Possibly to their surprise, he agreed and wrote a fifteen-minute piece of experimental music, 'Carnival of Light', which was played at the rave, but has never been released. Apparently, George Harrison forbade it being made public. McCartney has supposedly considered releasing it a number of times since. Beatles historian Mark Lewisohn, who has heard it, dismisses it as 'just loose random sounds'. If the YouTube upload calling itself 'Carnival of Light' is the real McCartney track (and I believe it is) then I have to disagree. In my view it's mesmeric, strangely brilliant, and reminds me of Stockhausen, Can and Pil, among others.

Members of BEV left their mark in other parts of the World's End. In 1967 Dudley Edwards teamed up with designer Michael McInnerney to form Om Tentacle, in order to design posters, book covers and other commissions, including painting a mural for Puss Weber's Flying Dragon Tea House at 436 King's Road. Puss Weber and her husband, Tommy, were exemplary figures of the London counterculture in the late 1960s. Both extraordinarily beautiful, connected and privileged, they led lives that were increasingly sad. Both became drug addicts, cocaine in his case, and heroin in hers. Tommy left Puss, dated Charlotte Rampling and became part of the Rolling Stones' inner circle. Puss, meanwhile, sought with ever decreasing success and ever greater lunacy, spiritual succour in various forms. Puss died by suicide in 1971.

In his account of Tommy and Puss Weber's glamorous tragic lives, Robert Greenfield describes the location of the Tea House as being at 'the epicenter of London's hip world, where everyone came to see and be seen on Saturdays'.[57] Puss was both taking a lot of LSD, which led her to make 'connections between events that others did not see as necessarily being related', and was also 'heavily involved with the I Ching'. The name of the Tea House came from the first hexagram Chi'en or 'The Creative', for which the judgement reads 'Flying dragon in the heavens. It furthers one to see the great man.'

McInnerney 'spent four very cold winter months perched on a scaffold painting the astonishing mural that covered the front of the tea shop', which Greenfield describes as

a twenty-by-thirty-foot representation of 'the heavenly dragon descended to earth, the symbol of God's compassion. A tear in its eye waters the earthly dragon in the form of a plant (the street door entrance), the symbol of God's presence on earth. The dragon's fiery breath parts the water on the beach to reveal the glass window and the interior.' Composed of several layers of hand-sanded primer with flamboyant coach paint mixed into it to produce a 'radiant' color, the snaking body of the heavenly dragon was prepared with silver leaf by F. G. Fowle, a well-known fairground artist, before being painted. As McInnerney noted, 'This was done to create a surface that would reflect the setting sun down the King's Road.'[58]

The interior of the Flying Dragon was also extraordinary, featuring a rising white horse on one wall and a descending white horse on the other. The background to the horses came from two large Anchor Butter posters, with the images of the butter cut out, leaving only the green grass. Finally, 'A moving cloud effect was created by two cloud machines placed in opposite corners of the room. Artificial grass was placed on the floor as a carpet with tables and cushions.' The Tea House soon rivalled the nearby Baghdad House, a Persian restaurant in the Fulham Road, as a major venue for those belonging to 'the crème de la crème of hip London society', including Mick Jagger and Donovan.[59]

[57] Greenfield, *A Day in the Life*, 109.
[58] Ibid., 110–11.
[59] Ibid., 112.

According to Nigel Waymouth, at the Baghdad House everyone

smoked joints and dropped Mandrax and acid while eating our kebabs. That was the first public place where people openly smoked joints in London. We did smoke joints at the Dragon, but we were a little more cautious because all those shops, my own included, would regularly get raided. The Dragon was a little phenomenon, and it was lovely. It was a sweet place, and Puss was there.[60]

Inspired by Mike McInnerney, Puss briefly became a devotee of Meher Baba, the Indian spiritual master, whose most famous countercultural follower was Pete Townshend of The Who, and the Dragon was a centre for his followers. The Dragon lasted eleven months, and closed down in December 1968. 'By then, Puss had embarked on a full-time search for meaning in her life. Her quest soon became so extreme that virtually no one she knew in London could keep up with her, much less understand what it was she was really trying to find.'[61] One of the places she sought meaning was at Trungpa Rinpoche's Kagyu Samye Ling Monastery in Scotland, dedicated to Tibetan Buddhism, where David Bowie and Leonard Cohen also spent time.

The World's End was also home to a different form of counterculture, less groovy and more hippy. In 1968 a shop and commune was started by Muz Murray in Dartrey Road. It was named Gandalf's Garden, apparently with Tolkien's blessing, and used *The Lord of the Rings* as a mythical basis for its ideas and activities, which including meditation, yoga and gardening. One of those activities was a magazine, also named *Gandalf's Garden*. The shop/commune's activities ceased in 1971 (or rather dispersed to various 'seed centres' around the world according to its members, by which time work was proceeding to knock down Dartrey Road and its surrounding roads to build the World's End Towers, then the largest social housing project in Europe).

In the 1960s Tolkien became a major cult figure for the English counterculture of the period. In his book *Electric Eden* Rob Young suggests that the enlightened clientele of Gandalf's Garden would 'have regularly slouched towards Middle Earth, the underground club started by John "Hoppy" Hopkins in November 1967 in the basement of a Covent Garden warehouse',

[60] Ibid.
[61] Ibid., 114.

to enjoy a 'total immersive environment in sound and light'.[62] For Young, that a commune shop and a night club should both be named after elements in Tolkien's confirms the centrality of his work, especially his 'three-volume legendarium' *The Lord of the Rings*, to the British Underground. He describes Marc Bolan handing his then producer Tony Visconti copies of *The Hobbit* and *The Lord of the Rings*, with the words 'If you're gonna record me, you gotta read this.' Bolan's partner in his band of the time, Tyrannosaurus Rex, named himself Steve Peregrine Took, after one of the hobbits in *The Lord of the Rings*. If the Shire was 'the Anglo-Saxon ideal of Merrie England, all rolling downs, village greens, and easeful plenty' then Mordor, with 'its engines of war and the fiery, white-heat technology of Mount Doom', is 'a military-industrial complex gearing up to wage a battle of evermore, forever disrupting the stability of the rest of Middle-earth'.[63] Young sees this as presenting a convincing enough analogy of a 'rough, fantastical mapping of the previous twenty years of world history', which 'certainly spoke to the children born in the middle of the real-life conflict who now just wanted to retreat to the Shires to do their own thing in peace'[64].

Michael Rainey opened Hung on You in 430 King's Road in 1967, having first located in the more staid Cale Street, further up the King's Road towards Sloane Square. Jonathan Aitken describes the shop's earlier incarnation, before it moved to the World's End, in *The Young Meteors*.

Just off the Kings [sic] Road in Cale Street stands Hung on You, perhaps the strangest of the young men's fashion establishments in London. The pop art designs in the shop front are worthy of a dipsomaniac's nightmare, a positive disincentive to purchase clothes one might think, but in fact this does not matter very much, since for all its apparently alluring décor and brightly-painted shelves, there was not, when I visited it, one single garment on sale in the shop front, nor any sign of an assistant.[65]

Aitken persists and notices 'a small hole in one corner of the shop floor, with steep precarious steps leading from it to unknown nether regions'. Having descended he finds himself in a 'large basement with rush matting on the floor, elaborate Morris wallpaper on the walls and chairs so large, and so

---

[62] Young, Rob, *Electric Eden: Unearthing Britain's Visionary Music* (London: Faber and Faber, 2011), 464.
[63] Ibid., 465–6.
[64] Ibid., 466.
[65] Aitken, *Meteors*, 22.

ornate that it would be more accurate to describe them as thrones'. He also encounters the two shop assistants, sitting in the chairs, one described as 'wearing a lace shirt and orange jeans too tight for him to move without appearing to be suffering from arthritis' and the other wearing a 'mini-skirt so short that it would not even have afforded decent coverage over a pigmy's buttocks, and this was topped by a transparent smock through which it was easy to see that she was wearing no other garment of any other kind'.[66] Aitken himself was all of twenty-four or twenty-five when he wrote this, despite channelling the authentic voice of a retired high court judge. This fogeyism is employed amusingly when he transcribes the words of a 'yellow-sweatered, purple-trousered, silver-buckle-shoed 19 year old I met in Carnaby Street' who 'claimed to have passed up a university entrance place to stay "on the scene"'.

University? Man, that's just dragsville. I want to stay where the action is, where the birds are, where the P.Y.P.s go [translation: pretty young people]. I'm a sceneman, jeansman [translation: I wear jeans on the scene]. It's the visual age. Read your Marshall McLuhan? The media is the message. My clothes are my message. They say – this man's the greatest, the most geared-up, the most with it. They say – birds, come and get screwed by this man, Harold Wilson, make this man one of your ministers, boozers buy this man a drink. I live for clothes, and I live on the scene. I'm happy. Why go and sweat over books in Latin for two years?[67]

Aitken suggests that 'in fact this sort of nonsensical hysteria seems to have quietened down considerably during the winter of 1966–67'.

---

[66] Ibid., 35.
[67] Ibid.

7

Them

Jon Savage suggests that by 1971 'the gloss had gone off the King's Road'.

> [A]s hippie bottomed out, the World's End became awash with drugs, a market centred on the "Golden Triangle" of pubs that followed the chicane: the Roebuck, the Man in the Moon on the corner with Beaufort Street, and the Water Rat.[1]

(I remember them all well, and their various reputations. Each one has gone, to be replaced with various up-market bars and restaurants.) Steve Jones claims that the Roebuck was 'where the classic Chelsea characters and the people who owned the shops down the King's Road tended to hang out', while the Markham Arms was the 'hippie pub in the area'. Among the Roebuck's clientele recalled by Jones was John Bindon, the 'actor/gangster who shagged Princess Margaret', and who also appeared in *Performance*.[2]

The connection between the World's End and the malign end of the counterculture finds an interesting expression in the Hammer film *Dracula AD 1972*, in which the eponymous vampire, calling himself Johnny Alucard, is now a King's Road hipster, with a gang of beautiful companions. They hang out at the Cavern coffee bar, situated on the north side of the King's Road, between Beaufort Street and the bend in the road. The Cavern was actually La Bersagliera, an Italian restaurant which was there for many years, and to which I went frequently. That Dracula/Alucard should hang out in Chelsea is appropriate, given that his creator, Bram Stoker, lived up the road, on St Leonard's Terrace.

---

[1] Savage, Jon, *England's Dreaming: Sex Pistols and Punk Rock* (London: Faber & Faber, 1992), 7–8.

[2] Jones, Steve, and Ben Thompson, *Lonely Boy: Tales from a Sex Pistol* (London: Windmill Books, 2016), 107.

After the exuberance of the 1960s the clothes people wore also tended to a kind of drab post-hippy phase. Lavinia Greenlaw nicely captures the grimness of youth fashion in the early 1970s.

To be a teenager in 1970 was to suffer an excess of gravity. I watched them move slowly along Camden High Street, boys and girls alike with faces half-closed behind long centre-parted hair. The shape their clothes made was that of something being pulled down into the earth: scoop-necked tops, pear-drop collars, flared or leg-of-mutton sleeves, and flared ankle-length skirts and trousers made of cumbersome corduroy, denim or hessian. They wore bare feet or sandals in summer and otherwise heavy boots or wedge platform shoes. In winter they wrapped in afghans, antique fur coats and greatcoats, hats and scarves. Their colours were vegetal – umber, ochre, aubergine, mushroom, sage. They looked damp.[3]

However, '[T]here was a higher realm, occupied by beautiful men who might be women, who wore feather boas and silver eyeshadow, their hair in ringlets, solid wedges and angular curtains, and who seemed remote, gentle and dangerous.'[4]

By the end of the 1960s the original founders of Granny's relinquished their interests in the business, to their manager Freddie Horninck, who brought in a couple of American habitués, Gene Krell and Marty Breslau, his partner. The stress of the musical side of things, along with other factors had left Waymouth, Pearse and Cohen all disaffected with running the shop and with each other. Interestingly, by this time Pearse was turning against the whole hippy style, and starting to produce 1950s revival clothing, thus anticipating the beginnings of Punk in the 1970s. Pearse's first major project after Granny's was to make a couple of films, a ten-minute short entitled *Jailbird* and an hour-long feature film, *Movie Makers*. The latter is hard to get hold of, but Pearse himself produced it as a DVD, which you can buy through his tailoring business in Soho. It's a strange film, somewhat slap-dash, with some terrible acting and some strangely moving and evocative scenes. Above all, it captures the sense of anomie and disillusion at the end of the 1960s. Despite not actually showing the area, Pearse describes it as a 'requiem for the King's Road', not least at the moment when, as Waymouth put it, 'the smack had moved in'. In his autobiography Steve Jones confirms this.

---

[3] Greenlaw, Lavinia, *The Importance of Music to Girls* (New York: Farrar, Straus and Giroux, 2008), 35.

[4] Ibid., 35–6.

The main shops the rock stars went to were Alkasura – I saw Marc Bolan wearing something from there – and especially Granny Takes a Trip. Granny's, as the cognoscenti called it, was a fantastic place with a Cadillac [sic] sticking out of the front window. It changed a lot over the years but it was fucking cool when I started going there. I didn't realise it at the time but the reason you could literally walk out of there with a velvet rhinestone suit you hadn't paid for was that the guys who were meant to be front of house were nodding out on smack out at the back.[5]

The new decade demanded a new style, exemplified in Hung On You's successor at 430 King's Road, Mr Freedom. Savage describes it as a 'gigantic playpen' with 'ice-cream sundae, Deco frontage' and 'a giant stuffed gorilla dyed fun-fur blue', later donated to Chelsea Football Club, 'the Blues'. A 'revolving silver globe in the ceiling gave an authentic Palais feel'[6]. Customers 'could buy sweets from the counters with inset televisions twinkling away'. The clothes were 'influenced by the 1950s' and were 'trivial, garish and fantastic, pastiching the past thirty years of "comic strip, Hollywood vulgar"'[7]. The jukebox played 'primal rock 'n' roll' rather than psychedelic and prog rock. A flag featured an image of Dick Tracy, while the clothes racks were in the shape of classic Elvis singles. Chairs, cushions and pouffes were in the shape of Liquorice Allsorts. There was a plastic version of the Statue of Liberty. Tommy Roberts, who designed the clothes at Mr Freedom, made T-shirts with appliqué lightning bolts, rockets, Mickey Mouse T-shirts, dresses with Mabel Lucy Attwell-style designs, or catchphrases such as 'Slip it to Me' and 'Pow', Superman jackets, and clothes made out of fake leopard skin. Savage characterises the mood of early seventies pop culture as a 'mixture of camp and infantilism'[8]. This was characterised by a nostalgia for older styles from the 1930s and 1950s. Roberts ordered brothel creepers from shoemakers George Cox, and sold Teddy boy clothing, drapes, trousers, socks etc... in lurid colours. Malcolm McLaren bought a pair of Brothel Creepers from Mr Freedom, a purchase that had a powerful effect on his future development. As he put it 'to buy a pair of suede shoes made a statement about what everyone else was wearing and thinking. It was a symbolic act to wear them; that's what I felt as I walked down the King's Road'[9].

[5] Jones, *Lonely Boy*, 68.
[6] Savage, *England's Dreaming*, 5.
[7] Ibid., 5–6.
[8] Ibid.
[9] Gorman, Paul, *The Life and Times of Malcolm McLaren* (New York: Little Brown, 2020), 142.

Mr Freedom also offered McLaren his first encounter with a Teddy boy, in the form of shop assistant Harry the Ted.

In *Me,* his autobiography, Elton John gives a vivid account of how Mr Freedom clothes represented a change of sensibility as the 1960s gave way to the 1970s. At his first appearance in the United States, at the Troubador in LA in 1970, he realises that the applause has a 'slightly odd quality... a surprised murmur, as if the audience were expecting someone else'. John realises that on the cover of his debut album he appears in a black T-shirt and a crocheted waistcoat, leading the audience to imagine they were going to see a 'brooding, introspective singer-songwriter'.[10] However, before flying out to the States, John had worked up the nerve to enter Mr Freedom, 'about which there was a real buzz developing: the designer Tommy Roberts was letting his imagination run riot, making clothes that looked like a cartoonist had drawn them'.[11] John continues that the 'clothes from Mr Freedom weren't outrageous because they were sexy or threatening, they were outrageous because they were larger than life, more fun than the world around them. I loved them.' He describes his outfit for that first concert; 'bright yellow dungarees, a long-sleeved T-shirt covered in stars and a pair of heavy workman's boots, also bright yellow, with a large set of blue wings sprouting from them'. As he points out, this is 'not the way sensitive singer-songwriters in America in 1970 looked. This was not the way anyone of sound mind in America in 1970 looked.' As he gives more concerts at the Troubador John 'rummaged deeper in my bag of Mr Freedom clothes', finally appearing 'wearing a pair of tight silver hot pants, bare legs and a T-shirt with ROCK AND ROLL emblazoned across it in sequins'[12].

According to Tommy Roberts's own account of his transformation in the early 1970s in Paul Gorman's *The Look*, 'I shaved my hair off and we went for an Indy 500 feel, a pop thing. We'd sell T-shirts with just one big star on the front in a vivid colour, or with lots of little stars all over them with a blue or a red trim.'[13] Roberts split from his business partner, Trevor Myles, and set up a bigger shop in Kensington High Street, while Myles renamed and restyled 430, calling it Paradise Garage, with green corrugated iron and Hawaiian-style bamboo lettering, and selling used jeans, Hawaiian shirts and Oshkosh

[10] John, Elton, *Me* (London: Pan Books, 2020), 73.
[11] Ibid.
[12] Ibid., 74.
[13] Gorman, Paul, *The Look: Adventures in Pop and Rock Fashion* (London: Sanctuary, 2001), 101.

dungarees. (Oshkosh dungarees and Kickers boots I remember as a favoured style of girls I knew in the early 1970s.) Roberts went on to open City Lights in Covent Garden, for which he designed the iconic 1940s-style suit with flared trousers and a box jacket, as worn by David Bowie on the front of his 1973 covers album *Pin-Ups*. Tommy Roberts remembers that it was Angie Bowie who first came into City Lights, and picked out clothes for her husband. Bowie's burgeoning success meant that anything he might have worn was immediately popular. Roberts claims that, if anyone came into the shop and asked if Bowie had worn it, he automatically said yes. As he puts it, 'why wouldn't I? By then he was already a cult.'[14]

Indeed, Bowie remained so all his life, and his creative surge just before his death made him even more so. In 1973, two days before the release of his album *Pin-Ups*, David and Angie Bowie moved from Beckenham to Chelsea, to 89 Oakley Street, a street of mid-Victorian terraces running from the King's Road to the River. Paul Trynka, in his life of Bowie, describes the house as being reworked as

a model of rock-star chic: stairs painted alternately matt and gloss black, a hallway lit by car headlamps, a sunken double bed, air-brushed murals in most of the rooms – a sun rise, based on the Sun Pat peanut butter logo for David, a tropical beach scene for Zowie's room on the top floor, alongside the office. The living room was in white shagpile, dominated by one of George Underwood's paintings and a larger Dali-style work. The sunken central area was surrounded by scatter cushions, with a spherical TV, a state-of-the-art video machine and Polaroids of 'exotic activities' remembers airbrush artist Mick Gillah.[15]

Bowie was central to 1970s. He represented another culture to that of my parents, strange, transgressive, a little frightening and deeply alluring. The first consciousness of this I can recall is seeing Bowie's *Diamond Dogs* in the window of a record shop in Edinburgh when staying there with my parents in what must be 1974, the year of the record's release, which means I must have been twelve. I remember I was both repelled and fascinated by Guy Peellaert's cover painting of Bowie as a kind of beautiful half man, half dog. I did not realise at the time that this creature actually lived in Chelsea.

[14] Jones, Dylan, *David Bowie: A Life* (London: Penguin, 2017), 173.
[15] Trynka, Paul, *Starman: David Bowie the Definitive Biography* (London: Sphere, 2011), 200.

Pellaert did the artwork for *Rock Dreams*, a book containing a series of highly evocative, sometimes bizarrely imagined representations of rock stars from the 1960s and 1970s. The name of the book is entirely appropriate as Pellaert has rendered the mythology of rock as a series of dream-like tableau and in doing so perfectly captured the oneiric nature of rock stardom. For me, the experience of looking at the book was perturbing and exciting, as it was published at the point at which I was just becoming aware of rock culture, and when, for me, it was still something beyond grasping. Thus *Rock Dreams* itself is part of the dream of rock I had as something vast and mythic.

I was always a fan of Bowie, though not excessively fanatical. I didn't like all his work, and am not that keen on Ziggy Stardust, or anything really between *Lodger* in 1979 and *Reality* in 2003. I find much of the Bowieolatry following his death a bit absurd. However, I think the five albums he released between 1974 and 1977, *Diamond Dogs*, *Young Americans*, *Station to Station*, *Low*, and *'Heroes'*, along with the final two releases, *The Next Day*, and *Blackstar*, are astonishing and among the best things ever produced in the genre of popular music. I was profoundly shocked when he died. It was a bit like a Lady Di moment for those of us who thought the fuss over her death was excessive. I had a sense of something major having gone from the world I knew, and that world being the less for it. It was his death, in part at least, that led me to think about writing about London in the 1960s and 1970s. I think of Bowie somewhat in the way Auden wrote of Freud after his death, as 'a whole climate of opinion'.[16]

The philosopher Simon Critchley, who is a Bowie fanatic, describes stealing *Station to Station* in 1976, from a bookshop in Letchworth. 'I was nearly sixteen', he writes 'and felt that something was beginning to change in both Bowie and myself.' He continues that the opening track 'seemed to open a door onto a new landscape of musical possibilities. Importantly, whatever this was didn't have a name. But it was no longer rock and roll. That's why I liked it.'[17]

The first David Bowie album I bought was *'Heroes'*, in 1977. I still consider it not just one of his best records, but one of the best rock albums ever made,

[16] Auden, W. H., *Another Time: Poems* (London: Faber and Faber, 1940), 118.
[17] Critchley, Simon, *On Bowie* (London: Profile Books, 2016), 92.

along with *Low*. Part of its greatness is that it has a kind of aesthetic perfection, both sonically and visually. The cover is a black and white photograph of Bowie in a contorted pose based, apparently, on the work of Austrian artist Egon Schiele. The cover, in particular, is an almost ideal representation of a certain ethos, something glamorously grey and European, and bound up with the Second World War and the Cold War. It is also astonishingly cool, channelling the ethos of the 20th-century avant-garde. In Agata Pyzik's *Poor But Sexy: Culture Clashes in Europe East and West*, the author tries to recover a sense of the dreamworld of Cold War Eastern Europe and analyse how it became an object of fascination for westerners such as Bowie. Pyzik has coined the useful word 'Berlinism' to capture this elusive set of phenomena.

What I'll be calling 'Berlinism' is the twentieth-century phenomenon of the German capital as a dreamland for both easterners and westerners. Arguably, it starts after the First World War, when the Weimar era turns it into a capital of all sorts of debauchery and transgression, in culture, politics, literature, art, music and theatre.[18]

Bowie went to Berlin in order to recuperate from his time in Los Angeles in the first part of the 1970s, where he was living on a diet of milk, peppers and cocaine, and was deeply involved with Crowleyan occult beliefs, exorcisms, the Kabbalah and suffering from delusions and paranoia.[19] It was, also, in this period that he flirted most fiercely with right wing ideas. As Simon Reynolds puts it in his history of Glam Rock, even if Bowie claimed his cocaine abuse as mitigating circumstances, his remarks of this sort 'don't read as addled provocations. They are so frequently, so articulately argued, so consistently *excited* in tone, it's hard to avoid concluding that Bowie had developed a morbid fascination with Fascism.'[20] As far back as 1969, he had proclaimed in an interview with *Music Now!* magazine that Britain was 'crying out for a leader' and named Enoch Powell as the best candidate. In later interviews he compared himself, or at least Ziggy Stardust, to Hitler. He goes on to muse that he 'should be prime minister of England', adding: 'I wouldn't mind being

[18] Pyzik, Agata, *Poor But Sexy: Culture Clashes in Europe East and West* (Zero Books, 2014), 78–9.

[19] Buckley, David, *Strange Fascination: David Bowie: The Definitive Story* (London: Virgin Books, 2005), 231, 240.

[20] Reynolds, Simon, *Shock and Awe: Glam Rock and Its Legacy, from the Seventies to the Twenty-first Century* (London: Faber & Faber, 2017), 548.

the first English president of the United States either. I'm certainly right wing enough.'[21]

Also, in 1976, Bowie informed a Swedish newspaper that 'Britain could benefit from a fascist leader', though he clarified this to explain that he meant fascism in its true sense.[22] It was in the same year that he returned to England on the Orient Express, arriving at Victoria Station to be met by an open-top Mercedes, a favoured form of transport for the Nazis. It was then that he may or may not have made a Nazi salute to the crowd.

All through his career Bowie was a profoundly eschatological figure. Peter Doggett suggests that no artist

offered a more incisive and accurate portrait of the troubled landscape of the 1970s than David Bowie.... he encapsulated many of the social, political and cultural themes that ran through this most fascinating of decades, from the elusive promise of scientific progress to the persistent fear of apocalypse that stalked the globe.[23]

He continued that

Through Ziggy, Bowie was also able to access themes that preoccupied the wider culture: the ominous hum of apocalypse, the fear of decay, the compulsive attraction of power and leadership, the search for renewed belief in a time of disillusion.[24]

Major Tom, the eponymous character in his first major commercial success, bears a great resemblance to J. G. Ballard's doomed astronauts. It was released five days before the launch of Apollo 11. In his story 'A Question of Re-entry', Ballard describes how the successful moon landing was only achieved after 'some half-dozen fatal attempts – at least three of the luckless pilots were still orbiting the moon in their dead ships'.[25] 'A Question of Re-entry' is the first story in Ballard's collection The Terminal Beach, first published by Victor Gollancz in 1964. The 1974 Penguin reprint was one of four Ballard books with covers by the great designer Dave Pelham. The cover of The Terminal Beach is a painting by Pelham of Little Man, the atom

[21] Simpson, Kate, "David Bowie Interview," Music Now!, 20 December 1969.
[22] Stewart, Tony, "Heil And Farewell," New Musical Express, 8 May 1976, 9.
[23] Doggett, Peter, The Man Who Sold The World: David Bowie And The 1970s (New York: Vintage, 2012).
[24] Ibid., 4.
[25] Ballard, J. G., The Terminal Beach (Harmondsworth: Penguin Books, 1974), 9.

bomb that destroyed Hiroshima, half buried in sand. Bowie's song offers a bleak vision of an astronaut who finds himself stranded in space. The producer who chose it to accompany the BBC's broadcast of the Apollo 11 launch clearly had not listened to the lyrics. Bowie returned to Major Tom several times during his career, and also continually evoked astral motifs in his work, including 'Starman' from 1972, which was a late inclusion on the album Ziggy Stardust and the Spiders from Mars (Ziggy's surname itself involving a star reference). Right at the very end of his career his final album, Blackstar, released two days before his death, returned to this motif. A couple of years before his musical, Lazarus, revisited the character Thomas Jerome Newton, from the 1975 film The Man Who Fell to Earth, made by Nick Roeg, who also co-directed Performance. It is this film that really captures the end of the dream of the cosmic sublime so prevalent in the 1960s. Bowie plays Newton, an alien from a dying planet, who arrives on earth with detailed technical knowledge of the advanced technologies of his species. He intends to use this to build a business empire in order to make enough money to build a spaceship and return to his home planet with water. According to Jon Savage the film

had a great impact on Punk, David Bowie as Newton begins to lose his precepts. He forgets why he is on earth and begins to succumb to the seduction of pleasure. In one of the film's most memorable scenes, Newton lolls back in his chair, booze-blitzed, and becomes immersed in a vast ocean of white noise emanating from dozens of television sets with a myriad moving pictures. In 1976 England, this was definitely futuristic – simultaneously exciting and terrifying – and this duality of response corresponded to Punk's simultaneous fascination with, and condemnation of, the media...[26]

Bowie was supposed to have contributed the soundtrack to the film, but in the end did not, owing to contractual wrangles. However, the presence of the character he plays is strongly felt in two of his best albums, Low and Station to Station, both of which feature him as Newton on their covers.

Exemplary of early 1970s London style was Barbara Hulanicki's boutique Biba, 'the quintessential fashion statement of early 1970s London, and

[26] Savage, Jon, England's Dreaming: Sex Pistols and Punk Rock (London: Faber & Faber, 1992), 178.

it styled the music scene that was succeeding the hippy underground'.[27] Originally at 124–126 Kensington High Street, in 1973 they moved to the old art-deco building that was once the home of the department store Derry and Tom's. I can just remember this incarnation of Biba, with its black-painted stairwells. Among those shopping there were Lou Reed, Freddie Mercury and Siouxsie Sioux. The most glamorous parts of Biba were the roof garden and the fifth floor Rainbow Room, which had been restored to its pre-war elegance. Paul du Noyer's description of what happened there presents an almost perfect picture of early 1970s pop culture.

Here appeared Ian Dury's Kilburn and the High Roads, Manhattan Transfer and Cockney Rebel. Bryan Ferry filmed his video for 'Let's Stick Together'; Liberace threw a party for his fans; David Bowie came to see the artist Guy Pellaert exhibit his Rock Dreams paintings and commissioned the Diamond Dogs sleeve from him. And the New York Dolls played a London showcase ('price including meal £2.50') which so enchanted the young Chelsea shopkeeper Malcolm McLaren that he came their manager.[28]

Biba infuriated the rather pathetic British radical terrorist group the Angry Brigade enough for them to bomb it in 1971, fortunately without any loss of life. They released a somewhat hysterical 'communiqué'.

If you're not busy being born you're busy buying.

All the sales girls in the flash boutiques are made to dress the same and have the same make-up, representing the 1940's. In fashion as in everything else, capitalism can only go backwards – they've nowhere to go – they're dead.

The future is ours.

Life is so boring there is nothing to do except spend all our wages on the latest skirt or shirt.

Brothers and Sisters, what are your real desires?

Sit in the drugstore, look distant, empty, bored, drinking some tasteless coffee? Or perhaps BLOW IT UP OR BURN IT DOWN. The only thing you can do with modern slave-houses – called boutiques – IS WRECK THEM. You can't reform profit capitalism and inhumanity. Just kick it till it breaks.

---

[27] Du Noyer, Paul, *In the City: A Celebration of London Music* (London: Ebury Publishing, 2009), 190.
[28] Ibid., 191.

Revolution,

Communique [sic] 8

The Angry Brigade[29]

A poignant detail about this communiqué is that it was printed using a John Bull printing set, which consisted of little rubber letters and trays in which to insert them to enable the printing of little documents. I had one and can remember how astonishingly fiddly they were. This may explain why, when the police raided the home of some members of the Angry Brigade, the printing set was in plain view, with the words 'Angry Brigade' still in place.[30]

Bowie's style, Tommy Roberts' designs, Biba, especially when it moved into the old Barker's department store building, a prime example of Art Deco, Ken Russell's film of the 1930s musical *The Boyfriend*, and the style of early seventies Bowie and Roxy Music, are, to some extent, the bridge between the hippy style of the 1960s and the Punk look of the mid-1970s. They retained the naivety of hippiedom but abandoned its utopian idealism in lieu of pure surface and style. To some extent it can be understood as the beginnings of what was already becoming known as 'postmodernism'.

One of the markers of this new style and all its implications was when Michael English 'abandoned the psychedelic style and had instead moved into environmental happenings, oil-lamp projections and the medium of airbrush'.[31] His most famous design, one of a series on the theme of rubbish, was a hyper-realistic airbrush image of a crumpled coke bottle lid, which sold millions of copies as an Athena poster. As Alistair O'Neill points out, these images 'harness an aesthetic that connects the late 1960s with the late 1970s'.[32]

Here the detritus of modern life, most specifically an American-inspired one, became the focus for an aesthetic that celebrated a hollowness that glorified surface over any desire for substance or idealism. It was a figuring of the 'flowers in the dustbin' as a desirable state before punk had appropriated it.[33]

[29] Carr, Gordon, *The Angry Brigade: A History of Britain's First Urban Guerilla Group* (Oakland, CA: PM Press, 2010), 87.

[30] Ibid., 137.

[31] O'Neill, Alistair, *London – After a Fashion* (London: Reaktion Books, 2007), 163–5.

[32] Ibid., 165–6.

[33] Ibid., 166.

In fact, the best description of this stylistic and cultural moment was written by one-time World's End resident Peter York. 'Them' was published in *Harpers and Queen* in 1976, and I am pretty sure I can remember reading it then. Rereading it is a reminder of what an astute cultural commentator York is, and how he could zone in on the minutiae of phenomena almost as brilliantly as Tom Wolf. 'Them' is an attempt to capture something extraordinarily elusive, what York calls the 'dominant high-style aesthetic of the seventies'.[34] In the beginning of the article York describes a number of examples of Thems he has seen. Though each is thoroughly different from each other they all share a clear obsession with style. Indeed, 'Thems are excessively literate in the language of style'.[35] They are also, mostly, apolitical, not least because 'Overly rigorous analysis depresses them', and also because they are, 'by instinct, elitist'.[36]

York cites *The Man Who Fell to Earth* as the exemplary film for Them (or Thems, perhaps). York, clearly not a fan of the film, suggests that spotting the Them allusions 'relieves the mild boredom of the film itself'. These include 'Bowie himself', sci-fi as a 'Them cult', 'prole Americana', 'Necro/Retro moments (such as Candy Clark looking like Annette Funicello), 'Homage to Warhol', and 'Suggestions of odd sex for the jaded palette'.[37] It turns out that Candy Clark was an early habituée of Malcolm McLaren and Vivienne Westwood's Sex boutique in the World's End, the centre of Punk in the mid-seventies.

York attributes the rise of Thems to two factors; the 'art school bulge and the assimilation of camp'. The former, a result of a massive increase during the 1960s and 1970s of those going into art education, gave hitherto neglected areas such as fashion far greater prominence, and produced a new, attractive self-image, that of the 'Applied Art media star, in particular The Designer'.[38] They 'were into clothes; and clothing was what many of them went into after they graduated. But many more spread their sensibility into ... music and films and magazines and restaurants.' Central to their ethos was Pop Art, and with it an interest in popular art forms, pastiche and a 'reverence

[34] York, Peter, *Style Wars* (London: Sidgwick and Jackson, 1980), 113.
[35] Ibid., 113.
[36] Ibid., 119.
[37] Ibid.
[38] Ibid., 114.

for prole and period Americana'.[39] Above all, Pop Art taught them to 'look at things in a cock-eyed way, i.e. in the way that someone else had already looked at them'. 'Thems were cognoscenti of trash, aficionados of sleaze.[40] This Pop sensibility along with the co-option of camp led to what York calls Art Necro, a 'quick-change revivalism, which came big business around the turn of the decade, when [...] people were looking for something *silly* to take their minds off depressing things'.[41] York's description of Art Necro is so evocative of a certain moment on the King's Road, I have to quote it in full.

The Necro industry gave employment to many Thems: designing new/old record sleeves, doing jackets for books about forties movie stars, working in Antiquarius in the King's Road, and so on. Send-ups or 'fun clothes' – fried egg appliques etc. – gave us the Mr Freedom/Paradise Garage/Tommy Roberts look... (In late 1970, Roberts started selling authentic-looking baggy overalls from Serena Shaffer's Electric Fittings. A harbinger of *anti-fashion* to come. Thems had been wearing real Osh Kosh B'Goshes and Pay-Days since 1968).[42]

For York the ultimate Them, the 'best possible example of the ultimate art-directed existence', is Bryan Ferry, the 'most important pasticheur in Britain today', who, despite being a 'big-time rock star' 'has a degree in Fine Art, and a very demanding Them sensibility'. 'He should hang in the Tate, with David Bowie.'[43] In a sense Ferry is the direct descendent in cultural terms of Whistler, not least as a straight man channelling a gay sensibility.

The cultural genesis of Bryan Ferry's group Roxy Music is the subject of what is probably the best book written about a rock band, not least because it's not really about rock music, Michael Bracewell's *Roxy: The Band That Invented an Era*.[44] In the book Bracewell carefully traces how Roxy Music and the sensibility they exemplified emerged out of the early 1960s world of Mod fashion, Pop Art, expanded art school curricula (especially at Newcastle, with teachers such as Richard Hamilton), and a fascination with contemporary American culture. Among the most important figures, strangely unmentioned by York, is the fashion designer Anthony Price, perhaps the most

[39] Ibid., 115.
[40] Ibid., 115.
[41] Ibid., 116.
[42] Ibid.
[43] Ibid.
[44] Bracewell, Michael, *Roxy: The Band that Invented an Era* (London: Faber and Faber, 2007).

gifted of his generation, who defined the style of the early 1970s. It's only now, researching for this book, that I understand the full meaning of the mysterious shop Price opened in the World's End in 1978. Named Plaza, its window displayed clothes that appeared to come from some future world. I cannot better Michael Bracewell's account, written in the third person, of going there.

When it opened, he felt that he'd been waiting for the changing room from the twenty-first century that was Anthony Price's shop, Plaza, at the top of the King's Road, below 20th Century Box and facing Beaufort Market. When Plaza finally opened – some time around 1978 – punk had fragmented into an eclectic array of sub-sections, from gobbing spike-tops to futurist industrial; Plaza was a minimalistic quartermaster store for the youth modern(e) who urged punk to renew itself from the instant cliché of a two-chord rant; fabric samples and garment samples were fastened to perspex sheets on the racks and then the human mannequin behind the mirrored counter handed you your chosen items. The changing rooms were totally mirrored, like a sex voyeur's dream or the nightmare of the insecure. Price was the genius behind Roxy Music's styling, and he caught an early post-punk sub-strand by creating clothes like fetishized sci-fi uniforms – girls in military shirts, with purple lurex and black crêpe epaulettes.[45]

I barely had the nerve to go into Plaza, let alone buy anything. I did go in a couple of times and I do remember the mirrored changing rooms. Plaza was too extreme in its aesthetics for me to fully understand it. I was an avid customer at 20th Century Box however. This was one of the many shops selling mostly American clothes from the 1950s and 1960s, sports jackets, drainpipe jeans, button-down shirts, Oxford shoes and other such items that evinced a nostalgia for earlier and supposedly simpler times.

The early to mid-1970s saw a considerable interest in the period before the rise of the counterculture. In 1973 my friend Paul's mother took us to see George Lucas' *American Graffiti*, set in 1962, the year we had gone to New York during the Cuban Missile Crisis. In the same year the musical *Grease*, set in an American high school in the late 1950s, started its London run, starring a young actor called Richard Gere. In 1974 the first episodes of the American sitcom *Happy Days* were broadcast, set in an idealised 1950s suburb. The American rock and roll revival band Sha Na Na had played at Woodstock, while, in Britain Shakin' Stevens and Showaddywaddy also

---

45 Kerr, Joe, and Andrew Gibson, eds, *London from Punk to Blair* (London: Reaktion, 2003), 304.

looked back to the music of that period. As Kim Levin pointed out in her 1974 article on the 1950s revival, 'Fifties Fallout: The Hydrogen Jukebox', the nostalgia for that period brought with it memories of the trauma of the threat of nuclear annihilation.[46] The nostalgia for the 1950s and early 1960s, however comforting it might have appeared, was also the harbinger of the nihilism of Punk. When they took over the lease of 430 King's Road in the World's End in 1971, Malcolm McLaren and Vivienne Westwood starting off by selling rock and roll records, 1950s clothes and memorabilia.

[46] Levin, Kim, *Beyond Modernism: Essays on Art from the '70s and '80s* (New York: Harper and Row, 1988), 36.

8

Culture and Anarchy in the UK

One of the most effective ways of understanding a period without recourse to idealised images of the past is by reading accounts written at the time, especially perhaps those written as fiction. One such is Zoe Fairbairn's *Benefits*, published in the late 1970s and set a little earlier in the decade. It is a dystopian fiction that anticipates the later work of Margaret Atwood, in chronicling the future repression of women and their rights. She starts the book with an account of the Great Drought of 1976, an event that seemed a plausible harbinger of apocalypse or dystopia. As she rightly points out, everyone who was in London in the summer of that year remembers the weather, much as those who were sufficiently aware in 1963 remember what they were doing when Kennedy was assassinated. Her continuing description rings entirely true.

From May to September, misty mornings preceded glaring debilitating days and dry airless nights. The Thames became unnavigable. Workers went on strike for better ventilation. Grass browned, trees drooped, earth subsided under foundations and buildings cracked. Commuters left jackets and cotton cardigans at home and adhered to each other in packed trains, licking ices. Umbrella sellers went out of business, shorts were worn in the staidest of offices, and Members of Parliament were outraged by the price of cold drinks in Oxford Street. Day followed incredible day and still the heat did not let up, still it did not rain. Once or twice a grey, brooding constipated sky rumbled and flashed and a few drops of water fell, but you could not call that rain; not when there was talk of standpipes in the streets and even Buckingham Palace (it was rumoured) had a sign up in the loo saying 'Don't pull for a pee.' It rained enough, it was true, to kill the Saturday of the Lords' Test against Australia (if it had to rain one day of the year, Londoners told each other wisely, that would be the one) but that was not enough to break the drought – an almost indecent word to be used about their city, thought Londoners, to whom drought meant sandy deserts and cracked farmland in places near the equator. In unaccustomed chats between strangers, sympathy for our own farmers (pictured each night on television running dust through their fingers and waving parched roots as if the government ought to do something about it) alternated only with contrived sighs of ecstasy: 'Isn't it glorious?' Londoners did not really believe in farmers.[1]

The year following the drought, 1977, was intended to be a celebration of the Queen's silver jubilee, but the whole decade was pervaded by a sense of doom and decay. The sense that some apocalyptic event was imminent found expression in roots reggae band Culture's 1976 song 'When Two Sevens Clash'. Culture singer Joseph Hill took his inspiration from a Rastafarian prophecy by Marcus Garvey, that the 1970s would be a watershed moment for Black people, to suggest that a momentous event would take place on the seventh day, of the seventh month of 1977. The liner notes to the album claims that, on the actual day 'a hush descended on Kingston [Jamaica]; many people did not go outdoors, shops closed, an air of foreboding and expectation filled the city'.[2]

The exemplary fictional account of the horror of the 1970s is Margaret Drabble's *The Ice Age*, a state-of-the-nation novel in which a number of characters find themselves adrift in the economic and social turmoil of the decade in which the promises of the 1960s have been failed. It is also a prescient look at the rise of the speculative and profiteering culture that would come into full view with the monetarism of Mrs Thatcher's government in the 1980s. One of the main characters, Anthony Keating, a clergyman's son, has repudiated his genteel background to become a property speculator, clearly operating at the edge of criminality. An associate, Len Wincobank, is in prison as the novel begins, for his own corrupt property dealings. Another associate has been killed, and his wife mutilated, in an IRA bomb. Through the travails of these and other characters, Drabble conveys the sense of a country and culture collapsed into despair, sleaze, shabbiness, and insecurity.[3]

Drabble's use of the IRA as a plot device is a useful reminder that, somewhere in the background of our lives, from the late 1960s through to the 1990s the 'Troubles' in Northern Ireland were always present, sometimes close, though usually more distant. Much of the time we either accepted or

[1] Fairbairns, Zoe, *Benefits* (London: Virago, 1979), 4–5.
[2] Hill, Joseph, Liner notes, *When the Two Sevens Clash*. Culture. Joe Gibbs, 1977. LP.
[3] Drabble, Margaret, *The Ice Age* (London: Weidenfeld and Nicolson, 1977).

ignored the fact that part of the United Kingdom was in a permanent state of armed conflict, and riven by terrorist atrocities, as well as state violence. It is a good example of what should be unthinkable becoming normalised. Mostly the Troubles impinged on our lives in a fairly remote manner, as a story in the newspaper, or a report on the six o'clock news on television. It was only when they came to the Mainland, in the form of bombing campaigns or other terrorist activities, that they suddenly came to the foreground of our lives.

The Ice Age was first published in 1977, the same year the Sex Pistols released 'Anarchy in the UK'. In an article in *Rolling Stone*, written in that year, Greil Marcus explicitly connects the two as showing how 'British society seems to have come to a dead end, to have turned back on itself, to be strangling on its own contradictions.' He suggests that the idea that 'the promises of the British Sixties', that of 'easy money, a spirit of high adventure and a revitalized popular culture shared by all' would dismantle the English class system 'seem like naive illusions'. He points to how the

pervasive sleaziness of the center of London today, the way Piccadilly has turned into one great den of pornography, seems to speak for an England that can no longer raise an image of itself that it wants to look at. England seems a vacuum, and ugliness, physical and spiritual, is filling it. Resentments are everywhere, and for the moment, blind, without satisfying objects.[4]

For Marcus, despite their differences, both Margaret Drabble and Johnny Rotten are 'scared, and both are responding to an overwhelming sense that their culture – political , economic, and aesthetic – has collapsed around them, leaving them stranded in a society that seems not only without prospects, but without meaning'. This is the reality the characters in the novel 'are confronting; their subject is the attempt of people in present-day England to live without a belief in the future'.[5] Marcus describes how, in *The Ice Age*, one of the characters, Alison, returns from a repressive Eastern bloc country where her daughter is incarcerated, and realises that London is 'shabby... mean-spirited, selfish, unfriendly and brutalized. Hideous new buildings have broken up communities that took centuries to form; people... can no longer connect to the landscape in which they grew up, because it speaks for things

---

[4] Marcus, Greil, *In The Fascist Bathroom: Punk in Pop Music, 1977–1992* (Cambridge, MA: Harvard University Press, 1999), 17.
[5] Ibid.

that no longer really exist, or that they do not want to know about'[6]. Marcus suggests that *The Ice Age* and the Sex Pistols both show that 'post-industrial society, the corrupt welfare state, has passed beyond its ability to order itself, to posit values worthy of respect and to maintain the kind of community that binds people rather than separates them'. What is left is 'the willingness to settle for what in the Seventies is called "survival"'.[7]

The proximate cause for Punk was the general decay of life in mid-seventies Britain. But the longer term reason for its existence is the deep existential horror of the Cold War and the sheer stupidity of a world that went on acting as if nothing was happening. Punk is the cultural manifestation, the salvaging of the ruins, the rubble of civilisation after Hiroshima and Nagasaki. It is not coincidental that the high point of Punk was also the year of the Queen's Silver Jubilee, an event of crushing inanity. The one good thing to emerge from the Jubilee was what has been proclaimed as the greatest single ever released, the Sex Pistols' 'God Save the Queen', which was kept off the top spot on the charts, where it should have been, in the week of the Jubilee, by record industry and broadcast machinations. Rotten famously sings that the 'fascist regime/They made you a moron/A potential H Bomb'.

The War returned in a kind of repressed form in popular music, especially in the 1970s, with Punk. Punks sported Nazi imagery such as Swastikas. Bands had names that alluded to aspects of the War and the Holocaust, such as Joy Division, and its successor New Order. More generally Germanness held a certain fascination, as if it contained the secret to the emerging world of new technologies and architectures. Germany's own rock music, *cosmische rock*, known, rather vulgarly in Britain as Krautrock, influenced New Wave here and in the States, not least in terms of style. Kraftwerk in particular epitomised, parodically perhaps, the idea of German machine-like efficiency and modernity. As described in a previous chapter, Bowie, ever alert to what was new and of the moment, spent a number of years in Berlin with Iggy Pop, producing some of his best work there, as well as that of Pop and Lou Reed. Writing on the film *Nightfall*, about the fall of Nazi Germany, Mark Fisher, blogging as K-punk, alludes to the Punk use of Nazi imagery.

[6] Ibid., 19.
[7] Ibid., 20.

While those scenes play out, you can almost hear Johnny Rotten leering, "when there's no future how can there be sin?" [...] As the Pistols pursue their own line of abolition into the scorched earth nihilism of "Belsen was a Gas" and "Holidays in the Sun", they keep returning to the barbed-wire scarred Boschscape of Nazi Berlin and the Pynchon Zone it became after the war. Siouxsie famously sported a swastika for a while, and although much of the flaunting of the Nazi imagery was supposedly for superficial shock effects, the punk-Nazi connection was about much more than trite transgressivism. Punk's very 1970s, very British fixation on Nazism posed ethical questions so troubling they could barely be articulated explicitly: what were the limits of liberal tolerance? Could Britain be so sure that it had differentiated itself from Nazism (a particularly pressing issue at a time that the NF was gathering an unprecedented degree of support)? And, most unsettling of all, what is it that separates Nazi Evil from heroic Good?[8]

'God Save the Queen' was released in the same year as Bowie's *'Heroes'* (note the ironic quotation marks). At the same time David Bowie was proclaiming his admiration for Adolf Hitler, the 'first rock star' and for the desirability of a Fascist dictatorship in Britain, Eric Clapton was drunkenly proclaiming that Enoch Powell was right about immigration. A number of young commentators felt sufficiently enraged to write a collective letter attacking Clapton's racism, which they sent to the NME and other music papers. They got hundreds of replies, which in turn encouraged them to Rock Against Racism, and, a year later, The Anti-Nazi League. At the end of 'White Noise Suprematicism', an article published in 1979 in *The Village Voice*, in which he castigated the would-be hipsters of the New York Punk scene for their casual racism, Lester Bangs mentions Rock Against Racism, which he describes as 'an attempt at simple decency by a lot of people whom one would think too young and naive to begin to appreciate the contradictions'.[9]

RAR and the ANL did a great deal to mobilise young people in opposition to racism, and to combat racist activity from the likes of the National Front, the most visible hard right political party, then seemingly advancing towards electoral success (much as UKIP was until recently). Like most of my friends I was too privileged and ignorant to have much exposure to this side of their activities. But I can claim to have been present at their most

---

[8] Fisher, Mark, *K-Punk: The Collected and Unpublished Writings of Mark Fisher* (London: Repeater, 2018), 132.

[9] Bangs, Lester, *Psychotic Reactions & Carburetor Dung: Literature as Rock and Roll Rock and Roll as Literature* (London: Minerva, 1990), 282.

famous moments, the two marches and free concerts they held in London in 1978. Or, rather, I know I went on the first, and I think I also went on the second, but cannot be entirely sure (and have no idea how to check whether I did or not).

The first march took place in April 1978 and was from Trafalgar Square in the centre of London to Victoria Park in the East End, a distance of about six miles, but also a journey from the imperial heart of the capital to what was then still a greatly impoverished part of town. I can recall, just, setting off from the Square, and the long stroll through increasingly down-at-heel streets, with the occasional barracking from hostile East Enders, and our arrival in the park for the concert. Of that I can remember almost nothing, except The Clash, who I had presumed to have been the headliners. I now know that the headliner was actually Tom Robinson, and his band, who finished their set with his anthemic 'Sing If You're Glad to be Gay', thus binding together anti-racism with gay liberation. I do remember that there were a lot of marchers on that first march, 100,000 apparently. More recent marches may have had far larger numbers, but, at the time, this number felt highly significant. At one point National Front members came out of an East End pub and started sieg heiling the marchers, but, confronted with such a large crowd passing slowly in front of them, lost heart and retreated back inside.

Punk was, in some senses at least, a product of the World's End and in particular of 430 King's Road. Through various machinations 430 King's Road fell into the hands of Malcolm McLaren, a would-be pop impresario, devotee of Situationism and other forms of radical-aesthetic politics, and his partner, Vivienne Westwood. They used the shop to enact a kind of Situationist detournement of hippy fashion. When they first opened the shop under the name Let It Rock, they had lighted upon the deeply reactionary and unfashionable Teds as clientele. Teds or teddy boys were the first rock sub-culture, emerging in the 1950s as an identity for rock and roll fans. Ted was short for Edwardian, after their imitation of post-war Guards officers' repudiation of austerity and gloom and adoption of the velvet collars of the beginning of the century. Teds wore velvet collared, long jackets, known as crepes, and rubber-soled shoes, brothel creepers, along with long watch chains, and hair greased into pompadours. They had somehow survived from the 1950s to the 1970s, but were not what McLaren and Westwood really wanted. They moved their allegiance to the more glamorous subculture of leather-clad rockers, and renamed the shop Too Fast To Live, Too Young To Die. Next they amped up the outrage, renamed the shop again, this time to Sex, and sold a mixture of bondage and fetish gear, and self-designed T-shirts, often displaying pornographic images or texts. As Sex, 430 was, of course, the birthplace of British Punk, the place where McLaren brought together the various elements that would become the Sex Pistols.

Part of that story involves the burgeoning New York Punk scene. In 1971 Sylvain Sylvain and Billy Murcia formed The New York Dolls, apparently named after The New York Doll Hospital, opposite a boutique at which Sylvain worked. They recruited Johnny Thunders, first on bass, then on guitar. The band went through a number of different groupings, not least as a result of the death of Murcia from an overdose in 1972. The Dolls were regarded as one of the earliest Punk bands, following The Velvet Underground and The Stooges. They are also a curious bridge between New York and the World's End. In 1975 McLaren went to New York, and was for a brief time and informally the Doll's manager. He was looking for something new and some other outlet for his Situationist-inspired desire to provoke. He tried to make the Dolls provocative by making them wear red leather outfits and have communist symbols such as the hammer and sickle as stage backdrops. This failed to extend the Dolls' existence, but their attitude and music, along with other emerging figures in New York, such as Patti Smith, and Richard Hell and Tom Verlaine, who formed their band Television in 1973, inspired McLaren to try to foster a similar scene in England.

Television were, at the time, my favourite band, and the manner in which they became so is indicative of my relation to music. For much of the 1970s I read the New Musical Express, usually known as the NME, with an almost religious devotion. One of the main music magazines in the United Kingdom, it was then going through an extraordinary phase of great, literate writing and criticism by some of the best music writers in the country and possibly even in the world. The NME was the magazine that engaged the most productively and enthusiastically with the coming of Punk and New Wave. The moment I saw the images and even the layout of their article about Television, I knew they were going to be my favourite band, before hearing a note of their music. It was because everything about them, the name with its invocation of mass media and culture, their look, especially the glamorously wasted Tom Verlaine, and even the fact that the NME had printed the article in televisual blue, was apt. It was brilliant as a statement about the increasingly obvious strangeness and mediated quality of life in the 1970s.

McLaren was particularly fascinated by Hell, and his idiosyncratic sartorial style and demeanour. Hell pioneered the idea of ripping up old clothes and putting them back together with safety pins, which became a staple of the British Punk look. McLaren wanted Hell to be the singer for the band he was planning to set up in England, though Hell demurred. In Hell's autobiography, *I Dreamt I was a Very Clean Tramp*, Hell describes the genesis of his look. It's fascinating to read as it would become fashionable and familiar in the late 1970s, but when he and Verlaine were developing it, it was entirely unprecedented.

We'd cut our hair short and ragged. I did mine in a style that poked up in shreds and thatches all over my skull. Our clothes were torn and frayed and sometimes held together by safety pins. I often wore a wrinkled baggy suit and an old tie that was pulled loose down my shirtfront.[10]

He also claims to be the first to wear 'pegged black jeans', and sported 'round horn-rimmed glasses, like Ivy League gone depraved or early Andy Warhol'. He 'arrived at the haircut by analysis', working out the semiotic signification in the haircuts of Elvis and the Beatles, before deciding on a '"butch" or "crew" cut that had gone ragged because kids didn't like going to barbers'. The clothes were based on cowboys and private detectives, and the 'ghetto rags the Bowery Boys wore in *Dead End*'.[11] Thus Hell's style was a kind of ironic detournement of the 1950s and early 1960s revival of the early 1970s.

If Mary Quant's Bazaar is the beginning of the boutique then Malcolm McLaren and Vivienne Westwood's Sex is perhaps its end, and the repudiation of its eroticisation of youth. Sex was in the World's End, at 430 King's Road, appropriately the other end from Bazaar. The clothes and those working in the shop also appeared in pornographic magazines, usually those devoted to fetishism. However, the pornography was intended to be resolutely unerotic, at least in terms understood in conventional girlie magazines. As Tony Parsons and Julie Birchall put it in *The Boy Looked at Johnny*, their obituary for Punk, published in 1978, the idea was 'not to cater for the secret

---

[10] Hell, Richard, *I Dreamed I was a Very Clean Tramp: An Autobiography* (New York: Ecco, 2014), 117.

[11] Ibid., 117–8.

desires of guilt-ridden respectable perverts but to shock indifferent and dismissive elders into white-knuckled, cardiac-arrest indignance'. None of the clothes

were either designed or worn to make the customer alluring; on the contrary, the flagrant fashion in which the clothes used sex as an offensive weapon required a certain asexuality on the part of the wearer. They used sex not to entice but to horrify, the perfect expression of which was found in Jordan 'don't call me Pamela' Hook, the Sex salesgirl who wore cutaway-buttock plastic leotards with black suspender belt and thigh boots while striving to make her hair, face and body as puke-promptingly repulsive as possible.[12]

Jordan plays one of the gang of Punk women and men in Derek Jarman's *Jubilee*, who seem to *détourné* traditional sex roles, particularly in the case of the women. The image of the 'girl' is taken apart and reconstituted as something far less comfortable than the passive objects of the male gaze and sexual attention of earlier times in pop culture. Punk, though by no means a particularly reconstructed movement, did offer new kinds of models of femininity, as evinced by Patti Smith, Cosey Fanni Tutti, Siouxsie Sioux, Poly Styrene, Chrissie Hynde, the Raincoats and the Slits, among others.

The possibilities of Punk style as a new form of sexual expression apparently caught Mariella Novotny's eye. In her life of Novotny, Lilian Pizzichini imagines her walking down the King's Road in 1976, and being inspired to change her look as a stripper, including a 'spiky punk wig, like Hazel O'Connor. High heels, skimpy clothes, and a swastika arm-band'.[13]

I wonder if Jordan and Christine Keeler ever met, or even saw each other. It seems perfectly plausible, given that Keeler moved to the World's End estate in 1978, when Jordan was still working at Sex. It was also when Joe Strummer was there. Keeler hated the estate, writing in her memoirs that 'In the spring of 1978 we moved into the World's End housing estate in London and the name tells you everything.'[14] However, she was able to leave after receiving payment for the film *Scandal*, about the Profumo

[12] Parsons, Tony and Julie Birchall, *The Boy Looked at Johnny* (London: Pluto Press, 1978), 259.

[13] Pizzichini, Lilian, *The Novotny Papers: 'A Bit Vulture, A Bit Eagle'* (Stroud: Amberley Books, 2021), 215.

[14] Keeler, Christine, *Secrets and Lies: The Trials of Christine Keeler* (London: John Blake, 2019), 271.

affair. Whatever her antipathy to the area, she was an esteemed figure for the early Punks. In late 1974 Bernie Rhodes, later manager of the Clash, designed a T-shirt to be sold in Sex, with the following text 'You're gonna wake up one morning and know what side of the bed you've been lying on!' followed by two lists, the first of things disapproved of, and the second of those approved by Rhodes. Among the former are Mick Jagger, The Liberal Party, Honey, *Harpers*, *Vogue*, in fact all magazines that treat their readers as idiots, YES, Leo Sayer, David Essex, John Osborne, Harry Pinter, the ICA and its symposiums, Andy Warhol, and Bibas, old clothes, old ideas and all this resting in the country business. Among the latter are Eddie Cochran, followed by Christine Keeler and then Valerie Solanis [sic], Kutie Jones and his SEX PISTOLS, Lenny Bruce, Joe Orton, Iggy Pop, Walt Whitman, Alex Trocchi – Young Adam, and 'John Lacey and his boiled book v. St Martin's Art School experiment to be seen in New York' (I think this must refer to John Latham's famous art piece involving getting students to chew pages of St Martin's copy of Greenberg's *Art and Culture* and preserving the result in test tubes (as cultures).

I can remember the appearance of Punk as a style on the King's Road and elsewhere in London in the mid-1970s. It was a curious mixture of a brico-lage of earlier subcultural styles from every era of rock music (save that of the hated hippies), and something more *sui generis*. Before the style got codified and commodified into the clichéd combination of Mohican haircut, leather biker jacket and bondage trousers, which happened very rapidly, the original Punks managed to look both startingly original and highly provocative. Within the spaces of 1970s London they stood out, disturbing the quotidian world of high street fashion, and provoking passers-by with their sartorial invocations of obscenity and revolt. As Jon Savage puts it

Punk announced itself as a portent with its polysemy of elements drawn from the history of youth culture, sexual fetish wear, urban decay and extremist politics. Taken together, these elements had no conscious meaning but they spoke of many things: urban primitivism; the breakdown of confidence in a common language; the availability of cheap, second-hand clothes; the fractured nature of perception in an accelerating, media-saturated society; the wish to offer up the body as a jumble of meanings.[15]

15 Savage, Jon, *England's Dreaming: Sex Pistols and Punk Rock* (London: Faber & Faber, 1992), 230.

Andrew Gallix sees in Punk the 'new hedonism' called for by Henry Wootton in Oscar Wilde's novel *The Picture of Dorian Gray*, as well as the drive for immaturity found in Witold Gombrowicz's *Ferdyduke*. He suggests that the main Punk club, the Vortex, could have derived its name from Ezra Pound's essay of the same name from 1914, or from Noel Coward's 1924 play. He quotes Oscar Wilde's witticism, that 'to be premature is to be perfect'. He also invokes Ronald Searle's work and even *The Beano*.

Early gigs frequently resembled a St Trinian's prom night gatecrashed by the Bash Street Kids. The ubiquitous school uniforms – all wonky ties and peekaboo stockings – were designed to rub punks' youthfulness in the wrinkled faces of the rock dinosaurs and other Boring Old Farts. One could also drag up the recurring theme of onanism ('Orgasm Addict' and 'Teenage Kicks' being the prime examples) as well as McLaren's dodgy flirtation with paedophilia (from the early nude boy T-shirt through Bow Wow Wow) to argue that the Blank Generation was more clockwork satsuma than orange. Bliss was it in that dawn to be young. But to be a punk rocker was very heaven![16]

I remember going into Sex, with some trepidation, at the age of fourteen or fifteen, and looking at the extraordinary and somewhat shocking clothes. Among the more memorable were the T-shirt with two naked cowboys, naked from the waist down, facing each other, with enormous penises, and the legend 'let's dance', and the one with the blue photo of breasts seen as if behind a letterbox, or an aperture in the shirt itself. Now, of course, I wish I had bought some of the clothes in Sex. Then I was confused by them, though definitely intrigued. I think I knew, or at least intuited, that this curious antiboutique was of cultural significance.

The other great, original Punk boutique was the legendary Acme Attractions, the clothes store founded by Steph Raynor and John Krivine that was sited, improbably, in the Antiquarius antique market. (Antiquarius, founded in the late 1960s, a wonderful and eclectic collection of antique dealers' stores, was closed down in 2009, to make way for a branch of Anthropologie. This is an enormous shame, though at least the building, originally a 1920s temperance hall, has been preserved.) Krivine had been an associate of Genesis P-Orridge and Cosey Fanni Tutti, founders of

---

[16] Gallix, Andrew (ed.), *Punk Is Dead: Modernity Killed Every Night* (Basingstoke: Zero Books, 2017), 17–18.

COUM Transmissions and Throbbing Gristle, in Hull in the early 1970s. In 1976 the performance group COUM Transmissions staged their exhibition *Prostitution* at the ICA, a harbinger of the coming of Punk rock, and famously featuring pornographic images of group member Cosey Fanni Tutti, who had entered the commercial pornographic world as a form of performance art. Also exhibited were props from COUM's performances ranging from a rusted knife to a jar of Vaseline to bloodied objects such as bandages, tampons and bottles of blood. The title *Prostitution* was just as much in reference to the art world as it was to the bodily act. COUM and TG are, in a sense, the bridge between the weirder end of the 1960s counterculture and Punk. Acme was first in the middle of the ground floor of the market, but soon moved to the basement, where I remember visiting it. They sold retro clothes, some of which were original and often in bright, vivid colours. Acme enabled and encouraged the revolt against hippie style, with singers such as Nick Lowe turning from denim and long hair to tailored suits. Gorman describes the 'distinctive Acme looks: vintage short-sleeved shirts, plastic sandals or winkle-pickers and brightly-coloured mohair jumpers' as well as demob suits.[17] Don Letts worked there, and his taste in Reggae helped to introduce that music to the protopunks of the King's Road. The shop in the basement came a major place for people to hang out, not least because of the amount of dope that was smoked there.

In 1976, Sex became Seditionaries and developed a stark, post-apocalyptic aesthetic, including a grey, industrial carpet, Adeptus chairs from the 1960s, a giant view of Piccadilly Circus, turned on its side, and photographs of Dresden after the allied bombing. The clothes were also developing in more original directions, including the famous, and overpriced bondage trousers designed by Westwood. In the same year, Acme Attractions shifted to a more Punk look, including encouraging Gene October to form a kind of house Punk band, called, appropriately, Chelsea. This in turn led Raynor and Krivine to open a more commercial version of Acme, and a more downmarket rival to Seditionaries, on the King's Road, called BOY. Taking its cue perhaps from Acme customer Genesis P-Orridge, the original shop was made to look as if it had been burnt, and featured fake charred body parts, and T-shirts with slogans and images about the IRA and

---

17   Gorman, Paul, *The Look: Adventures in Pop and Rock Fashion* (London: Sanctuary, 2001), 128.

Gary Gilmore, as well as used syringes and contraceptive packs. I bought stuff from BOY, including fluorescent socks in green and yellow, and a T-shirt, also fluorescent, sleeveless with black tiger stripes on a green background.

One final site for Punk clothing is worth mentioning, not least as it tends to get forgotten. The Beaufort Market was in the World's End, just west of Beaufort Street. It is best known as the place in which Poly Styrene of X-Ray Spex had a stall, selling, in her words, 'plastic trash'. I don't remember her stall, though I did hang around the Market, mostly at Jock McDonald's stall. McDonald, often described as a kind of cut-price Malcolm McLaren, was busy promoting John Lydon's post-Sex Pistols project, Public Image Ltd, or PiL. Lydon himself was living in the World's End, SW10, at 45 Gunter Grove. Lydon started renting there in 1977, bought the house in the following year, and sold it in 1981. In his autobiography he described how McLaren had got him the house, and how it had possibly belonged to rock star Steve Winwood. From Lydon's own account and from images of the interior it seems that 45 Gunter Grove was a classic rock residence, run as 'an open house', with a party held every Friday, with guests including, surprisingly perhaps, Joan Armatrading, and 'everyone in the Reggae world'.[18] It was actually part of what was almost a rock ghetto, with, according to Lydon, Peter Grant, Led Zeppelin's manager, living opposite, and Brian Eno in a converted church at the top of the road. Grant probably lived there because of its close proximity to the offices of Swansong, Led Zeppelin's record company on the King's Road, almost next door to where Granny's had been. Bowie's management company, MainMan, also had their London offices on the Grove. Poly Styrene was a frequent visitor to no. 45, sometimes when escaping from mental health institutions. The police also made regular visits, largely to try to bust Lydon for drugs.

Eventually, this all became too much and Lydon left for New York and then Los Angeles, and sold the house. Now, it would cost several thousand pounds a month to rent, and several million to buy. Of course, it seems entirely right that the most demonic representative of the most apocalyptic music genre, the one who proclaimed himself the Antichrist, should live in the World's End. In his strange book on Punk, *Lipstick Traces*, Greil Marcus takes advantage of the serendipity of the coincidence of

---

[18] Lydon, John, *Anger is an Energy* (New York: Simon and Schuster, 2015), 182.

names to compare Lydon to eschatological medieval mystic and revolutionary John of Leydon, one of many figures in the late middle ages
proclaiming the end of days.[19] Lydon's post-Pistols work with PiL is incredibly impressive, and still seems vital and relevant. Writing in *The Quietus*
about listening to *Flowers of Romance*, PiL's third studio album, during
lockdown, writer Richard V. Hirst describes it at first as 'the sound of the
abyss'. He goes on to suggest that

Abyss isn't quite the word though, implying as it does an unplumbable darkness,
almost luxurious in its despair. Think Joy Division, think The Cure at their most baroque,
think *goth*. The Flowers Of Romance has moments where it attires itself handsomely
in the gothic, but it feels markedly un-camp, always circling back to its aggressively
stripped-down base, the sound of starkness itself. The musical terrain here is the
audio equivalent of bare concrete, the glare of the mortuary slab, or perhaps of the
brightly lit hospital ward. Listening to *The Flowers Of Romance* in our present times –
and listening to it *over and over* – is to be brought face to face with the denuded lives
we have become accustomed to living, shorn of almost all ornamentation, reduced
to their bare, repeated elements, coloured only by glimpses of some inconceivable
cosmic horror controlling things from beyond.[20]

Derek Jarman's *Jubilee* (1978) is the most enduring film to come out of the
Punk movement. Jarman imagines Queen Elizabeth I transported by John
Dee to a dystopian version of 1970s, in which London has collapsed into
lawlessness and ruin. The film follows the adventures of a kind of nihilistic,
messianic child commune of Punk rockers, a bit like a savage version of
the children in *Here Come the Double Deckers*. Far from being a reaction
against the transformations of the 1960s, the film shows that the anarchy
and destructiveness of Punk was its logical end. When the film gets to
modern London, it is a hilariously dystopian version, with youths wandering
past fires and rubble, with wrecked cars and walls daubed with graffiti such
as 'POST MODERN'. We are shown the view of the driver of a Rolls-Royce
as they go down a street with corrugated iron on either side, where a gang
of Punks are seen beating someone up. They are interrupted by Toyah

[19] Marcus, Greil, *Lipstick Traces: A Secret History of the Twentieth Century* (London: Faber and
      Faber, 2011), 182.
[20] Hirst, Richard V., 'The Sound of Freedom: PiL's Flowers of Romance Forty Years On', *The
      Quietus*, 26 April 2021, https://thequietus.com/articles/29813-pil-public-image-ltd-flowers-
      of-romance, accessed 1 May 2021.

Wilcox in a boiler suit brandishing a submachine gun. As the camera pulls back we see a pram in flames. This cuts to a scene with a spinning globe, in which countries have been blackened, and the words NEGATIVE WORLD STATUS, NO REASON FOR EXISTENCE, and OBSOLETE, handwritten. I am amused to discover that, in Jarman's original script, this scene is named 'THE WORLD'S END'.[21]

---

[21] Jarman, Derek, *Jubilee: Six Film Scripts* (Minneapolis: University of Minnesota Press, 2011), 47.

9

Learning to Love the Bomb

In 1978 the Afghanistan government was overthrown in a Marxist coup. In late 1979, in order, ostensibly, to support the government against the mujahideen, the Soviet Union invaded the country. This in turn caused alarm in the West, and seemed to be a return to the hottest days of the Cold War in the early 1960s. Along with everyone of my generation, I can distinctly remember the extreme anxiety about the possibility of nuclear war we all felt. It coloured everything, or rather greyed everything out, made the world gloomy with foreboding. The government actually prepared pamphlets and information films about what to do in the event of nuclear attack, the notorious Protect and Survive campaign, countered by the CND with their slogan of 'Protest and Survive'. Both the *Protect and Survive* and *Protest and Survive* pamphlets are available online, as is the *Advising the Householder* pamphlet from 1963, described in an earlier chapter. The later government pamphlet differs little in content from its predecessor, and the main difference between the two is in the design. They could work as useful teaching materials about the development of graphic design over the period of the long 1960s. In *Protect and Survive* the faux naïve coloured images have been replaced by bolder two tone drawings, showing, for example, the paterfamilias of the putative family being advised on building the inner fallout refuge. He is wearing flared trousers and sports sideburns. The inner fall-out refuge itself is constructed out of doors leaning against the wall, bolstered by bags and boxes filled with sand. The most striking image shows the family, father, mother, son and daughter, about to enter the refuge. Their heads are bowed, and the father's right hand is on the shoulder of the son, and his left hand grasps the essential transistor radio.[1] This image is reproduced in *Protest and Survive*, illustrating its forensic critique of the fabulous rhetoric of nuclear war then being bandied about by politicians, with the sardonic caption 'the nuclear family'.[2] The BBC also got newsreader Peter Donaldson to record a message to be broadcast in the event of nuclear war. The transcript is worth quoting in full.

This is the Wartime Broadcasting Service. This country has been attacked with nuclear weapons. Communications have been severely disrupted, and the number of casualties and the extent of the damage are not yet known. We shall bring you further information as soon as possible. Meanwhile, stay tuned to this wavelength, stay calm and stay in your own house.

Remember there is nothing to be gained by trying to get away. By leaving your homes you could be exposing yourself to greater danger.

If you leave, you may find yourself without food, without water, without accommodation and without protection. Radioactive fall-out, which follows a nuclear explosion, is many times more dangerous if you are directly exposed to it in the open. Roofs and walls offer substantial protection. The safest place is indoors. Make sure gas and other fuel supplies are turned off and that all fires are extinguished. If mains water is available, this can be used for fire-fighting. You should also refill all your containers for drinking water after the fires have been put out, because the mains water supply may not be available for very long.

Water must not be used for flushing lavatories: until you are told that lavatories may be used again, other toilet arrangements must be made. Use your water only for essential drinking and cooking purposes. Water means life. Don't waste it.

Make your food stocks last: ration your supply, because it may have to last for 14 days or more. If you have fresh food in the house, use this first to avoid wasting it: food in tins will keep.

If you live in an area where a fall-out warning has been given, stay in your fall-out room until you are told it is safe to come out. When the immediate danger has passed the sirens will sound a steady note. The 'all clear' message will also be given on this wavelength. If you leave the fall-out room to go to the lavatory or replenish food or water supplies, do not remain outside the room for a minute longer than is necessary.

Do not, in any circumstances, go outside the house. Radioactive fall-out can kill. You cannot see it or feel it, but it is there. If you go outside, you will bring danger to your

---

[1] Great Britain. Central Office of Information, *Protect and Survive* (London: H.M.S.O., 1980), 23.
[2] Thompson, E. P., *Protest and Survive* (London: The Campaign for Nuclear Disarmament, 1980), 16.

family and you may die. Stay in your fall-out room until you are told it is safe to come out or you hear the 'all clear' on the sirens.

Here are the main points again: Stay in your own homes, and if you live in an area where a fall-out warning has been given stay in your fall-out room, until you are told it is safe to come out. The message that the immediate danger has passed will be given by the sirens and repeated on this wavelength. Make sure that the gas and all fuel supplies are turned off and that all fires are extinguished. Water must be rationed, and used only for essential drinking and cooking purposes. It must not be used for flushing lavatories. Ration your food supply – it may have to last for 14 days or more.

We shall be on the air every hour, on the hour. Stay tuned to this wavelength, but switch your radios off now to save your batteries. That is the end of this broadcast.[3]

From the mid-1970s onwards the United Kingdom produced a series of public information films about preparing for nuclear war. They are now, of course, viewable online. They are both terrifying and comic and involve a combination of simplified graphics, models and photographs. What is particularly striking and sinister is the soundscape of the films. Each one starts with a fairly crude animation of a mushroom cloud and the rumble of an explosion, over which a pink circle is superimposed and into which a highly stylised image of a 'nuclear' family of a mother and a father and a boy and a girl appears. Even stranger is the little animation at the end of each film. The same image of the family appears again, this time against a blue background, with the words 'Protect and Survive'. This is accompanied by what I can only describe as a kind of screech/drone noise followed by five descending notes all played on some kind of early synthesiser. As the five notes are played the words 'Protect and Survive' wrap around the family and then solidify into a ring. It seems, then, that the UK government thought that nuclear war needed a jingle.

The advice given in the films is all delivered by a man with a measured BBC-accented voice, that I imagine is meant to be reassuring. This makes the films even more surreal, given the horrifying prospects of post-apocalyptic life about which he is advising us. In the film about 'Food Consumption', there is something almost Beckettian about the suggestion that 'most of the time you will be resting in your fall-out room and you will not need to eat much

[3] BBC News Magazine, 'Who, What, Why: What Would the BBC Broadcast in a Nuclear War', www.bbc.co.uk/news/magazine-34711497, accessed 11 February 2021.

food'. The final film on the reel I found online is entitled 'Casualties' and offers laconically matter-of-fact advice about what to do if someone dies.

If anyone dies while you are kept in our fallout room move the body to another room in the house. Label the body with name and address and cover it as tightly as possible with polythene, paper, sheets, or blankets. Tie a second card to a covering. The radio will advise you what to do about taking the body away for burial. If, however, you have had a body in the house for more than five days and if it is safe to go outside then you should bury the body for the time being in a trench or cover it with earth and mark the spot of the burial.

It is the wrenching tension between these kind of warnings and the banal normality of everyday life that produced what is arguably the greatest work of art to come out of the possibility of nuclear war, Raymond Briggs' graphic novel *When the Wind Blows*, published in 1982, at the height of nuclear fear. It tells the story of Jim and Ethel Bloggs, a retired couple, and their futile attempts to follow the instructions for surviving nuclear war. When it was made into an animated film in 1986, David Bowie sang the theme song.

It is hard to overstate how terrifying the early 1980s felt, especially in Britain. This fear found its most forceful cultural expression in rock and pop music. Writing in the *New York Times* in 1985, Stephen Holden suggested that there was a great difference between American and British pop music attitudes towards nuclear war with the British being far more anxious,

In American pop, nuclear war and the end of the world are often presented as an ultimate fireworks display – inevitable but exciting. Trans-Atlantic groups like the Police, U2, Culture Club, and Frankie Goes to Hollywood, on the other hand, are expressing a more fearful and realistic concern. Recently, both Culture Club and Frankie Goes to Hollywood enjoyed No. 1 English hits with explicit warnings about the horrors of nuclear war. Though heavily promoted in America, neither of these songs became significant hits here.[4]

He ends his article by suggesting that

If the sales of pop records are any kind of indicator of youthful conviction, one might conclude that there is a fundamental difference in the American and British outlooks. American youth would seem to feel so powerful and prosperous that its pop culture

---

[4] Holden, Stephen, 'Rock Music: Or Songs for the End of the World', *New York Times*, 17 January 1985, 16.

can afford to be oblivious to real nuclear peril. Less economically robust, and with a far less rosy future, British youth are expressing their sense of vulnerability.[5]

William M. Knoblauch concurs:

British artists stand out for their unique Cold War perspective. Scarred by the bombings of World War II, sceptical of UK civil defense propaganda, and scared of conservatives' brazen rhetoric at home and in America, these British artists created a unique brand of antinuclear pop.[6]

He continues that 'Having lived through the German "Blitz," Britons knew first hand the horrors of urban warfare. While it is impossible to quantify the psychological impact of this collective experience, wartime bombing undoubtedly shaped British perspectives in the nuclear age.' It was exactly at this moment, the end of the 1970s and the beginning of the '80s, that the Blitz club-night in Covent Garden on Tuesdays and the Blitz Kids, made the New Romantic movement possible. In his book *The British Pop Dandy* Stan Hawkins succinctly defines the Blitz Kids as a

group that frequented the Blitz nightclub in the early 1980s, including Boy George and his friend Marilyn, Steve Strange, Martin Degville, Philip Sallon and others. As a reaction to the punk movement, the Blitz Kids, androgynous by all counts, sought a new direction by wearing garish home-made costumes and clothing and buckets of make up.[7]

Reading the names of the songs of that period that dealt with nuclear war brings back the sense of extreme fear and anger of the period with great vividness.

A play list of such British nuclear songs might include 'Two Tribes' by Frankie Goes to Hollywood, 'Breathing' by Kate Bush, 'Everyday is Like Sunday' by The Smiths, 'Shout' and 'Everyone Wants to Rule the World' by Tears for Fears, 'Dancing with Tears in my Eyes' by Ultravox and 'Living Through Another Cuba' by XTC. Going back a little earlier than the 1980s I might include 'A Bomb in Wardour Street' and 'Going Underground' by The

---

[5] Ibid.

[6] Knoblauch, William, 'Will You Sing about the Missiles?' In *Nuclear Threats, Nuclear Fear and the Cold War of the 1980s*, edited by Eckart Conze, Martin Klimke and Jeremy Varon (Cambridge, New York: Cambridge University Press, 2016), 103.

[7] Hawkins, Stan, *The British Pop Dandy: Masculinity, Popular Music and Culture* (Farnham: Ashgate, 2009), 60.

Jam. I am not sure the latter is directly about nuclear war, but its title vividly suggested the need to find underground shelter in such an event, with obvious echoes of the Blitz.

However, for my money, the best 1980s Cold War song is by the largely forgotten post-Punk pioneers Television Personalities, who were from the World's End. To begin with they claimed to be the actual television personalities Bruce Forsyth, Russell Harty, Hughie Green and Nicholas Parsons. 'Parsons', whose real name was Dan Treacy, was interviewed by Garry Bushell in *Sounds* in 1979, where he gives his actual address, which is in the 1950s block on the south side of the King's Road, opposite Seditionaries. Treacy describes his routine watching the King's Road.

Yeah, I just sit here some days watching people. You see everything walking down the Kings [sic] Rd – that's where I get all my songs from. Y'know, you see someone walk into a shop to buy the *News Of The World* and everyone in front of them's buying *The Observer* so they buy *The Express*. I ain't got any 'O'-levels but I notice these things.[8]

Bushell asks about what it's like living opposite a famous institution such as Seditionaries.

Oh yeah, my mum used to do their dry cleaning... you see all the stars up here. I must see Steve Jones five times a week. Gene October. They all go in there, Charlie Watts, Diana Dors, Reggie Bousanquet [sic]. I wrote a song about that, 'I Saw Reggie Bousanquet Yesterday'.[9]

(Reggie Bosanquet was a hard-drinking newsreader who lived in the World's End, on the King's Road, and was a regular visitor to Seditionaries, and indeed a customer. He liked the rubber underwear.) Released in 1986, The Television Personalities' song 'How I Learned to Love the Bomb' takes its title from that of Stanley Kubrick's film *Dr Strangelove: Or How I Learned to Love the Bomb*. Unlike the more angry and fearful songs listed above, it is sardonic and ironic and suggests, sarcastically perhaps, accepting the necessity of nuclear deterrence.

> Well there's no more sleepless nights for me
> Now it's easier from now on

[8] Bushell, Garry, 'These Men Are Part-Time Punks', *Sounds*, 20 January 1979.
[9] Ibid.

'cause I've realised exactly where I've been going wrong
Well I've been lying awake at night
Worrying about the Russians
But the Russians are my friends
'cause we've got a love that will never end
cause now I've learned to love the bomb
Now I've learned to love the bomb.

The late 1970s and early 1980s saw the election of Mrs Thatcher in this country and Ronald Reagan in the United States. You can watch footage online of Thatcher leaving Flood Street and Chelsea to go to Downing Street. By 1986 summits between Gorbachev and Reagan lessened the tensions of the renewed Cold War. In the same year the Chernobyl nuclear reactor in the Ukraine exploded, which was not just the world's most catastrophic nuclear incident but also evidence of the sclerotic nature of Soviet society. A few years later, the Berlin Wall fell and the Soviet Union collapsed. Despite Chernobyl and other indications, this caught almost everyone by surprise. However, this did not stop hubristic declarations concerning the triumph of capitalist liberal democracy and the 'End of History'. Once again, it looked as if Armageddon had been averted. However, another kind of Armageddon took place, a neoliberal apocalypse, beautifully described by the late Mark Fisher in his book *Capitalist Realism*, in which the whole of the world is subsumed by capitalism, which is 'very much like the Thing in John Carpenter's film of the same name: a monstrous, infinitely plastic entity, capable of metabolizing and absorbing anything with which it comes into contact'.[10]

Harbingers of this new apocalypse were visible in the late 1970s, in the form of the Sloane Ranger, a term made famous by style columnist Peter York in the late 1970s. York, or his editor at *Harpers and Queen*, had noticed a distinct tribe of young people wearing unashamedly old-fashioned upper-class clothes. The Sloane Ranger, male and female, represented the full-on embrace of a privileged class identity, something that had been more or less unacceptable in the 1960s and early 1970s. A vestigial sense of honesty compels me to admit that, as a public school boy, I was on the edges of the Sloane Ranger world. I went, along with many of my friends, to one of the main Sloane pubs, the Admiral Codrington (the Cod), near Sloane Square (of course). What I did not realise I was then witnessing was the emergence of a

---

[10] Fisher, Mark, *Capitalist Realism: Is There No Alternative?* (Winchester: Zero Books, 2009), 6.

newly confident ruling class. Decades later, the kind of person who went to the Cod would end up running the country, disastrously as it happens.

Not so long ago, walking with my mother in the King's Road at the World's End I saw a most bizarre sight, in the form of what can only be described as a motorcade. In the middle of this line of cars were two Rolls-Royce Mansorys, each of which would have cost nearly £300,000, and a sports car. Flanking them were two top-end Range Rovers. All were black and all had personalised number plates, variations on STUNT. This absurd sight was made more comic by the fact that they had missed their turning up Limerston Street, so the whole motorcade was laboriously and clumsily having to back up, much to the rage of other traffic. This was the normal mode of urban travel of James Stunt, erstwhile husband of Petra, daughter of Formula One boss Bernie Ecclestone. Stunt, whose name begs to become a piece of rhyming slang, is a gold dealer, self-proclaimed billionaire and art collector, and, as is obvious from his preferred mode of transport, a fool. (This was a view shared, incidentally, by his now ex-father-in-law who is quoted as saying that 'James is a lovely lad. He's harmless, but he's an idiot.'[11] After the divorce and an unfortunate interview with Stunt in *Tatler*, it's likely that Ecclestone will be less generous now.) In his sad neediness and desperate showing off Stunt is similar to a certain recent occupant of the White House. Together they are both symptoms of a toxic form of weak masculinity that tells us something disturbing about our current cultural moment.

Stunt's grotesque and pointless display of wealth is just a more obvious marker of the considerable and increasing inequality in London. In a recent article in *The Guardian*, the World's End itself was described, in the words of Labour MP for Kensington Emma Dent Coad as a 'fault line of dramatic inequality' in 'the most unequal borough in Britain. This fault line runs across the King's Road, dividing the 'brick towers of the World's End estate in Chelsea and the £5m Georgian houses over the road'.[12] (The article, as

[11] Scott, Paul, 'His-and-hers Rollers. Armed Bodyguards. Wild Champagne Sprees in Nightclubs... Why Bernie Ecclestone Thinks his "Billionaire" Son-in-law's too Flash for His Own Good', *Mailonline*, 26 April 2014, www.dailymail.co.uk/news/article-2613504/His-Rollers-Armed-bodyguards-Wild-champagne-sprees-nightclubs-Why-Bernie-Ecclestone-thinks-billionaire-son-laws-flash-good.html, accessed 15 December 2020.

[12] Booth, Robert, 'World's End Estate Exemplifies Fault Lines of Dramatic Inequality', The Guardian, 13 November 2017, www.theguardian.com/society/2017/nov/13/worlds-end-estate-exemplifies-fault-lines-of-dramatic-inequality, accessed 15 January 2021.

originally published in the print version of *The Guardian*, placed the World's End in Fulham, though this was corrected in the online version. That the houses are not Georgian as the article also stated but mid-Victorian terrace houses intended for artisans and lower middle-class families remains uncorrected.) The inequalities that are a mark of the neoliberal order are also part of the New Cold War that is being waged between Russia and the West. It is widely believed that Vladimir Putin ordered billionaire oligarch Roman Abramovich to buy Chelsea Football Club as a means of infiltrating London society.[13]

The idea of neoliberalism as a kind of Armageddon found accidently ironic expression in a site in Chelsea in 2020. Among the more ostentatious markers of wealth recently has been the fashion for digging extra basements in which home gyms or cinemas, or even swimming pools, can be installed. Often these are built in terrace houses, with accompanying disturbance to neighbours, and the constant sense that, one day, one of these projects would cause structural damage. In early November two houses in Durham Place, near the Royal Hospital and dating from the late 18th century and worth millions of pounds, collapsed. They were being made into one property, and having their basements extended. We went to look at the remains. It was exactly, and eerily, like an image from the Blitz, a bombsite, as if the area's traumatic past had come to haunt its present.

On 14 June 2017 fire broke out at Grenfell Tower, a twenty-four-storey block of social housing in North Kensington. Seventy-one died. It was widely thought that a combination of factors had led to the fire being so destructive of life, including the advice that, in the event of a fire, tower block occupants should remain in their flats, inadequate sprinkler systems, and a form of cladding on the outside of the building that helped to spread the flames. All this seemed to suggest a neglect of and contempt for the occupants, especially in the context of their comparative poverty in one of the richest areas in Britain. Certainly the Inquest, which is taking place as I write, suggests criminal levels of deceit and chicanery in the name of profit on the part of the suppliers of the cladding. It was thought that Kensington and Chelsea Borough Council were far more concerned with their rich constituents than

---

[13] Belton, Catherine, *Putin's People: How the KGB Took Back Russian and Then Took on the West* (New York, London: HarperCollins, 2020).

those in places such as Grenfell. All this was understood as a disastrous consequence of seven years of Coalition and then Tory rule nationally, in which a ruthless policy of austerity had been pursued. The extraordinarily powerful and apocalyptic image of the burning tower became an icon for the anger many felt at the contemptuous attitude of the ruling elite towards ordinary people. Theresa May compounded her reputation for insensitivity by refusing to meet with residents and victims, opting for a private visit to the site instead, thus giving Jeremy Corbyn an easy PR victory when he did make a public visit and embraced residents and survivors.

A curious aspect of the Grenfell in light of earlier parts of this book is that the councillor supposedly responsible for the shortcomings of the tower's safety arrangements was Rock Feilding-Mellen, son of Chelsea trepanners Joe Mellen and Amanda Feilding. Feilding-Mellen, as deputy leader of the Tory-led Kensington and Chelsea Borough Council, had overseen the £10 million refurbishment of the tower, including the cladding. (Strangely, Feilding-Mellon, at least in photographs, is a dead ringer for the young Malcolm McLaren.) According to the newspapers, shortly after the Grenfell fire, protestors gathered outside his 'luxury £1.2 million home', also described as a 'three-storey townhouse', necessitating his and his family's hasty departure.[14]

Grenfell was a symbol not just of neglect and even the suspicion that the council were engaging in a kind of social cleansing but also of the rapid and dramatic transformation of London's built environment. This was intimately bound up with the increasing inequality symbolised by Stunt and the fault line of the King's Road at the World's End. Instead of the social housing that had proliferated since the early part of the 20th century and even the late 19th century in the form of Peabody and Guinness estates, or the post-war cities in the sky, what was now being built was almost entirely speculative, purely profit-driven developments. Perhaps more shockingly, at a time when there is considerable homelessness, and young people find it almost impossible to get on the property ladder in London, because of the price of houses, many

14 Lake, Emma, 'Grenfell Cllr Flees Tory Councillor Who Oversaw Grenfell Tower Cladding Refurb Flees £1.2m Family Home after "Threats and Vandalism"', *The Sun*, 25 June 2017, www.thesun.co.uk/news/3879245/tory-councillor-who-oversaw-grenfell-tower-cladding-refurb-flees-1-2m-family-home-after-threats-and-vandalism/, accessed 30 June 2017.

such speculative developments remain empty. Often they have been bought by investors as safe places to keep money in the form of property. There are rumours that in some such houses the entire interiors are shrink wrapped in order to keep them in good condition.

There is also a sense that much of this development is almost entirely unregulated. Almost any development, however unnecessary and however aesthetically misjudged, is given the go-ahead. This can be seen clearly from the river at World's End. On both the Chelsea and Battersea sides going west there are endless, ill-thought out blocks in various geometric or undulating shapes, almost all glass cladding steel structures.

This is even more evident from a vantage point such as Waterloo Bridge, where, looking east, one can see an uncoordinated mishmash of tall developments, all bearing some nickname based on their shape. There is the Shard, the Cucumber, the Cheese Grater and the Razor. The net effect is that of an unimaginatively realised science fiction city as might have featured in the comic *2000AD* twenty years ago – except that it is real and it is here, now. What is most curious about this is the sense that what, when I look at this new London, I am seeing is the future past, the future as imagined from my past. It is a kind of nostalgic future vision of the city, prefigured in endless utopian and dystopian schemes from those of the Futurist Sant'Elia, to Metropolis, Dan Dare, J. G. Ballard, Moebius, *Blade Runner* and so on. I have lived to see the dream of the future from my youth become something of a nightmare of the present. I realise that the dates of almost all the futures of my past have already arrived, Kubrick's *2001: A Space Odyssey* has come and gone, as has October 2015, the time in which *Back to the Future Part II* is set. Even more disturbing is that the first *Blade Runner* is set in 2019, the year in which I am writing these words. The year 2001 brought not the future that Kubrick foresaw but a present in which the threat from above returned, in the form of hijacked airliners crashing into skyscrapers. I remember walking home from Birkbeck College, where I then worked, on the afternoon of 11 September, with a sense, familiar from the Cold War, of London as a target.

In his *Ghosts of My Life: Writings on Depression, Hauntology and Lost Futures*, Mark Fisher quotes Franco 'Bifo' Berardi referring to 'the slow cancellation of the future [that] got underway in the 1970s and 1980s'. Fisher continues that

If the late 1970s and early 80s were the moment when the current crisis of cultural temporality could first be felt, it was only during the first decade of the 21st century that what Simon Reynolds calls 'dyschronia' has become endemic.[15]

Fisher invokes Jacques Derrida's notion of hauntology to understand how our present is constitutively haunted by lost and unrealised pasts. This can be seen in the egregious use of the idea of the 'Blitz Spirit' and the Second World War more generally in discussions about Brexit. However, Fintan O'Toole diagnoses the roots of Brexit in a more recent cultural moment. He points out that 60 per cent of English men and women between fifty and sixty-four, the Punk generation in other words, and 'if not an actual punk, then a vicarious one, living off the thrills of the most powerful and original English cultural movement of modern times', voted for Brexit[16]. As if confirming O'Toole's thesis, John Lydon declared himself a supporter of Brexit in an interview on the BBC breakfast show *Good Morning Britain*. In his words, 'Where do I stand on Brexit? Well, here it goes, the working class have spoke and I'm one of them and I'm with them. And there it is.' He then went on to suggest that Donald Trump was a 'political Sex Pistol'.[17]

[15] Fisher, Mark, *Ghosts of my Life: Writings on Depression, Hauntology and Lost Futures* (Winchester: Zero Books, 2014), 21.
[16] O'Toole, Fintan, *Heroic Failure: Brexit and the Politics of Pain* (New York: Apollo, 2019), chap 5, Kindle.
[17] Brittan, Luke Morgan, 'Watch John Lydon Defend Brexit, Nigel Farage and Donald Trump', *NME*, 27 March 2017, www.nme.com/news/music/john-lydon-brexit-nigel-farage-donald-trump-2028596, accessed 26 May 2021.

10

The Drowned World

During the early part of writing this book I took my daughter to California for three weeks. I had been invited to give a paper at a conference at Chapman University in Orange County. This gave me an excuse to spend some time with my daughter and my sister, who lives in California, and to visit parts of the state that I had not been to. In OC we were close (in the relative, Californian sense) to Disneyland, but we decided not to go there. Apart from being the location of Disneyland, I also remembered that Philip K. Dick lived in Orange County at various points in his life, and we were near to his last home in Santa Ana, where he had his final, fatal stroke. It seemed to me that Dick living in the middle class suburbs of OC was as perverse as J. G. Ballard choosing to live in Shepperton in West London. While in OC I realised I was as close as I will probably ever be to the location of the philosopher Jacques Derrida's actual archive (or at least part of it) at UC Irvine, and thus also near to where Derrida lived when teaching at Irvine, Laguna Beach. Since there was nothing at all to do where we are staying and there was a day before the conference started, I persuaded my daughter that we would take a bus (or rather two buses) to Laguna Beach. It was a journey of about an hour and three quarters, and a vivid demonstration of the fact that no one takes a bus in OC if they have any alternative. The journey through Santa Ana to the Huntington bus interchange in the June gloom was truly dispiriting, mile after mile of dun or ochre-coloured sheds covered in plastic logos for fast food outlets. Things got better after Huntington as the bus travels along the Pacific Coast on Highway 1.

Laguna Beach was a relief from the horrors of inland OC but fairly banal. I find it strange to think of Derrida here. Even stranger is the idea that at one point Laguna was a centre of LSD culture, boasting the presence of Timothy

Leary and the manufacturers of the famous Orange Sunshine brand of acid.[1] Perhaps that is an appropriate juxtaposition in relation to Derrida's interest in the idea of the *pharmakon*, the drug that can be both poison and remedy. The light and space in California put the zap on my head, to quote Colonel Willard's description of the effect of Vietnam on Mr Clean in *Apocalypse Now*. It seems a place without shadow, as far as I can see, just light and blue. It is also strangely sexless, despite the abundance of exposed young flesh. I wonder if this is something to do with the disavowal of ageing and death that I take to be part of the SoCal culture. In this sense this part of the world is a kind of Garden of Eden, in that it seems to lack a sense of both sex and death, but is also an end, a final point. In *Call Me Ishmael*, his book on Melville and Moby Dick, the poet Charles Olson sees the Pacific Ocean as the last American frontier. 'Of waters as Russia of land, the Pacific gives the sense of immensity. She is the HEART SEA, twin and rival of the HEARTLAND. The Pacific is, for an American, the Plains repeated, a 20th century Great West.'[2] It feels to me like an end or ending, a *finis terrae*, an end of the land or even world.

The French for World's End can be either '*les extrémités de la terre*', if we take the phrase to mean the ends of the earth, or '*la fin du monde*' (or '*fin de globe*' as in Wilde's *The Portrait of Dorian Gray*) if understood in a more apoc-alyptic way. In 2003 the French publishing house Galilée published a selec-tion of Derrida's eulogies for and essays about friends and colleagues of his who had died. The title of the English translation is *The Work of Mourning*, but the French title is far better. *Chaque fois unique, la fin du monde*, 'each time uniquely, the end of the world' (or perhaps the world's end).[3] The title expresses the idea, found elsewhere, in Derrida's work, that an indi-vidual death is no less a catastrophic loss of an entire world than a nuclear holocaust. In 'No Apocalypse, Not Now', his essay of nuclear criticism, he suggests that 'there is no common measure adequate to persuade me that a personal mourning is less serious than a nuclear war'.[4] He repeats this thought in his final seminar before he died, proclaiming that

---

[1] Schou, Nicholas, *Orange Sunshine* (New York: Thomas Dunne Books, 2010).

[2] Olson, Charles, *Call Me Ishmael* (San Francisco: City Lights, 1996), 114.

[3] Derrida, Jacques, *The Work of Mourning* (Chicago: Chicago University Press, 2001).

[4] Derrida, Jacques, *Psyche: Inventions of the Other, vol. 1* (Stanford: Stanford University Press, 2007), 403.

each time the end of the world, the end, the whole end of the world... not a particular end of this or that world, of the world of so and so, of this one or that one, male or female, of this soldier, this civilian, this man, this woman, this child, but the end of the world in general, the absolute end of the world.[5]

For Derrida, one of the consequences of nuclear war would be the 'remainderless destruction of the archive', and he later wrote on what he called '*mal d'archive*', archive sickness or archive fever. This book is perhaps a symptom of my archive fever or sickness, and knowledge that my end is the end of my world, my world's end. But it is also the condition for being able to write at all. Derrida's friend 'Hélène Cixous remarks that 'writing is learning to die'.

So it gives us everything, it gives us the end of the world; to be human we need to experience the end of the world. We need to lose the world, to lose a world, and to discover that there is more than one world and that the world isn't what we think it is. Without that, we know nothing about the mortality and immortality that we carry. We don't know that we're alive as long as we haven't encountered death: these are the banalities that have been erased. And it *is* an act of grace.[6]

'End' also means aim or intention and any consideration of ending is also a thinking about what one's activities in life have been for. What has been my end in this world as I come nearer to the end of my world. The answer in the end is always, 'very little... almost nothing'. But, as Simon Critchley suggests, in his book that takes those words as its title, the key word here is 'almost'. For Critchley Beckett offers a way of 'redeeming us from the temptations of redemption' and of returning 'us to the ordinary or the everyday'.[7] 'However,' Critchley continues 'the ordinary is not something we can simply turn to by taking a walk in the street or a break from our work. On the contrary, the ordinary is not something we can simply turn to by taking a walk in the street or a break from our work. On the contrary, the ordinary is an achievement.'[8] It is even more of an achievement, in my view, in the light of the horrors of the 20th and 21st centuries, especially after what

---

[5] Derrida, Jacques, *The Beast & the Sovereign. Volume II* (Chicago: University of Chicago Press, 2011), 259–60.

[6] Cixous, Helene, *Three Steps on the Ladder of Writing* (New York: Columbia University Press, 1993), 10.

[7] Critchley, Simon, *Very Little... Almost Nothing: Death, Philosophy and Literature* (London, New York: Routledge, 2004), xxiv.

[8] Ibid.

Peter Wyden calls 'Day One', the historical break initiated by the bombing of Hiroshima. This is the ordinary maintained in the condition of the deferred death sentence of living in a nuclear world.

At Laguna Beach itself, my daughter went swimming, and I sat on the beach and listened to the surf. I find it strange to hear a noise that I have heard all my life – in Suffolk, Greece, Italy, Dorset, Cornwall, China and India. There is an added poignancy here as many of those memories, particularly from Cornwall, are also those of being with my daughter, on holiday, throughout her childhood. Somehow, I think of the sea, and the beach, as a kind of archive, of sounds. The artist Ruth McLennan responded to a Facebook post I made about this experience, in which I connected that experience with Derrida's notion of archive fever.

I like the idea of coastal archive fever. The shifts and erosion of coastlines covering and uncovering traces of humans trying to keep the sea out make a difficult archive to keep track of. The land itself seems to have less authority here than elsewhere. But also the way people congregate along coastlines, staring out at the horizon, or making a living from the sea, or putting up buildings with a view of the sea, seems somehow to dare the sea to sweep them away.[9]

Beaches and the edges of the sea always make me think of nuclear war. On the front of *The Picture Post* for 25 August 1945, there is a picture of a small boy in dungarees, seen from the back, on a beach, looking out to the sea and cloudy sky. Beneath is the legend 'MAN ENTERS THE ATOM AGE'. Perhaps this is why Nevil Shute called his 1957 post-apocalypse novel, in which survivors of a nuclear war await their fate in Australia, *On the Beach*. J. G. Ballard's most melancholy story, 'The Terminal Beach', plays with this too, in its account of a man, Travers, mourning his wife and child, wandering the deserted Eniwetok Atoll, site of American atomic bomb testing. There the 'series of weapons tests had fused the sand in layers, and the pseudogeological strata condensed the brief epochs, microseconds in duration, of thermonuclear time'.[10] This connection between nuclear apocalypse and the beach is also found in the title of Colin Self's brilliant sculpture from 1966, 'Beach Girl', which is made out of a shop dummy made to look like an incinerated female body. Self's sculpture is in the Cold War gallery in the Imperial War Museum in London, next to a case with some of the apparatus of

9   McLennan, Ruth, personal correspondence.
10   Ballard, J. G., *The Terminal Beach* (Harmondsworth: Penguin Books, 1974), 139.

British nuclear warning systems, including hand-operated sirens, telephone units and radiation monitors – the stuff of Cold War nightmares. It is also near a full-scale replica of Little Boy, the bomb that was dropped on Hiroshima. (When I posted a picture of the last on Instagram, somebody remarked that it looked in good condition, considering.)

In London during the first lockdown, walking around the backstreets of Hammersmith at dusk, looking up from the canyons of terrace houses to the purple evening sky, I felt myself underwater, subaquatic. The dusk light is a kind of underwater light. This connects to the fact that, for me, my birth city is both nurturing, maternal and suffocating. It makes perfect sense that the word 'metropolis' comes from the Greek for mother state. I feel I am drowning in it. I know why Michael Moorcock named his great novel of London life *Mother London*. One of his epigraphs is from Robert Downes' 1914 book, *Cities which Fascinate*.

LONDON! There is a resonant sound and roll in the very name of the world's greatest city. It affects us like the boom and reverberation of thunder. There is a note of majesty in it, accompanied by a throb as of doom. It is the fullness of life which impresses us most in London – the pathos, the passion and the power of restless, striving multitudes. This it is which thrills and fills us, as sea-captains are thrilled and filled by the vastness, might and mystery of the sea.[11]

This is perhaps why the image of the drowned city is so alluring or fascinating. For example, Richard Jeffrey's *After London* is profoundly dystopian, imagining London abandoned and overgrown into a great marsh.

At the eastern extremity the Lake narrows, and finally is lost in the vast marshes which cover the site of the ancient London. Through these, no doubt, in the days of the old world there flowed the river Thames. By changes of the sea level and the sand that was brought up there must have grown great banks, which obstructed the stream. I have formerly mentioned the vast quantities of timber, the wreckage of towns and bridges which was carried down by the various rivers, and by none more so than by the Thames. These added to the accumulation, which increased the faster because the foundations of the ancient bridges held it like piles driven in for the purpose. And before this the river had become partially choked from the cloacæ of the ancient city which poured into it through enormous subterranean aqueducts and drains.[12]

---

[11] Moorcock, Michael, *Mother London* (London: Weidenfeld and Nicholson, 2016), 59.

[12] Jefferies, Richard, *After London: Or, Wild England* (Oxford; New York: Oxford University Press, 1980), 65.

J. G. Ballard's *The Drowned World* was published in 1962, the year after I was born. Reading it nearly 60 years after its publication in order to write about London in the past, Ballard's future drowned London offered some fascinating reflections on memory and the act of remembering a city from my past. *The Drowned World* is set in the 22nd century in which what we would now call global warming has rendered almost the entire earth uninhabitable, with major cities overrun with water and vegetation. For a recent lecture about pluralising the Anthropocene, I invented some new 'cenes' to add to the already proliferating number, one of which was the Ballardocene. Most of the remaining five million humans left have retreated to the Arctic Circle, leaving a few scientific expeditions surveying the drowned cities, before making their own retreats, and a handful of obdurate remainers. At the beginning of the book the main protagonist, a scientist named Kerans, doesn't even know where he is; 'had it once been Berlin, Paris or London? Kerans asked himself'.[13] 'Curiously, though, despite the potent magic of the lagoon worlds and the drowned cities, he had never felt any interest in their contents, and never bothered to identify which of the cities he was stationed in.' The cities themselves are intensely, explicitly surreal.

Sixty feet below the cutter a straight grey promenade stretched away between the buildings, the remains of some former thoroughfare, the rusting humped shells of cars still standing by the curb. Many of the lagoons in the centre of the city were surrounded by an intact ring of buildings, and consequently little silt had entered them. Free of vegetation, apart from a few drifting clumps of Sargasso weed, the streets and shops had been preserved almost intact, like a reflection in a lake that has somehow lost its original. The bulk of the city had long since vanished, and only the steel-supported buildings of the central commercial and financial areas had survived the encroaching flood waters. The brick houses and single-storey factories of the suburbs had disappeared completely below the drifting tides of silt. Where these broke surface giant forests reared up into the burning dull-green sky, smothering the former wheatfields of temperate Europe and North America. Impenetrable Matto Grossos sometimes three hundred feet high, they were a nightmare world of competing organic forms returning rapidly to their Paleozoic past, and the only avenues of transit for the United Nations military units were through the lagoon systems that had superimposed themselves on the former cities. But even these were now being clogged with silt and then submerged.[14]

---

[13]   Ballard, J. G., *The Drowned World* (London: Fourth Estate, 2014), 36.
[14]   Ibid., 19.

Ballard often spoke of his debt to Surrealism, especially in relation to his wartime experiences as a child interned in a Far Eastern prison camp. The Surreal nature of the drowned world is made explicit in the description of the luxury apartment lived in by Beatrice, a young woman who refuses to leave the city, and who is also Kerans' mistress.

Over the mantelpiece was a huge painting by the early 20th century surrealist Delvaux, in which ashenfaced women danced naked to the waist with dandified skeletons in tuxedos against a spectral bonelike landscape. On another wall one of Max Ernst's self-devouring phantasmagoric jungles screamed silently to itself, like the sump of some insane unconscious.[15]

The latter painting sounds like 'Europe After the Rain', Ernst's attempt to come to terms with the Second World War, and also, incidentally, the inspiration for the name and for the cover image for another dystopian fiction of the same period as *The Drowned World*, Alan Burns' *Europe After the Rain*, published in 1965. The Ballardian conceit at the heart of the book is that the altered climactic conditions are returning the world to a primeval condition, and that this is triggering deep forms of inherited memory in the remaining humans. More interesting to me is the more immediate effect the cities have on those old enough to remember them before they were inundated. For example, Kerans' colleague Dr Bodkin,

twenty-five years his senior, had actually lived in several of them, both in Europe and America, and spent most of his spare time punting around the remoter water-ways, searching out former libraries and museums. Not that they contained anything other than his memories.[16]

It is Bodkin who tells Kerans where they actually are.

'Do you know where we are?' he asked after a pause. 'The name of this city?' When Kerans shook his head he said: 'Part of it used to be called London, not that it matters. Curiously enough, though, I was born here. Yesterday I rowed over to the old University quarter, a mass of little creeks, actually found the laboratory where my father used to teach.'[17]

[15] Ibid., 29.
[16] Ibid., 20.
[17] Ibid., 75–6.

When the scientific expedition to which he is attached leaves, Kerans, along with Bodkin and Beatrice, contrive to stay, despite the dangers of doing so. Over time each becomes

increasingly preoccupied with their own descents through total time. Bodkin had become lost in his private reverie, punting aimlessly around the narrow creeks in search for the submerged world of his childhood. Once Kerans came across him resting on an oar in the stern of his small metal scow and gazing vacantly at the unyielding buildings around him. He had stared straight through Kerans, failing to acknowledge his call.[18]

Bodkin's melancholy 'search for the submerged world of his childhood' really resonated with me. It struck me as an apt metaphor for what I am trying to do in this book. Part of its resonance is that that world is drowned, gone, dead and unrecoverable. It is that very unrecoverability that makes it so compelling. Later on in the book some pirates invade the lagoon in which Kerans, Bodkin and Beatrice are staying, and manage to pump out the water to reveal the city below. This turns out to be extraordinarily disquieting. As Beatrice puts it to Kerans, 'But it's all so hideous. I can't believe that anyone ever lived here. It's like some imaginary city of hell. Robert, I need the lagoon.'[19]

The Drowned World may have been written as an oblique response to the prospect of nuclear holocaust, but its account of planetary ecological catastrophe seems at least as plausible as the latter as the way the world ends. There can be no doubt at all that we are in the midst of a massive environmental catastrophe, right now. Ballard's vision of a superheated planet looks far more prescient than I suspect it did in the early 1960s, as David Wallace-Wells' recent work has made starkly clear.[20] Wallace-Wells suggests that the 'threat from climate change is more total than that from the Bomb'. Writing a book partly about the world's end, which plays on the coincidental naming of the area known as the World's End, it is hard for me to resist the obvious quotation from T. S. Eliot's 'The Hollow Men', a poem one of the epigraphs of which comes from Joseph Conrad's *Heart of Darkness*, 'Mistah Kurtz – he dead', and in which the eponymous hollow men are 'Gathered on this beach of the tumid river'.

[18] Ibid., 84.
[19] Ibid., 123.
[20] Wallace-Wells, David, *The Uninhabitable Earth: Aa Story of the Future* (London, New York: Penguin Books, 2019).

In a sense this brings us full circle as Conrad's novel itself starts and ends on the same river with which this book begins. *The Heart of Darkness* opens in the Thames estuary, where my cremated remains might find themselves eventually.

The sea-reach of the Thames stretched before us like the beginning of an interminable waterway. In the offing the sea and the sky were welded together without a joint, and in the luminous space the tanned sails of the barges drifting up with the tide seemed to stand still in red clusters of canvas sharply peaked, with gleams of varnished sprits. A haze rested on the low shores that ran out to sea in vanishing flatness. The air was dark above Gravesend, and farther back still seemed condensed into a mournful gloom, brooding motionless over the biggest, and the greatest, town on earth.[21]

Just before he starts recounting the story of Mr Kurtz, Marlow comments on the Estuary. "'And this also," said Marlow suddenly, "has been one of the dark places of the earth."'[22] The final words of the book also let us know, in no uncertain terms, that the supposedly civilised imperial capital was no less dark than the Africa in which the novel's action mainly takes place. This is returned to in the book's last sentence.

The offing was barred by a black bank of clouds, and the tranquil waterway leading to the uttermost ends of the earth flowed sombre under an overcast sky – seemed to lead into the heart of an immense darkness.[23]

The name 'Thames' may well derive from an Indo-European word for dark. If so, it was probably given its name in reference to the colour of the water. But there is something dark about the Thames at a more metaphorical level. It has never been a light-hearted river. It has been far too bound up with the bloody history of empire, conquest and trade to be so. That, at its end, it more or less dissipates, rather than flows into the sea seems appropriate. Ultimately, this darkness is not just that of the horror at the heart of civilisation, but death itself, for which the river dissipating itself into the sea has always been a figure. In D. H. Lawrence's *Women in Love* Birkin distinguishes between the 'silver river of life, rolling on and quickening all the world to a

---

[21] Conrad, Joseph, *Heart of Darkness* (London, New York: Penguin Books, 2007), 3.
[22] Ibid., 5.
[23] Ibid., 96.

brightness, on and on to heaven, flowing into a bright eternal sea, a heaven of angels thronging', which is what we think our lives are, and what they are in reality, a 'river of darkness', a 'black river', a 'dark river of dissolution'.[24]

'The Hollow Men' famously finishes with the suggestion that the world ends not with a bang but a whimper.[25] Perhaps Ballard and Eliot were right. This is how the world will end. But I am not sure that that fact is a cause for sadness. Your world and my world will end. All worlds come to an end. All worlds are impermanent, and fleeting. Things arise, abide, change, and perish. The astrophysicist Adam Frank suggests that '*This* – meaning everything you see around you in our project of civilization – has quite likely happened thousands, millions, or even trillions of times before'. For David Wallace-Wells, though Frank's claim 'sounds like a parable from Nietzsche' it 'is really just an explication of the meaning of "infinity" and how small and insignificant the concept makes humans and everything we do in the space of such a universe'.[26] As the Zen teacher Dogen Eihei puts it

> To what shall
> I liken the world?
> Moonlight, reflected
> In dewdrops,
> Shaken from a crane's bill.[27]

This is why in the title of this book there might as well be no apostrophe in the word Worlds. What might be construed as a name or as an event, can also be a sentence:

Worlds end.

---

[24] Lawrence, D. H., *Women in Love* (London, New York: Penguin Books, 1995), 172.

[25] Eliot, T. S., *Collected Poems 1909–1935* (London: Faber & Faber, 1936), 90.

[26] Wallace-Wells, *The Uninhabitable Earth*, 223.

[27] Heine, Steven, *Existential and Ontological Dimensions of Time in Heidegger and Dōgen* (Albany: State University of New York Press, 1985), 91.

Bibliography

Acton, William. *Prostitution, Considered in Its Moral, Social and Sanitary Aspects in London and Other Large Cities and Garrison Towns, with Proposals for the Control and Prevention of Its Attendant Evils*. London: Cass, 1972.

Aitken, Jonathan. *The Young Meteors*. London: Secker and Warburg, 1967.

Allingham, Margery. *The Tiger in the Smoke*. Harmondsworth: Penguin Books, 1957.

Auden, W. H. *Another Time: Poems*. London: Faber and Faber, 1940.

Bailey, Anthony. *Standing in the Sun: A Life of J. M. W. Turner*. London: Pimlico, 1998.

Ballard, J. G. *The Terminal Beach.* Harmondsworth: Penguin, 1974.

Ballard, J. G. *The Drowned World*. London: Fourth Estate, 2014.

Bangs, Lester. *Psychotic Reactions & Carburetor Dung: Literature as Rock and Roll Rock and Roll as Literature*. London: Minerva, 1990.

BBC News Magazine. 'Who, What, Why: What Would the BBC Broadcast in a Nuclear War.' www.bbc.co.uk/news/magazine-347497, accessed 15 February 2021.

Beckett, Samuel. *Murphy*. London: Calder, 1963.

Beckett, Samuel. *The Complete Short Prose*. New York: Grove Press, 1995.

Beer, Gillian. *Meredith: A Change of Masks: a Study of the Novels*. London: Athlone, 1970.

Benjamin, Walter. 'Central Park.' *New German Critique*, 34 (Winter 1985): 32–58.

Benjamin, Walter. *Selected Writings. Vol 3*. Cambridge, MA: Belknap Press, 2002.

Birchall, Danny. 'Food for a Blush.' BFI Screenonline, www.screenonline.org.uk/film/id/452792/index.html, last accessed 4 February 2021.

Blunt, Reginald, ed. *The Crown & Anchor: a Chelsea Quarto*. London: The Chelsea Publishing Company, 1925.

Blunt, Reginald, ed. *Red Anchor Pieces.* London: Mills and Boon, 1928.

Booth, Robert. 'World's End Estate Exemplifies Fault Lines of Dramatic Inequality.' *The Guardian*, 13 November 2017, www.theguardian.com/society/2017/nov/13/worlds-end-estate-exemplifies-fault-lines-of-dramatic-inequality, accessed 15 January 2021.

Bracewell, Michael. *Roxy: The Band That Invented an Era*. London: Faber and Faber, 2007.

Bracewell, Michael. 'The Thrill of It All.' 2009. www.frieze.com/article/thrill-it-all-0, last accessed 4 February 2021.

Bradshaw, David, and Kevin J. H. Dettmar (eds). *A Companion to Modernist Literature and Culture. Blackwell Companions to Literature and Culture*. Malden, MA: Blackwell, 2006.

Braune, Sean. 'From Lucretian Atomic Theory to Joycean Etymic Theory.' *Journal of Modern Literature*, 33, no. 4 (2010): 167–181.

Bret, David. *Diana Dors: Hurricane in Mink*. London: JR, 2010.

Brittan, Luke Morgan. 'Watch John Lydon Defend Brexit, Nigel Farage and Donald Trump.' *NME*, 27 March 2017. www.nme.com/news/music/john-lydon-brexit-nigel-farage-donald-trump-2028596, accessed 26 May 2021.

Brooks, Roy. *Mud, Straw and Insults: Confessions of an Honest Estate Agent*. London: John Murray, 2001.

Bryher. *Days of Mars: A Memoir 1940–1946*. New York: Harcourt, Brace, Jovanovich, 1972.

Buckley, David. *Strange Fascination: David Bowie: The Definitive Story*. London: Virgin Books, 2005.

Buning, Marius, Matthijs Engelberts, and Sjef Houppermans. *Samuel Beckett: Crossroads and Borderlines = L'oeuvre Carrefour/l'oeuvre Limite. Samuel Beckett Today/aujourd'hui*; 6. Amsterdam: Rodopi, 1997.

Burroughs, William S. *The Soft Machine: the Restored Text*. London, New York: Penguin, 2014.

Bushell, Garry. 'These Men Are Part-Time Punks.' *Sounds,* 20 January 1979.

Butler, A. S. G. *Recording Ruin*. London: Constable & Co, 1942.

Byrne, Peter. *The Many Worlds of Hugh Everett III Multiple Universes, Mutual Assured Destruction, and the Meltdown of a Nuclear Family*. New York, London: Oxford University Press, 2010.

Carlyle, Thomas. *Collected Letters of Thomas and Jane Welsh Carlyle. Vol 7: October 833 to December 1834*. Durham, NC: Duke University Press, 2007.

Carr, Gordon. *The Angry Brigade: A History of Britain's First Urban Guerilla Group*. Oakland, CA: PM Press, 2010.

Cartwright, Garth. *Going for a Song: A Chronicle of the UK Record Shop*. London: Flood Gallery Publishing, 2018.

Chisholm, Dianne. *H. D.'s Freudian Poetics: Psychoanalysis in Translation*. Ithaca, NY: Cornell University Press, 1992.

Christopher, John. *The World in Winter*. London: Penguin, 2016.

Cixous, Helene. *Three Steps on the Ladder of Writing*. New York: Columbia University Press, 1993.

Collins, Marcus. 'The Pornography of Permissiveness: Men's Sexuality and Women's Emancipation in Mid Twentieth-Century Britain.' *History Workshop Journal*, 47 (1999).

Congreve, William. *Love for Love*. London: Benn, 1969.

Connolly, Cyril. *The Condemned Playground. Essays: 1927–1944*. London: Routledge, 1945.

Conrad, Joseph. *Heart of Darkness*. London, New York: Penguin Books, 2007.

Costello, Elvis. *Unfaithful Music & Disappearing Ink*. London, New York: Viking, 2015.

Crisp, Quentin. *The Naked Civil Servant*. London: Flamingo, 1996.

Critchley, Simon. *Very Little... Almost Nothing: Death, Philosophy and Literature*. London, New York: Routledge, 2004.

Critchley, Simon. *On Bowie*. London: Profile Books, 2016.

Dahl, Roald. *Sometime Never: A Fable for Supermen*. New York: C. Scribners Sons, 1948.

Décharné, Max. *King's Road: The Rise and Fall of the Hippest Street in the World*. London: Weidenfeld & Nicolson, 2005.

Defoe, Daniel. *A Tour through England and Wales. Vol II*. London: New York: J. M. Dent & Sons; E. P. Dutton & Co., 1928.

Deighton, Len. *The London Dossier*. Harmondsworth: Penguin Books, 1967.

Deleuze, Gilles and Félix Guattari. *Anti-Oedipus: Capitalism and Schizophrenia*. London: Athlone Press, 1984.

Derrida, Jacques. *The Work of Mourning*. Chicago: Chicago University Press, 2001.

Derrida, Jacques. *Psyche: Inventions of the Other. Vol. 1*. Stanford: Stanford University Press, 2007.

Derrida, Jacques. *The Beast & the Sovereign. Volume II*. Chicago: University of Chicago Press, 2011.

Doggett, Peter. *The Man Who Sold The World: David Bowie And The 1970s*. New York: Vintage, 2012.

Doolittle, Hilda (H. D.). *The Gift: The Complete Text*. Gainesville: University of Florida Press, 1998.

Drabble, Margaret. *The Ice Age*. London, Weidenfeld and Nicolson, 1977.

Du Noyer, Paul. *In the City: A Celebration of London Music*. London: Ebury Publishing, 2009.

Edmonds, Richard. *Chelsea. From the Five Fields to the World's End... With Eighteen Drawings by Dennis Flanders*. London: Phene Press, 1956.

Elborough, Travis. *The Bus We Loved: London's Affair With The Routemaster*. London: Granta, 2005.

Eliot, T. S. *Collected Poems 1909–1935*. London: Faber & Faber, 1936.

Fairbairns, Zoe. *Benefits*. London: Virago, 1979.

Faviell, Frances. *A Chelsea Concerto*. London: Dean Street Press, 2016.

Ferguson, Rachel. *Royal Borough*. London: Jonathan Cape, 1950.

Fisher, Mark. *Capitalist Realism: Is There No Alternative?* Winchester: Zero Books, 2009.

Fisher, Mark. *Ghosts of My Life: Writings on Depression, Hauntology and Lost Futures*. Winchester: Zero Books, 2014.

Fisher, Mark. *K-Punk: The Collected and Unpublished Writings of Mark Fisher*. London: Repeater, 2018.

Fussell, Paul. *Wartime: Understanding and Behaviour in the Second World War*. New York: Oxford University Press, 1989.

Gallix, Andrew (ed.). *Punk Is Dead: Modernity Killed Every Night*. Basingstoke: Zero Books, 2017.

Gamble, Rose. *Chelsea Child*. London: BBC Books, 1982.

Gardiner, Philip. *The Bond Code: The Dark World of Ian Fleming and James Bond*. London: New Page, 2008.

Gascoyne, David. *Selected Poems*. London: Enitharmon, 1994.

Glover, Edward. War. *Sadism and Pacifism: Further Essays on Group Psychology and War*. London: Allen and Unwin, 1946.

Goldberg, Alf, and Barry McLoughlin. *World's End for Sir Oswald: Portraits of Working-class Life in Pre-war London*. Blackpool: Progressive, 2006.

Gorman, Paul. *The Look: Adventures in Pop and Rock Fashion*. London: Sanctuary, 2001.

Gorman, Paul. *The Life and Times of Malcolm McLaren*. New York: Little Brown, 2020.

Great Britain. Central Office of Information, *Protect and Survive*. London: H.M.S.O., 1980.

Green, Jonathan. *Days in the Life: Voices from the English Underground, 1961–1971*. London: Pimlico, 1998.

Greenfield, Robert. *A Day in the Life: One Family, the Beautiful People, and the End of the '60s*. Cambridge, MA: Da Capo Press, 2009.

Greenlaw, Lavinia. *The Importance of Music to Girls*. New York: Farrar, Straus and Giroux, 2008.

Hanley, James. *No Directions*. London: Nicholson & Watson, 1946.

Hawkins, Stan. *The British Pop Dandy: Masculinity, Popular Music and Culture*. Farnham: Ashgate, 2009.

Heine, Steven. *Existential and Ontological Dimensions of Time in Heidegger and Dōgen*. Albany: State University of New York Press, 1985.

Hell, Richard. *I Dreamed I Was a Very Clean Tramp: An Autobiography*. New York: Ecco, 2014.

Hill, Joseph. Liner notes. *When the Two Sevens Clash*. Culture. Joe Gibbs, 1977. LP.

Hennessy, Peter. *Winds of Change: Britain in the Early Sixties*. London, New York: Allen Lane, 2019.

Hirst, Richard V. 'The Sound of Freedom: PiL's Flowers of Romance Forty Years On.' *The Quietus*, 26 April 2021, https://thequietus.com/articles/29813-pil-public-image-ltd-flowers-of-romance, accessed 1 May 2021.

Hoggart, Richard. *Permissive Society: The Guardian Inquiry*. London: Panther, 1969.

Holden, Stephen. 'Rock Music: Or Songs for the end of the World.' *New York Times,* 7 January 1985.

Home Office, and Central Office of Information. *Advising the Householder on Protection against Nuclear Attack.* London: H.M.S.O., 1963.

Jarman, Derek. *Jubilee: Six Film Scripts.* Minneapolis: University of Minnesota Press, 2011.

Jefferies, Richard. *After London: Or, Wild England.* Oxford; New York: Oxford University Press, 1980.

John, Elton. *Me.* London: Pan Books, 2020.

Johnson, Pamela Hansford. *World's End. A Novel.* London: Chapman & Hall, 1937.

Jones, Dylan. *David Bowie: A Life.* London: Penguin, 2017.

Jones, Steve, and Ben Thompson. *Lonely Boy: Tales from a Sex Pistol.* London: Windmill Books, 2016.

Joyce, James. *Finnegans Wake.* London: Faber, 1964.

Keeler, Christine. *Secrets and Lies: The Trials of Christine Keeler.* London: John Blake, 2019.

Kennedy, Caroline, and Philip Knightley. *How the English Establishment Framed Stephen Ward.* Scotts Valley, CA: CreateSpace, 2013.

Kerr, Joe, and Andrew Gibson (eds). *London from Punk to Blair.* London: Reaktion, 2003.

Knoblauch, William. 'Will You sing about the Missiles?' In *Nuclear Threats, Nuclear Fear and the Cold War of the 1980s,* edited by Eckart Conze, Martin Klimke and Jeremy Varon. Cambridge, New York: Cambridge University Press, 2016, 101–115.

Lake, Emma. 'Grenfell Cllr Flees Tory Councillor Who Oversaw Grenfell Tower Cladding Refurb Flees £1.2m Family Home After "Threats and Vandalism"', *The Sun,* 25 June 2017, www.thesun.co.uk/news/3879245/tory-councillor-who-oversaw-grenfell-tower-cladding-refurb-flees-1-2m-family-home-after-threats-and-vandalism/, accessed 30 June 2017.

Larkin, Philip, and Thwaite, Anthony. *Collected Poems.* London: Marvell Press and Faber and Faber, 1988.

Lawrence, D. H. *Women in Love.* London, New York: Penguin Books, 1995.

Levin, Kim. *Beyond Modernism: Essays on Art from the '70s and '80s.* New York: Harper and Row, 1988.

Lewis, Wyndham. *Blast* No. 1: *Review of the Great English Vortex,* p. 11, 20 June 1914.

Lydon, John. *Anger Is an Energy.* New York: Simon and Schuster, 2015.

Macaulay, Rose. *The World Is My Wilderness.* London: Collins, 1968.

MacInnes, Colin. *England, Half English: The Life and Times of Colin MacInnes: A Polyphoto of the Fifties.* London: Faber and Faber, 2012.

Mandell, Charlotte. 'The Gift: A Review'. *English Literature in Transition 1880–1920*, 42, no. 3 (September 1999): 344–348.

Marcus, Greil. *In The Fascist Bathroom: Punk in Pop Music, 1977–1992*. Cambridge, MA: Harvard University Press, 1999.

Marcus, Greil. *Lipstick Traces: A Secret History of the Twentieth Century*. London: Faber and Faber, 2011.

Marcus, Steven. *The Other Victorians: A Study of Sexuality and Pornography in Mid-nineteenth-century England*. London: Weidenfeld and Nicolson, 1966.

Martin, Benjamin Ellis. *Old Chelsea. A Summer-day's Stroll.* London: T. Fisher Unwin, 1889.

Marx, Karl, and Friedrich Engels. *The Communist Manifesto*. New York: Pocket Books, 1964.

McCarthy, Fiona. *The Last Curtsey*. London: Faber and Faber, 2007.

Mellen, Joe. *Bore Hole*. London: Strange Attractor Press, 2015.

Moorcock, Michael. *Mother London*. London: Weidenfeld and Nicholson, 2016.

Moraes, Henrietta. *Henrietta*. London: Hamish Hamilton, 1994.

Mumford, Lewis. *The Culture of Cities*. New York: Harcourt, Brace & Jovanovich, 1970.

Nead, Lynda. *The Tiger in the Smoke: Art and Culture in Post-War Britain*. New Haven: Yale University Press, 2017.

Noel-Tod, Jeremy. *The Penguin Book of the Prose Poem: from Baudelaire to Anne Carson*. London, New York: Penguin Books, 2019.

Norman, Frank. *Norman's London*. London: Secker and Warburg, 1969.

Novotny, Mariella. *King's Road*. London: New English Library, 1973.

Nuttall, Jeff. *Bomb Culture*. London: McGibbon and Kee, 1968.

Oldham, Andrew Loog. *Stoned*. New York: Vintage, 2008.

Olson, Charles. *Call me Ishmael*. San Francisco: City Lights, 1996.

O'Neill, Alistair. *London – After a Fashion*. London: Reaktion Books, 2007.

O'Toole, Fintan. *Heroic Failure: Brexit and the Politics of Pain*. New York: Apollo, 2019.

Orton, Joe, and John Lahr. *The Orton Diaries: Including the Correspondence of Edna Welthorpe and Others*. London: Methuen, 1986.

Overy, Richard. *The Bombing War: Europe 1939–1945*. London: Allen Lane, 2013.

Painter, Peter D. *The World's End: Chelsea Unplugged*. Morrisville, NC: Lulu, 2012.

Parsons, Tony, and Julie Birchall. *The Boy Looked at Johnny*. London: Pluto Press, 1978.

Pearsall, Ronald. *The Worm in the Bud: The World of Victorian Sexuality*. Harmondsworth: Penguin, 1971.

Peppiatt, Michael. *Francis Bacon in the 1950s*. New Haven: Yale University Press, 2008.

Pizzichini, Lilian. *The Novotny Papers: 'A Bit Vulture, A Bit Eagle'*. Stroud: Amberley Books, 2021.

Pocock, Tom. *Chelsea Reach: The Brutal Friendship of Whistler and Walter Greaves*. London. Hodder & Stoughton, 1970.

Pritchett, V. S. and Evelyn Hofer. *London Perceived*. London: Chatto & Windus, 1962.

Pynchon, Thomas. *Gravity's Rainbow*. New York: Viking Press, 1973.

Pyzik, Agata. *Poor But Sexy: Culture Clashes in Europe East and West*. Zero Books, 2014.

Quant, Mary. *Quant by Quant*. London: Cassell and Co., 1966.

Raphael, Phyllis. *Off the King's Road: Lost and Found in London*. New York, Roadswell Editions, 2014.

Report from the Select Committee of the House of Lords on the Law Relating to the Protection of Young Girls: Together with the Proceedings of the Committee, Minutes of Evidence and Appendix: 9 August 1882. London: House of Commons, 1882.

Reynolds, David. *Swan River*. London: Picador, 2002.

Reynolds, Simon. *Shock and Awe: Glam Rock and Its Legacy, from the Seventies to the Twenty-first Century*. London: Faber & Faber, 2017.

Ritchie, Charles. *Siren Years: Undiplomatic Diaries, 1937–1945*. London: Macmillan, 1974.

Ross, Geoffrey Aquilina. *Day of the Peacock: Style for Men 1963–1973*. London: V. & A. Publishing, 2011.

Ruskin, John. *Complete Works of John Ruskin*. New York; Chicago: National Library Association, 1903.

Saint-Amour, Paul K. *Tense Future: Modernism, Total War, Encyclopedic Form*. London, Oxford: Oxford University Press, 2015.

Samuel, Raphael. *Theatres of Memory. Vol. 1, Past and Present in Contemporary Culture*. London: Verso, 1994.

Sassoon, Siegfried. *Meredith*. London: Constable, 1948.

Savage, Jon. *England's Dreaming: Sex Pistols and Punk Rock*. London: Faber & Faber, 1992.

Savage, Jon. *Teenage: The Creation of Youth Culture*. London: Pimlico, 2008.

Savage, Jon. *Uninhabited London* . London: Rough Trade Editions, 2018.

Schell, Jonathan. *The Fate of the Earth*. New York: Knopf, 1982.

Schou, Nicholas. *Orange Sunshine*. New York: Thomas Dunne Books, 2010.

Scott, Paul, 'His-and-hers Rollers. Armed Bodyguards. Wild Champagne Sprees in Nightclubs... Why Bernie Ecclestone Thinks His 'Billionaire' Son-in-law's too Flash for His Own Good.' *Mailonline*, 26 April 2014. www.dailymail.co.uk/news/article-2613504/His-Rollers-Armed-bodyguards-Wild-champagne-sprees-nightclubs-Why-Bernie-Ecclestone-thinks-billionaire-son-laws-flash-good.html, accessed 15 December 2020.

Searle, Ronald. *Souls in Torment*. London: Perpetua, 1953.

Serres, Michel. *Hermes – Literature, Science, Philosophy*. Baltimore: Johns Hopkins University Press, 1982.

Simpson, Kate. 'David Bowie Interview.' *Music Now!*, 20 December 1969.

Smith, Chris L. *Bare Architecture: A Schizoanalysis*. London: Bloomsbury, 2017.

Sontag, Susan. "Notes on 'Camp'". *Partisan Review*, 31, no. 4 (Fall 1964): 515–530.

Spark, Muriel. *The Girls of Slender Means*. London: Macmillan, 1963.

Sutherland, Douglas. *Portrait of a Decade: London Life 1945–1955*. London: Harrap, 1988.

Stewart, Tony. 'Heil and Farewell.' *New Musical Express*, 8 May 1976.

Tate Britain. *Joseph Mallord William Turner: The Angel Standing in the Sun*. www.tate.org.uk/art/artworks/turner-the-angel-standing-in-the-sun-n00550, accessed 15 June 2020.

Theroux, Paul. *World's End and Other Stories*. New York: Houghton Mifflin Harcourt, 1980.

Thompson, E. P. *Protest and Survive*. London: The Campaign for Nuclear Disarmament, 1980.

Thornbury, George Walter, and Edward Walford. *Old and New London; Illustrated. A Narrative of Its History, Its People, and Its Places. Vol V.* London, Paris: Cassell, Petter, & Galpin, 1873.

Trynka, Paul. *Starman: David Bowie the Definitive Biography*. London: Sphere, 2011.

Wallace-Wells, David. *The Uninhabitable Earth: A Story of the Future*. London, New York: Penguin Books, 2019.

Webster, Augusta, Mathilde Blind, and Amy Levy. *Out of My Borrowed Books: Poems by Augusta Webster, Mathilde Blind and Amy Levy*. Manchester: Fyfield Books/Carcanet, 2006.

Wheal, Donald James. *World's End: Memoirs of a Blitz Childhood*. London: Arrow Books, 2005.

Whistler, James McNeill. *The Gentle Art of Making Enemies*. London: William Heinemann, 1890.

Willans, Geoffrey, and Ronald Searle. *The Compleet Molesworth*. London: Max Parrish, 1958.

Williams, Evan Calder, *Combined and Uneven Apocalypse*. Ropley, Hants: Zero Books, 2011.

Wilson, Elizabeth. *Adorned in Dreams: Fashion and Modernity*. London: Virago, 1985.

Woolf, Virginia. *Street Haunting*. San Francisco: Westgate Press, 1930.

Woolf, Virginia. *The Years*. New York: Harcourt, Brace & Co, 1937.

Woolf, Virginia. *Collected Essays. Vol 6*. London: Hogarth Press, 1966.

Wyden, Peter. *Day One: Before Hiroshima and After*. New York: Simon and Schuster, 1984.

Wyndham, Joan. *Love Lessons: A Wartime Diary*. London: Heinemann, 1985.

York, Peter. *Style Wars*. London: Sidgwick and Jackson, 1980.

Young, Rob. *Electric Eden: Unearthing Britain's Visionary Music*. London: Faber and Faber, 2011.